HIGH IMPACT RESUMES
AND LETTERS

By Ron Krannich

CAREER AND BUSINESS BOOKS AND SOFTWARE

201 Dynamite Job Search Letters
The $100,000+ Entrepreneur
America's Top 100 Jobs for People Without a Four-Year Degree
America's Top Jobs for People Re-Entering the Workforce
America's Top Internet Job Sites
Best Jobs for the 21st Century
Change Your Job, Change Your Life
The Complete Guide to Public Employment
The Directory of Federal Jobs and Employers
Discover the Best Jobs for You!
Dynamite Salary Negotiations
Dynamite Tele-Search
The Educator's Guide to Alternative Jobs and Careers
The Ex-Offender's Job Hunting Guide
Find a Federal Job Fast!
From Air Force Blue to Corporate Gray
From Army Green to Corporate Gray
From Navy Blue to Corporate Gray
Get a Raise in 7 Days
High Impact Resumes and Letters
I Can't Believe They Asked Me That!
I Want to Do Something Else, But I'm Not Sure What It Is
Interview for Success
The Job Hunting Guide: Transitioning From College to Career
Job Hunting Tips for People With Hot and Not-So-Hot Backgrounds
Job Interview Tips for People With Not-So-Hot Backgrounds
Job-Power Source and *Ultimate Job Source* (software)
Jobs and Careers With Nonprofit Organizations
Military Transition to Civilian Success
Military Resumes and Cover Letters
Moving Out of Education (with William J. Banis)
Moving Out of Government
Nail the Cover Letter!
Nail the Job Interview!
Nail the Resume!
No One Will Hire Me!
Re-Careering in Turbulent Times
Savvy Interviewing
The Savvy Networker
The Savvy Resume Writer
Win the Interview, Win the Job

TRAVEL AND INTERNATIONAL BOOKS

Best Resumes and CVs for International Jobs
The Complete Guide to International Jobs and Careers
The Directory of Websites for International Jobs
International Jobs Directory
Jobs for Travel Lovers
Mayors and Managers in Thailand
Politics of Family Planning Policy in Thailand
Shopping and Traveling in Exotic Asia
Shopping in Exotic Places
Shopping the Exotic South Pacific
Travel Planning On the Internet
Treasures and Pleasures of Australia
Treasures and Pleasures of Bermuda
Treasures and Pleasures of China
Treasures and Pleasures of Egypt
Treasures and Pleasures of Hong Kong
Treasures and Pleasures of India
Treasures and Pleasures of Indonesia
Treasures and Pleasures of Italy
Treasures and Pleasures of Mexico
Treasures and Pleasures of Paris
Treasures and Pleasures of Rio and São Paulo
Treasures and Pleasures of Santa Fe, Taos, and Albuquerque
Treasures and Pleasures of Singapore and Bali
Treasures and Pleasures of Singapore
Treasures and Pleasures of South America
Treasures and Pleasures of Southern Africa
Treasures and Pleasures of Thailand and Myanmar
Treasures and Pleasures of Turkey
Treasures and Pleasures of Vietnam and Cambodia

HIGH IMPACT RESUMES AND LETTERS

How to Communicate Your Qualifications to Employers

9th Edition

Ronald L. Krannich and William J. Banis, Ph.Ds

IMPACT PUBLICATIONS
Manassas Park, VA

HIGH IMPACT RESUMES AND LETTERS:
How to Communicate Your Qualifications to Employers

Ninth Edition

Library of Congress Cataloguing-in-Publication Data

Krannich, Ronald L.
    High impact resumes and letters: how to communicate your qualifications to employers/ Ronald L. Krannich, William J. Banis. — 9th ed.
        p.   cm.
    Includes bibliographical references and index.
    ISBN 1-57023-243-1
    1. Resumes (Employment) I. Banis, William J. II. Title.

HF5383.K7   2006
650-14'2—dc2   2005937966

Publisher: For information on Impact Publications, including current and forthcoming publications, authors, press kits, online bookstores, catalogs, news, and submission requirements, visit our website: www.impactpublications.com.

Publicity/Rights: For information on publicity, author interviews, and rights, contact the Media Relations Department: Tel. 703-361-7300, Fax 703-335-9486, or query@impactpublications.com.

Sales/Distribution: All bookstore sales are handled through Impact's trade distributor: National Book Network, 15200 NBN Way, Blue Ridge Summit, PA 17214, Tel. 1-800-462-6420. All other sales and distribution inquiries should be directed to the publisher: Sales Department, IMPACT PUBLICATIONS, 9104 Manassas Drive, Suite N, Manassas Park, VA 20111-5211, Tel. 703-361-7300, Fax 703-335-9486, or e-mail: query@impactpublications.com.

Contents

Preface

YOU ARE WHAT YOU WRITE. At least to employers who don't know much about you, how and what you write – both form and content – tells them whether or not you are worth seeing in person. Indeed, you usually make your first impression with employers on paper or on a computer screen in the form of a letter and resume. And first impressions are extremely important with employers. They make the difference between being immediately accepted or rejected for a job interview.

Whether you are first entering, re-entering, or changing jobs and careers within the job market, there's a 90 percent chance you will join millions of other job seekers in sending resumes and letters to more than one potential employer. How well you write, produce, distribute, and follow up your resumes and letters will largely determine if you will receive an invitation to interview for a job you really want.

Resumes and job search letters may well be the most important written communication of your life. Failure to communicate your qualifications loud and clear to employers will affect your future job satisfaction, career advancement, and potential earnings.

Few people know the secrets to writing high impact resumes and letters. Lacking clear goals, strong organization, and a sense of direction in their job search, they flounder in the job market with poorly written resumes and letters. They communicate their weaknesses rather than demonstrate their strengths. Not surprisingly, such job seekers receive few invitations for job interviews.

However, our readers and users have learned how to better organize and target their job search by following the practical resume and letter advice offered in the past eight editions of this book. Unlike other books on resumes and letters, this one walks you through two closely linked processes simultaneously in order to develop powerful communication skills: (1) the job search process and (2) the resume and letter writing process. But we don't just show you how to write nice looking resumes and letters – that would be form with little function or a product without an outcome. We also show you how to market and manage your written communication for maximum impact. In contrast to other resume books, this one emphasizes producing outcomes and results **after** you complete your resume and letter writing exercises. Thus, when you finish this book, you should be in a much better position to open the doors of potential employers and get those interviews that lead to excellent job offers and satisfying jobs.

This edition of *High Impact Resumes and Letters* again places resumes and letters within a larger context – career planning and job search processes. It includes in Chapter 12 the latest information on using electronic resumes and the Internet in today's rapidly changing job market. This ninth edition also provides new insights in Chapter 14 on the 110 most frequently asked questions concerning resumes and letters. Through this Q&A format, we quickly answer numerous questions asked by our readers. We've showcased in Appendix D a new section of exciting resumes produced by four professional resume writers, including 10 examples with corresponding analyses and a collection of blue-collar resumes. While not immediately apparent, the work of these exceptionally talented professionals has made a major difference in the lives of their clients. While this book is designed to help you write your own resume, we also recognize that there are times when you are best served by working with such professionals who can save you a great deal of time, money, and frustration by getting you headed in the right direction.

Based on years of experience in training and counseling thousands of job seekers as well as writing, revising, and reviewing hundreds of resumes, we've learned the best resumes and letters – those that move employers to interview the "best qualified" candidates – must reflect the "unique you." If written according to our advice, such resumes and letters will clearly communicate **your goals** as well as **your pattern of performance to employers** who want to minimize the risks of hiring strangers. Such resumes and letters translate your goals, skills, and achievements as being the employer's hiring needs. They tell employers that you are someone who has the best potential for solving their problems.

While much has changed since we first wrote this book in 1982, especially the role of the Internet and e-mail in the recruitment and job finding processes, certain things also have remained the same. The most important constant is this:

Employers want to hire talented individuals who can solve their problems and move their organizations to new levels of productivity and profitability.

Talented individuals who are also enthusiastic, dependable, loyal, and likable are always in short supply. As you craft your resume and letters and engage in other job search activities, don't forget this enduring need of employers. It will serve you well as you focus on communicating your qualifications to employers. Indeed, in the midst of all the technological changes affecting the recruitment and job search processes, the needs of employers are very simple. Make sure your resumes and letters respond to those basic needs.

Join us as we take you on an important journey into what should become one of the most exciting and rewarding adventures – writing high impact resumes and letters that persuade employers to invite you to job interviews. If you follow this book carefully and implement each chapter, you should join thousands of our other readers who report greater success in their job search efforts.

We wish you the very best as you create your own high impact resumes and letters. Whatever you do, make sure you go beyond just creating pretty paper filled with nice sounding keywords and phrases. Your resumes and letters must have impact. If you can achieve such impact, you should be well on your way to increased job and career success!

Ron Krannich
krannich@impactpublications.com

HIGH IMPACT RESUMES
AND LETTERS

1

Communicate Your
Qualifications
With Impact

W E'VE HEARD ALL THE RESUME and letter writing stories, principles, and do's and don'ts from seemingly well-meaning individuals, including many so-called experts. They often go like this:

- When looking for a job, the first thing you should do is write a resume.

- Blue-collar workers don't need resumes – they only complete applications.

- Paper, mailed, and faxed resumes are obsolete. Just go online with an electronic resume to conduct your job search.

- Don't put an objective on your resume.

- Functional and combinational resumes are better than chronological resumes.

- It's not necessary to send a cover letter with your resume.

- Use lots of action verbs. No, try nouns and keywords instead.

- Don't use a resume – they're old-fashioned and less effective than portfolios, leadership profiles, websites, networking, letters, e-mail, and just "showing up."

- Don't send your resume to personnel offices.

- Employers prefer e-mailed resumes in the form of attachments or ASCII documents rather than mailed or faxed resumes.

- Blast your resume to as many employers as possible.

- Follow up with second and third copies of your resume.

1

- You should always write your own resume.

- Put as much information as possible on your resume about your education and work history.

- Your resume should not run more than one page.

The list of resume and letter do's and don'ts – supposedly honed from years of research and experience – goes on and on. Constituting part of today's job search folklore, these principles of effective communication are anything but tried, tested, or trustworthy. They should be viewed with suspicion. Like much of what passes as sound job search advice, this folklore lacks a firm foundation in reality. Like urban legends, it's basically a set of beliefs that gets passed down from one true believer to another, most of whom incestuously quote each other as authorities on the subject.

So what is the job seeker to make of all this advice, much of which seems contradictory? Let's cut through the folklore and fuzzy thinking surrounding the subject of resume and job search letters. In so doing, we'll sharpen your focus on what's really important in conducting an effective job search vis-a-vis you and potential employers who are shopping for unique talents.

The World of High Impact Resumes and Letters

So you're getting ready to look for a job you hope you'll really love, one that pays good money and leads to a rewarding career. You're about to engage in a curious ritual shared, and dreaded, by millions of people each year. But you're different from others. Rather than languish in the job market for weeks peddling a weak resume, beating on numerous doors, or sitting idly in someone's over-hyped resume database, you're going to cut through the chaos with high impact resumes and letters designed to quickly open employers' doors. Armed with such resumes and letters, you'll soon land a terrific job!

Welcome to the world of high impact resumes and letters. It's a different world from the usual sea of paper and electronic communication received by most employers. Unlike other job seekers who lack strong writing, production, distribution, and follow-up skills, you want to clearly communicate your qualifications to employers with a particular type of resume – one that immediately grabs their attention and results in job interviews, and eventually job offers. To navigate the job market with anything less than high impact resumes and letters is to do a real disservice to yourself and to potential employers.

It's About Effectively Communicating Qualifications

Communicating your qualifications to employers should be the single most important goal of your job search. After all, employers want to see you on paper or on a computer screen before they decide to meet you in person. They want to know who you are and what you can do for them rather than what they can do for you. In other words, your qualifications should come together as a **predictable pattern of performance**. Therefore, if you want to get invited to job interviews, you need to clearly communicate to employers that you have the right combination of experience, skills, interests, and attitudes to add value to their operations. You must appear competent, enthusiastic, and likable on paper **before** you can communicate these same qualities in the all-important job interview.

Expertly crafted and intelligently distributed resumes and letters produce the most desired job search outcomes – interviews that eventually turn into job offers and satisfying jobs. To be most effective, these resumes and letters must be employer-centered rather than self-centered.

But not everyone knows the secrets to writing and distributing high impact resumes and letters. That's our task in the following pages – to make sure you know how to put the maximum **impact** into your written job search communications so that you can get interviews for the jobs you want.

> *Your resumes and letters must be employer-centered rather than self-centered.*

Focus On the Process

Please be forewarned that this is not your normal reflective resume and letter writing guidebook crammed with examples of so-called "outstanding" or "winning" resumes and letters. The market is full of such guides that assume you can write good resumes and letters through a process of emulation or osmosis. Just visit your local bookstore or library and you will be assaulted with such books rich with examples. Most of these guides present the final products with little useful advice on how you get to point A – identify your goals – and then proceed on to points B, C, D, E, and F – specify skills and experience and target organizations, jobs, and employers.

Using previous editions of this book has been a very rewarding experience for many of our readers. They discovered *High Impact Resumes and Letters* was much more than just another resume and letter writing guide filled with numerous writing principles and a scattering of examples. Focusing on the whole job search process, the book helped them travel along the road to discover their "real self" as well as communicate their qualifications loudly and clearly to potential employers.

We purposefully designed this book to put you to work creating, distributing, and following up your own high impact resumes and letters. Our primary focus is on the **job finding process**. We stress the importance of having explicit goals and strong organization and management skills for achieving the most desired job search outcomes – job interviews and offers. In this sense, high impact resumes and letters become the central driving force around which you will create and manage an effective job search campaign.

We don't just explain how to write effective resumes and letters and then "fill up" the book with lots of unrelated examples that may or may not be relevant to your situation. Instead, we start with the most important element in the whole job search process – **you** as defined by your particular mix of interests, skills, abilities, values, and goals. Above all, you need to become better acquainted with yourself **before** you can introduce yourself to strangers who want to know what it is you have done, can do, and will do for them. You'll need to become conversant in a special language that succinctly speaks about your achievements and future job performance in reference to employers' needs.

We'll take you on an important and revealing **journey of self-discovery** as you discover the "unique you" and explore the "ins" and "outs" of one of the most important steps in any job search. You'll discover how this step is critically related to other equally important steps in your job search. We'll show you not only how to write and produce powerful resumes and letters, but also how, when, and where to distribute and follow them up for maximum impact.

If you follow our advice in this book, you should be in a powerful position to get the job you want. Not only will you quickly find a job, you'll find one you really love – one that is literally "fit" for you.

Most important of all, you will learn how to **present your best self** prior to being invited to a formal job interview. While this may not be an easy task, it is much less painful than many people believe it is, or make it to be. For in creating high impact resumes and letters you also present an image of yourself that helps direct every stage of your job search. As such, writing, producing, distributing, and following up high impact resumes and letters should become central activities in your whole job search.

Yes, Anyone Can Find a Job

It's no big secret. Almost anyone can find a job, especially in an economy where unemployment is less than 6 percent. But finding a really good job – one you do well, enjoy doing, and look forward to each day as well as see yourself doing for many years to come – is not the usual outcome of most job searches. People find jobs, leave jobs, and go looking for other jobs in a cycle of job-hopping that is commonplace in our employment culture. Part of the reason for making these changes goes back to the **methods** people use for finding and keeping jobs, from the very moment they write a resume to when they negotiate a job offer.

> *Everything you do should be aimed at linking your capabilities to employers' specific needs.*

How well you make job and career changes will largely depend on what job search methods you use. These methods will be reflected in the way in which you write, produce, distribute, and follow up your resumes and letters.

Finding a good job involves much more than responding to want ads and vacancy announcements with attractive pieces of paper called resumes and letters. Above all, it requires communicating qualifications to employers in the most efficient and effective manner possible. Resumes and letters are only two means – albeit the most popular and frequently used – of doing so. Whether they are efficient and effective depends on both **what** you communicate and **how** you communicate your message.

You should learn how to best develop and target your written communication in conjunction with other forms of communication for maximum impact on employers. That is the subject of this book. Everything you do – be it identifying your skills, formulating an objective, conducting job research, writing resumes and letters, or networking – should be aimed at linking your capabilities to employers' specific needs.

You Must Communicate Your Value to Employers

Communication in the job market is all about being effective – having a positive impact on employers and your employment future. You want others to take action, based on your perceived benefits to them, that will result in a really good job.

To be most effective, you must formulate a high quality **message** and then **disseminate** it through specific **communication channels**. In so doing, you develop **strategies** – either implicitly or explicitly – for communicating your message to employers.

The message, channels, and strategies come together in a well-defined **process** when you write resumes and letters. This process – the formulation and dissemination of formal written communication – plays a critical role in your job search. You want to write high quality resumes and letters to:

1. Quickly uncover job leads.
2. Succinctly communicate the "unique you" to employers.
3. Get invited to job interviews that hopefully will lead to job offers.

Without such resumes and letters, you will have difficulty gaining access and communicating your qualifications to employers. Above all, resumes and letters lend legitimacy to your job search as well as provide you and employers with a central focal point for examining your qualifications in reference to specific job requirements. If you develop high quality messages and disseminate them properly, you will indeed communicate your qualifications to employers with impact. Employers will select you amongst the very few to be invited to a job interview.

Key Products Promoting a Process

The purpose of this book is to clarify how you can make this process best work for you – from beginning to end. Let's be perfectly clear what we are and are not doing here. We emphasize the whole **process** rather than examine only a few discrete elements within the process. We provide examples of resumes and letters but only within the context of the larger career planning and job search processes, as outlined in Chapter 4, as well as in direct reference to the key principles for writing different types of resumes and letters.

> *Your resume will become the single most important calling card you will need to land a job.*

Resumes and job search letters are some of the most controversial and abused forms of communication. Most career counselors, for example, advise you to write a one- to two-page resume and use it frequently throughout your job search. Others claim resumes are unnecessary and thus you should use alternative means of communication, especially portfolios, networking, or the Internet, to gain access to employers. Still others concentrate on developing individual resume elements with little regard for the function and use of resumes in the overall job search process. What is one to make of all this conflicting advice?

Frankly, there is a lot of nonsense written about resumes and letters by people who should know better – or better know what goes on in the job search process. This book is based upon a very simple fact of employment life: **resumes and letters are important parts of the job search process that are here to stay, and in a very big way.** They are here to stay because they are wonderful double-edged swords for cutting through other less organized forms of communication: employers find them efficient for screening candidates; candidates know they are acceptable pass cards for opening employers' doors and communicating qualifications to strangers. Resumes will become even more important in the years ahead as more and more employers use resume databases for screening resumes and encourage candidates to submit resumes and profiles online. The resume will become the single most important piece of paper and electronic document you will need for getting jobs today and in the decade ahead.

Put another way, resumes and letters are written **products** used for furthering an important **process**. If written well and used intelligently, they can open the doors to job and career success. They lead to job interviews and offers and set the tone for productive work relationships with employers. If written poorly and used inappropriately, resumes will be useless, if not negative, for one's job search campaign and future employment.

Use the Right Resources

Each year millions of job hunters turn to books for job search assistance. They usually turn to three books which address three key elements in the job search – resumes, cover letters, and interviews. Some go directly to software programs or visit various Internet sites for producing resumes and preparing for job interviews.

If this book represents your first career planning book, you may want to supplement it with a few other key books, especially Ron's comprehensive career planning guides – *Change Your Job, Change Your Life* and *No One Will Hire Me!* – and his eight other resume and letter writing books – *The Savvy Resume Writer, Nail the Resume!, Nail the Cover Letter!, Best Resumes and CVs for International Jobs, Best Resumes and Letters for Ex-Offenders, Military Resumes and Cover Letters, 201 Dynamite Job Search Letters,* and *Resume, Application, and Letter Tips for People With Hot and Not-So-Hot Backgrounds.*

Several other books examine various stages in the job search: *Job Hunting Tips for People With Hot and Not-So-Hot Backgrounds, Nail the Job Interview, Savvy Interviewing, Interview for Success, Job Interview Tips for People With Not-So-Hot Backgrounds, Dynamite Tele-Search, The Savvy Networker, Salary Negotiation Tips for Professionals, Dynamite Salary Negotiations,* and *I Want to Do Something Else, But I'm Not Sure What It Is.*

He also addresses particular job and career fields and Internet sites in the following books: *The Best Jobs for the 21st Century, Jobs for Travel Lovers, America's Top 100 Jobs for People Without a Four-Year Degree, America's Top Jobs for People Re-Entering the Workforce, America's Top Internet Job Sites,* and *The Directory of Websites for International Jobs.*

Many of these books are available in your local library and bookstore, or they can be ordered directly from Impact Publications (see the "Career Resources" section at the end of this book). These and hundreds of other resources are available online at:

www.impactpublications.com

This website contains almost every important career and job finding resource available today, including many titles that are difficult, if not impossible, to find in bookstores and libraries. You will find everything from additional resume and cover letter books to resources on assessment, interviewing, government and international jobs, military, women, minorities, students, ex-offenders, and entrepreneurs, as well as videos, computer software programs, and posters. This is an excellent website for keeping in touch with the major resources that can assist you with every stage of your job search as well as with your future career development plans. Impact's site also includes downloadable catalogs and flyers for keeping you in touch with the latest in career products. In addition, you also can request a free copy of their job resource flyers by sending a self-addressed stamped envelope (#10 business size). Send your request to:

IMPACT PUBLICATIONS
ATTN: Free Career Flyers
9104 Manassas Drive, Suite N
Manassas Park, VA 20111-5211

Impact Publications also operates two additional websites, that provide advice on finding jobs and developing careers:

www.winningthejob.com
www.exoffenderreentry.com

Power Up Your Job Search

Whatever you do, make sure you put the power of high impact resumes and letters into your job search. You should go into the job search equipped with the necessary knowledge and skills to be most effective in communicating your qualifications to employers.

As you will quickly discover, the job market is not a place to engage in wishful thinking nor wasteful activities. It is at times impersonal, frequently ego deflating, and often unforgiving of errors. It requires a positive attitude, clear thinking, strong communication skills, and effective strategies for making the right moves with employers. Above all, it rewards individuals who follow through in implementing each job search step with enthusiasm, dogged persistence, and the ability to handle rejections.

May you soon discover this power and incorporate it in your own high impact resumes and letters!

2

Focus on Employers' Needs

S O YOU'RE LOOKING FOR A JOB. How do you plan to get one? Whom will you contact? How will you go about meeting potential employers? What do you have to offer them? Do you really know what employers want from you? Will this be the right job for you? How should you get started?

Let's discuss some of these initial job search questions so we know we're going in the right direction. We need to make sure we're talking the same language about resumes, letters, jobs, and employers.

Get Started Right

Let's look at the way most people go about writing resumes and letters and positioning themselves in the job market. Here's a typical approach:

"I'm really excited about finding a job. What I thought I would do first is write my resume. That shouldn't take long – maybe two or three hours. Once I finish it, I'll send it to employers along with a cover letter. Isn't that what most people do?"

You're right. Most people do start with a resume. Perhaps you could expand a little more by explaining what you plan to put into your resume.

"I really haven't given that much thought. I have a copy of a friend's resume. She also loaned me a resume book filled with examples. I'll look at these examples for some guidance. I guess I'll include what most people put on their resumes – education, work history, special interests, references, salary expectations. Isn't that what's supposed to go on a resume?"

Yes, most resumes include much of that information. But we're more interested in how you are conducting your job search. We want to know how **you** will write, produce, distribute, and follow up **your** resume. What will your resume say about you in terms of

8

your interests, goals, skills, experience, strengths, and future productivity for the employer? How many pages will it be? How will you produce it? Will it be word processed using attractive fonts and special graphic design elements? What about the color and weight of the paper? How many copies will you run? Whom will you send it to? What type of response do you expect to receive? How long will you wait before you contact the employer about the status of your application?

You'll have to address many of these and other questions as you get into the details of writing, producing, distributing, and following up your resumes.

> *"Yeah, that's a lot to think about. I haven't really given those questions much thought. I've been most concerned about just getting my resume written! I can see there are several things I need to consider once I finish writing my resume. Or maybe I need to answer those questions **before** I write my resume. What do you think?"*

We think you're beginning to ask the right questions. In fact, the solution to most problems is found in asking the right questions. If you ask the right questions about your resume, letters, and job search, chances are the answers will come more easily. But if you don't ask those questions up front, you may end up doing what so many other job seekers do – head off with inappropriate baggage which results in conducting an ineffective job search. We think you can and should do better. Let's do first things first.

What we want you to do is consider writing high impact resumes and letters. These will take more than two or three hours to write, and they cannot be written by just modifying others' examples. They require you to do first things first. And one of the first things you should **not** do is write a resume. If you are to write it right, you first need information about

> *Make your resume the central focus or driving force around which you will organize each step of your job search.*

yourself, jobs, employers, and organizations. This information will be the basis for carefully constructing each section of your resume. You also must think in terms of developing and managing a resume and letter **process** involving distinct writing, production, distribution, and follow-up principles and activities. This process identifies and relates each activity that must be performed sequentially in order to achieve desired outcomes with your resume and letters – get job interviews and offers.

More importantly, let's make an important strategic decision at this point: make your resume the central focus or driving force around which you will organize each step of your job search. In so doing, your resume becomes more than just a piece of pretty paper for passing your history on to employers. Carefully crafted, it represents you, your job search, and your future. It's a particular type of product, based upon a well defined process, which should have a tremendous impact on your future.

Interested? Let's see what we can do in the next few hours to properly pack your bags as you journey along a new road to career success. We'll begin by doing first things first – assessing your interests, skills, and abilities – and then proceed to build each section of your resume based upon sound career planning and job search principles. The end result will be a high impact resume that reflects your greatest strengths and communicates the "unique you" to employers. It tells them what you have done, can do, and will do in the future. That's what employers want to know.

Make the High Impact Difference

Each year millions of anxious souls engage in a curious paper ritual. They write resumes and cover letters, send them to prospective employers, and wait to be called for a job interview and/or receive a job offer. Some even hire a professional to write and distribute their resumes and letters for them – thinking an expert might have better success than they themselves will.

While most people hope to write resumes and letters that will put them on the road to job search success, few have the knack to put it all together with impact. But what exactly are high impact resumes and letters?

> *High impact resumes and letters grab the attention of employers and move them to invite you to interviews. They accurately represent your strengths.*

High impact resumes and letters are ones that grab the attention of employers and move them to invite you to interviews. They are an accurate representation of you, your strengths, and your future productivity. Communicating what it is you have done, can do, and will do, high impact resumes and letters make the critical difference between getting no response or getting a positive response. That positive response is an invitation to a job interview, which, in turn, may result in a job offer and a satisfying job.

Take Employers Seriously

Let's turn the tables for a moment to see exactly what is being communicated in today's world of work. Put yourself in the shoes of the employer who receives numerous resumes and letters and who must develop a system for screening the good, the bad, and the ugly. Your problem is similar to that of other employers: You are inundated with resumes. But you've decided to handle the mail, faxes, and e-mail yourself rather than rely on outside employment firms, headhunters, or a resume database to screen applicants. Suppose, for example, you received 150 resumes and letters this week in response to your vacancy announcement. After spending four hours sorting these paper qualifications into three piles – *"yes," "maybe," "no"* – you discover your stack of *"yeses"* is relatively thin. Altogether, you spent less than 30 seconds reading each resume and accompanying letter. Most resumes landed in your *"no"* pile, from where they will next find a final resting place in your trash can. In fact, 75 percent of these resumes and letters should never have been sent to you because they didn't include the required skills and experience you specified in your ad, or they were very difficult to interpret in reference to the position under consideration. Perhaps the candidates didn't read the ad carefully or they were hoping you wouldn't see their obvious lack of qualifications. Out of 150 resumes and letters, you have found only seven people whom you will consider inviting for an interview. But you just want to see three. You'll telephone this pool of candidates tomorrow to see if they **sound** as promising as they **look** on paper. Then you will be able to decide whom you wish to **see** in person.

Having gone through this sorting ritual, you reflect on the crucial resume and letter writing step in the job search. You're surprised at what you discovered in the process of screening the candidates:

1. How poorly people portray themselves on paper.

2. What they are willing to tell strangers who have the power to hire.

3. Why they think they can get a job primarily by using the postal system, faxes, and e-mail.

Is this the best they can do? After all, you are offering a good job with potential for career advancement – your money for their talent. You would think applicants would be more serious about themselves, their futures, and employers' needs. If these resumes and letters are any indication, few seem to really care.

Transcend Communication Rituals

We're not anthropologists, but we know a communication ritual when we see one. Resume and letter writing is a kind of ritual, complete with a set of beliefs about how one should relate to the job world with pieces of paper for communicating one's qualifications to employers. As with most rituals, this one is a mixture of myths, magic, and mysterious movement. Thus, resume and letter writing becomes an accepted "rite of passage" in the process of finding a job.

> *Employers want to know what you will do for them in the future. They are looking for someone who can **add value** to their operations.*

While most people feel they must write resumes and letters to get a job, few fully understand what they are doing or how they can best improve their communication skills. Only these few know the secrets to writing, producing, and distributing resumes and letters that spur the right people to invite them to job interviews.

The way most people write and distribute resumes and letters in today's job market would lead one to believe they are not really serious about finding a job nor are they concerned about the needs of employers. After all, why would anyone develop a resume or write a letter based upon someone else's examples? Or why would someone just list employment dates, positions, and job duties and responsibilities on their resume? And some even go so far as to include such personal information as their height, weight, hobbies, and children! Don't they know what they're doing? Have they no sense of focus? What is it they want – other than this job? Don't they know employers have very specific needs – someone who has potential for adding value to their operations?

Above all, employers want to know what you will do for them in the **future**. They want to **hire your capabilities** to solve their present and future problems. Since they want someone who can **add value** to their operations, your resume should clearly reflect your potential to add such value. Therefore, it's important that you clearly state an objective with corresponding capabilities relating to employers' needs. At the very least, your resumes and letters should indicate your value-added behavior.

Go for High Impact Communication

Few job seekers know how to write effective resumes and letters in today's job market. They have yet to learn the secrets to writing and distributing high impact resumes and letters that reflect their value in relation to employers' specific performance needs.

Since high impact resumes and letters are designed to grab the attention of employers who, in turn, invite you to job interviews, these documents must clearly communicate a message – your qualifications and capabilities – in relation to employers' needs. In contrast to the "canned" language found in resumes and letters produced from others' examples, high impact resumes and letters tell employers that you have the requisite skills and abilities to do the job. Moreover, these resumes and letters **persuade** employers to invite you to an interview where you will be asked to elaborate on the content of your resume.

To have **impact** in a sea of job search paper should be your single most important goal when writing and distributing resumes and letters. For to produce ritual documents and distribute them in the traditional manner is the best way **not** to be taken seriously in today's job market.

Become a Successful Communicator

Maybe you've wondered about differences in human abilities and how you compare to others. Why, for example, do some people know how to open the right doors to career success while others seem to struggle to get ahead? Are they more experienced or better qualified? Are they inherently more intelligent? Maybe they are just luckier. Or do they know something about the hiring process and employers that others do not?

Be it ability, intelligence, knowledge, drive, or sheer luck, getting ahead in today's job market at the very least requires key **communication skills**. Successful job hunters – those who find jobs that are right for them – do things differently from the typical job seeker. Among other things, they are skilled at writing and distributing high impact resumes and letters that open the doors to job interviews, offers, and career advancement. They also demonstrate excellent conversation skills that enable them to successfully network and interview. Overall, they are excellent communicators at each stage of their job search.

It is these writing and dissemination skills you, too, can learn. Within several hours, you can be communicating some of the most important messages of your life. Once you learn to develop a proper **message** and use the right **channels** to get the attention of employers, you will have unlocked the secrets of clearly communicating your capabilities to employers who, in turn, will invite you to job interviews. Transferring this important skill to you is our central purpose in writing this book.

The following pages are designed to put you into the class of successful job seekers. If you follow the steps in this book, you should become an effective resume and letter writer who also knows how to best distribute resumes and letters to the right people. You will gain important knowledge and skills for opening doors that once seemed closed to you. Better still, luck will come your way as you become better prepared to take advantage of new opportunities in today's highly competitive job market.

Use a Different Approach

Why produce another resume and letter writing book in an already crowded sea of such books? When we published the first edition of this book 24 years ago, we wrote it because we found few effective books on these subjects. While hundreds of resume and cover letter books have been published since then, few meet our standards of effectiveness. Most are compilations of resume and letter examples that primarily focus on writing and language;

few provide useful guidance on how to write, produce, distribute, and follow up your own written job search communication. Consequently, we still see a need for a different type of resume and letter writing book which does 13 things not commonly found in other books:

1. It should be **comprehensive and complete**, including each step in the resume and letter writing, production, distribution, and follow-up process.

2. It should include **alternative methods** for creating different types of resumes and letters rather than offer only "one best way."

3. It should be **linked to the larger career planning and job search** process as well as based upon the most advanced career development **methods**.

4. It should be **based on self-assessment**, which provides the building blocks for creating resumes and letters that reflect the "unique you" as well as clearly communicate interests, skills, abilities, goals, and predictions for future performance.

5. It should treat resume and letter writing as a **skill** that can be quickly learned and applied.

6. It should examine resume and letter writing and distribution as key **communication processes** requiring attention to the details of communication.

7. It should include **production, distribution, and follow-up skills** along with the more traditional writing skills.

8. It should deal with the **form, structure, content, and process** of writing, producing, distributing, and following up resumes and letters.

9. It should incorporate **self-evaluation mechanisms** in order to be a truly self-directed guide.

10. It should include **examples** of effective resumes and letters, but these examples must be designed to illustrate important principles.

11. It should be **easy to use and effective**, with a generous inclusion of self-directed exercises, illustrations, examples, and resources interspersed throughout a readable text.

12. It should be **up to date** in terms of including the latest information on paper and electronic resumes along with the increasing role of the Internet in writing and distributing resumes and letters.

13. It should **answer the most important questions** concerning the writing, production, distribution, and follow-up of resumes and letters.

Above all, you will find this is not another typical book on how to write "job-winning" resumes. Let's talk truth about what we are dealing with here. Most such books present page after page of examples of supposedly outstanding resumes for numerous occupational groups. Some make exaggerated claims of effectiveness – their examples represent resumes that resulted in real jobs, even though we know resumes don't get jobs and that most people eventually get jobs regardless of the presence, absence, or quality of their resumes. While some resume books include cover letters, only a few tell you what to do with your resume once you finish the writing exercise. Falsely claiming performance, most such books completely fail to address the real basis for performance – resume distribution and follow-up. Many implicitly or explicitly urge you to creatively plagiarize their questionable examples.

> *Employers want to know about the "unique you." If you write high impact resumes and letters, you will communicate a refreshing "unique you" to employers.*

Many of these traditional resume books do a disservice to both job seekers and employers. Quite frankly, they are a plague on the house of employers who must read hundreds of similar "model" products. For job seekers, these books are at best incomplete and at worst inaccurate; most are misleading. Imitated models simply are not the types of resumes and letters employers wish to receive. They want to know about the "unique you" in reference to their needs. They want to learn about **your predictable pattern of performance**. If you write high impact resumes and letters, you will communicate a refreshing "unique you" to employers.

What we find most incomplete and misleading is a failure to relate resume and letter writing skills to the larger career planning and job search processes. Resume and letter writing is only one step among other equally important job search activities, which include:

1. Identifying interests, skills, and abilities.
2. Specifying an objective.
3. Conducting research.
4. Networking for job leads.
5. Interviewing for jobs.
6. Negotiating terms of employment.

This book includes these other job search components in its examination of resumes and letters. In addition, the following pages are based upon years of successful experience with thousands of clients and in close collaboration with employers who read hundreds of resumes each year.

Uses and Users

Given the self-directed format of this book, you can learn to effectively write, produce, distribute, and follow up resumes and letters at your own pace, without external guidance. At the same time, we designed this book for use in classrooms where career planning and job search methods are taught. It requires no skills other than what most people already possess – the ability to learn, communicate, organize, analyze, and engage in new activities. If you want to achieve the maximum benefit from this book, you must demonstrate discipline, persistence, and creativity – the same qualities important to conducting an effective job search.

Many individuals should find this book useful. We purposefully wrote this book for a general audience, but it also will assist people with specialized needs. If you are a high school graduate or a college student entering, re-entering, or advancing in the job market, this book will respond to your needs. It can be used productively by anyone regardless of age, educational background, occupation, or employment situation. Young and old, new employees as well as retirees, can use this book effectively. Given the strong process and database orientations of this book, page after page will respond to the job and career needs of engineers, lawyers, teachers, students, auto workers, civil servants, salespersons, secretaries, and most other occupational groups. The inexperienced, underemployed, unemployed, and soon-to-be-displaced will find this book especially helpful in facing an uncertain and disquieting, yet hopeful, future.

What Comes Next

The remainder of the book is organized to be comprehensive, integrated, and easy to use. It begins with basic concepts, develops specific production steps and techniques, and ends with effective distribution and follow-up strategies. The next four chapters set the framework for writing resumes and letters from which all subsequent chapters flow.

- **Chapter 3** addresses 32 myths and 48 mistakes preventing individuals from effectively writing and distributing resumes and letters. The myths are challenged with corresponding realities for improving your effectiveness in the job search.

- **Chapter 4** introduces the concept of the resume in relation to a dynamic seven-step career development process embedded in philosophy, ethics, and methods.

- **Chapter 5** focuses on important organizational principles. It explains the overall time frame for producing, targeting, and distributing the resume, as well as outlines a hypothetical action plan for organizing your job search.

- **Chapter 6** examines alternative types of resumes and formats. It also outlines the internal structuring of resume elements, including the use of resume language.

- **Chapter 7** begins the actual production phase. This chapter takes you step-by-step through each section of the resume – statement of objective, summary of experience, functional abilities and skills, education, experience, personal information, etc. It includes the necessary worksheets so you can generate the key information for each section.

- **Chapter 8** guides you through the process by pulling your resume together, evaluating it according to both internal and external criteria, and producing and distributing it for maximum impact. This chapter also gives you useful hints for producing high quality at low cost.

- **Chapter 9** is your letter writing chapter. Here you examine resume, cover, approach, and thank-you letters in terms of their purpose, structure, production, and distribution.

- **Chapter 10** is the critical action chapter. Here you examine the best distribution methods for getting your resumes and letters in both the publicized and hidden job markets, with special emphasis on direct mail and networking techniques.

- **Chapter 11** addresses the key issues of implementation and follow-up. It stresses the importance of taking action and discusses when and how to follow up your resume and letter distribution activities. It includes important tips on telephone and letter writing follow-up methods to help you further reinforce and redirect your marketing strategies for maximum effect.

- **Chapter 12** concludes with a discussion of anticipated results, the importance of further integrating the resume and letter writing phases into your overall job search campaign, and the need for persistence, discipline, and follow-through.

- **Chapter 13** addresses the special case of electronic resumes – plain-text, formatted, HTML, video, and multimedia. In contrast to conventional resumes, this chapter outlines a separate set of principles for producing and distributing such resumes, as well as critiques the effectiveness of these resumes in a rapidly changing technology-driven job market.

- **Chapter 14** pulls together over 100 major issues relevant to resumes and letters and addresses each within a handy question/answer format. Examining 110 key questions, this chapter provides the latest advice on writing, producing, distributing, and following up resumes and letters. The chapter serves as a quick advisory for answering many of the most difficult questions concerning resumes, letters, and the job search.

- **Four appendices** provide examples of resumes and letters that follow the principles outlined in previous chapters. Each example illustrates how these principles are incorporated into finished high impact products, including the transformation of a weak traditional chronological resume into improved chronological, functional, and combination resumes and a resume letter. The final appendix includes a unique collection of resumes and letters produced by leading career professionals.

- **The final section** of the book includes a listing of job search resources that can be conveniently ordered through Impact Publications or accessed through their online bookstore. This is your career planning resource center, offering many titles that may be difficult to find in local libraries and bookstores.

Implement and Follow Through

Resumes and letters are key communication **products** for promoting a larger job search **process**. You produce and distribute them in order to get job interviews which hopefully lead to job offers. If produced and marketed properly, resumes and letters have desired results. They especially work well for individuals who are committed to following through with the step-by-step procedures outlined in this book.

Learning how to write a resume and letter tells you little about actual effectiveness in **using** them in the job market. The single most important reason many job seekers fail to achieve success is their inability to **implement and follow through**. Understanding a process as well as knowing how to put good form and content into your resume and letters are critical first steps for achieving success – but they are not enough. Success comes to those who follow through in practicing each step in the process. At the very least, this means sharpening your pencils, completing the exercises, drafting resumes and letters, evaluating the drafts, producing, distributing, and following up the final product. This takes time and effort; it involves mundane mechanical activities as well as higher-level analytical, problem-solving activities.

Taking shortcuts is the sure way to cut short your job search effectiveness! The benefits you will reap from this book are in direct proportion to the amount of time you devote to producing the final product. As is so often the case, there are no such things as free lunches or quick and easy ways to job placement.

We wish you well in your job search and hope that you **implement** with gusto! In so doing, you may also experience what many of our students and clients report with increasing frequency – greater self-confidence, self-esteem, career direction, and job satis-faction. Most importantly, they get **results** from their high impact resumes and letters.

We're convinced the additional time and effort you devote to making your resumes and letters more effective are well worth the investment. At the very minimum, the quality of resumes and letters you produce reflects how you feel about yourself – and employers. Employers know this and they interpret your resumes and letters accordingly.

3

32 Myths and 48 Mistakes You Shouldn't Make

NUMEROUS MYTHS AND MISTAKES surround the writing, production, distribution, and follow-up of resumes and job search letters. Many are harmless misunderstandings about how the job market works. Others are more embarrassing and result in job search mistakes that prevent individuals from becoming effective in today's job market. This should not happen to you.

Major Myths and Realities

Many job seekers muddle through the job market with questionable perceptions of how it works. Few understand how to conduct an effective job search, from writing a resume to negotiating compensation. Even fewer understand the perspectives of employers: what they expect from candidates, how they screen resumes, and why they choose to interview candidate X over candidates Y and Z. Combining facts, stereotypes, myths, and folklore – gained from a mixture of logic, experience, and advice from well-meaning individuals – many job seekers engage in random acts that take them down several unproductive paths.

Numerous myths are responsible for some of the major errors involved in writing and distributing resumes and letters. Understanding these myths and corresponding realities, as well as how they relate to the larger job search, is the first step toward building effective resume and letter writing skills.

Over the years we have discovered 32 recurring myths and corresponding realities relating to resumes, letters, and the job search. Let's take a look at these myths and realities as we prepare for writing and distributing your written communication to potential employers. Examined individually, the corresponding realities illustrate **key principles** to guide you in writing, distributing, and following up your resumes and letters. Taken together, the realities make up an important part of a larger American job search folklore which continues to guide – rather than misguide as did the myths – many job hunters.

Getting a Job

MYTH 1:   **Anyone can find a job; all you need to know is how to find a job.**

REALITY: This "form versus substance" myth is often associated with career counselors who were raised on popular career planning exhortations of the 1970s
and 1980s that stressed the importance of having positive attitudes and
self-esteem, setting goals, dressing for success, and using interpersonal
strategies for finding jobs. While such approaches may work well in an industrial society with low unemployment, they constitute myths in a post-in-
dustrial, high-tech society which re-
quires employees to demonstrate both
intelligence and concrete work skills
as well as a **willingness to relocate** to
new communities offering greater job
opportunities. For example, many of today's unemployed are highly skilled in
the old technology of the industrial
society, but they live and own homes in
economically depressed communities.
These people lack the necessary **skills
and mobility** required for getting jobs
in high-tech, growth communities.
Knowing job search skills alone will not
help these people. Indeed, such advice and knowledge will most likely frustrate highly motivated individuals who possess skills appropriate for old
technology.

> *This is a highly
> decentralized, frag-
> mented, and chaotic
> job market where job
> information is at best
> incomplete. Most of
> the best jobs are un-
> covered through
> word-of-mouth.*

MYTH 2:   **The best way to find a job is to respond to classified ads, use
employment agencies, submit applications, and mail and e-mail
resumes, cover letters, and employment data to personnel offices
and online databases.**

REALITY: Many people do get jobs by following such formalized application and
recruitment procedures. However, these are not necessarily the most effective ways to get the best jobs – those offering good pay, advancement opportunities, and an appropriate "fit" with one's abilities and goals. For this
approach makes two questionable assumptions about the structure of the
job market and how applicants should relate to it. The first assumption
deals with how the job market operates:

> **Assumption #1:** There is an organized, coherent, and centralized
> job market "out there" where one can get information and job
> vacancies.

Despite periodic efforts to create a centralized job market – including recent
electronic job bank initiatives organized through the U.S. Department of
Labor (America's Job Bank – www.ajb.dni.us) and aggressively developed
through Monster.com – in reality no such market exists in either the public

or private sector. Instead, the so-called "job market" is highly decentralized, fragmented, and chaotic. Job vacancy information in this market is at best incomplete, skewed, and unrepresentative of available job opportunities at any particular moment. Classified ads, agencies, and personnel offices tend to list low paying yet highly competitive jobs. Most of the best jobs – high level, excellent pay, least competitive – are neither listed nor advertised; they are primarily uncovered through word-of-mouth and executive recruiters. When seeking employment, your most fruitful strategy will be to conduct research and informational interviews on what is called the "hidden job market."

The second assumption deals with how you should relate to this job market:

> **Assumption #2:** You should try to alter your goals and abilities so they will better fit into existing vacancies rather than find a job directly related to your strengths.

This may be a formula for future job unhappiness. If you want to find a job fit for you rather than try to fit yourself into a job, you must use another job search strategy based upon a different set of assumptions regarding how you should relate your goals and abilities to the world of work.

MYTH 3:	**A good resume and cover letter will get me a job.**
REALITY:	Resumes and letters don't get jobs – they advertise you for interviews. Your resume and letters are **marketing tools** designed to communicate your qualifications to employers. From the perspective of employers, resumes and letters are used to screen candidates – who are basically strangers to employers – for interviews. Few people ever get hired on the basis of their resume and letters. In fact, over 95 percent of employers indicate they hire on the basis of a personal interview. If you believe your cleverly crafted resume and letters have some magical quality, you may end up engaging in a whole series of useless – and embarrassing – resume and letter writing activities.
MYTH 4:	**The candidate with the best education, skills, and experience will get the job.**
REALITY:	Employers hire individuals for many different reasons. Education, skills, and experience – major information categories appearing on your resume – are only a few of their hiring criteria. Surprising to some candidates, these criteria may **not** be the most important in the eyes of many employers. If, for example, employers only hired on the basis of education, skills, and experience, they would not need to interview candidates. Such static and redundant information is available in applications and resumes. Employers interview because they want to see a warm body – how you look and interact with them and how you will fit into their organization. They can get other information from additional sources. Indeed, the most important reason for hiring you is that the employer "likes" you. How "likes" is defined will vary from one employer and organization to another. In some

cases the employer "likes" you because your educational background, demonstrated skills, and experience are perfect fits for the position. In other cases the employer "likes" you because of your style and personality, as well as a gut feeling that you are the right person for the job. The employer will determine or confirm these feelings in the actual job interview. So be prepared in the interview to communicate a great deal of information about yourself other than what the employer already knows – education, skills, and experience.

> *The most important reason for hiring you is that the employer "likes" you.*

MYTH 5: **Paper resumes are obsolete in today's new high-tech job market. Employment websites and employers primarily want to receive electronic and e-mailed resumes.**

REALITY: You need to produce **both** a paper and an electronic resume. You are well advised to start by producing a paper resume and then create an electronic resume. Electronic and e-mailed resumes are designed by job seekers for high speed distribution to resume databases and employer. They enable employers to quickly store, retrieve, and analyze large numbers of resumes. Paper resumes still play an important role in the job search. Many small businesses, which employ 85 percent of workers, handling paper resumes. Indeed, companies with fewer than 50 employees, can easily deal with paper resumes. Job seekers need paper resumes when networking for information, advice, and referrals; when attending job fairs; and when interviewing for a job.

MYTH 6: **You can plan all you want, but getting a job is really a function of good luck.**

REALITY: Luck is a function of being in the right place at the right time to take advantage of opportunities that come your way. But how do you plan your luck? The best way to have luck come your way is to plan to be in many different places at many different times. You can do this by putting together an excellent resume and marketing it within both the advertised and hidden job markets. If you are redundant, persistent, and tenacious – rather than aggressive, obnoxious, and a pest – in implementing your plans, luck may strike you many times!

Planning Resume Content

MYTH 7: **The best type of resume is one that outlines employment history by job titles, responsibilities, and inclusive employment dates.**

REALITY: This is one type of resume which may or may not be good for you. It tends to be the traditional chronological or "obituary" resume. It's filled with historical "what" information – what work you did, in what organizations, over what period of time. This type of resume may tell employers little about what you can do for them. You should choose a resume format that clearly communicates your major strengths – not your history – to employers in relation to your goals and skills as well as the employer's needs. Your choices include variations of the chronological, functional, and combination resumes – each offering different advantages and disadvantages.

MYTH 8:   **It's not necessary to put an objective on the resume.**

REALITY: Survey research (McLean Group and Career Masters Institute) with employers validates the importance of objectives on resumes: employers are especially attracted to resumes including objectives that either state an applicant's career goal (what he or she wants to do career-wise) or what an applicant can do for the organization. These findings are not surprising when viewed from organizational and screening perspectives. Employers prefer coherent resumes that are easy to read and interpret. After all, what quickly ties your resume together in communicating to employers what it is you both want and can do? An objective, presented at the very top of your resume, becomes the central focus from which all other elements in your resume should flow. The objective gives the resume organization, coherence, and direction. It tells employers exactly who you are in terms of your goals and skills.

> *An objective becomes the central focus from which all other elements in your resume should flow.*

If properly written, your objective will become one of the most powerful and effective statements on your resume. Without an objective, you force the employer to "interpret" your resume. He or she must analyze and synthesize the discrete elements in each of your categories and draw conclusions about your capabilities and goals which may or may not be valid. This can be a very time-consuming exercise, something few employers feel motivated to do.

Thus, it is to your advantage to set the agenda – control the flow and interpretation of your qualifications and capabilities by stating the objective. Most people who object to including an objective on a resume (1) do not understand the importance of integrating all elements in the resume around key goals and skills, (2) do not know how to develop a good employer-centered objective, or (3) are misinformed because they believe they must change the objective for each employer – an obvious confession they do not know what they really want to do. Developing a resume objective is not a difficult task. If nothing else, stating an objective on your resume is a thoughtful thing to do for the employer. And always remember, employers "like" to hire such thoughtful people!

MYTH: 9:   **Most employers appreciate long resumes because they include more information for screening candidates than short resumes.**

REALITY: Employers prefer receiving one- or two-page resumes. Longer resumes lose the interest and attention of readers. They usually lack a focus, are filled with extraneous information, need editing, and are oriented toward the applicant's past rather than the employer's future. If you know how to write high impact resumes, you can put all of your capabilities into a one- to two-page format. These resumes only include enough information to persuade employers to call you for an interview. But this one- to two-page rule does not apply to all employment situations. Individuals applying for academic and international jobs, for example, may be expected to write a five- to ten-page curriculum vitae (CV) rather than a one- to two-page resume. In these special situations the CV is actually a traditional chronological resume prominently displaying dates, job titles, responsibilities, and publications.

MYTH 10:   **It's okay to put salary expectations on a resume.**

REALITY: One of the worst things you can do is to mention salary on your resume. Remember, the purpose of your resume is to get an interview. Only during the interview, preferably toward the end, should you discuss salary. And before you discuss salary, you want to demonstrate your **value** to employers as well as learn about the **worth** of the position. Only after you make your impression and gather information on the job, can you realistically talk about salary. You can't do this if you prematurely mention salary on your resume.

> *The purpose of your resume is to get an interview. Salary should be a subject for the interview – not your resume.*

MYTH 11:   **Contact information (name, address, and phone numbers) should appear in the left-hand corner of your resume.**

REALITY: You can choose from a variety of resume formats which place the contact information in several different positions at the top of the resume. Choose the one that best complements the remaining layout and style of the resume.

MYTH 12:   **You should not include your hobbies or any personal statements on a resume.**

REALITY: In general this is true. However, there are exceptions which would challenge this rule as a myth. If you have a hobby or a personal statement that can strengthen your objective in relation to the employer's needs, do include it on your resume. For example, if a job calls for someone who is outgoing and energetic, you would not want to include a hobby or personal statement that indicates that you are a very private and sedentary person, such as *"enjoy reading and writing"* or *"collect stamps."* But *"enjoy organizing community fund drives"* and *"compete in the Boston Marathon"* might be very appropriate statements for your resume. Such statements further emphasize the "unique you" in relation to your capabilities, the requirements for the position, and the employer's needs. Again, your resume should be a quick and coherent read for the employer who is trying to screen you in reference to his or her hiring criteria. Personal statements that contribute to such a quick and easy read, and emphasize your unique qualifications, should be included on your resume. They can enhance your candidacy.

MYTH 13: **You should list your references on the resume so the employer can check them before conducting the interview.**

REALITY: Never include references on your resume. The closest you should ever get to doing so is to include this statement at the very end: "References available upon request." **You** want to control your references for the interview. You should take a list of references appropriate for the position you will interview for with you to the interview. The interviewer may ask you for this list at the end of the interview. If you put references on your resume, the employer might call someone who has no idea you are applying for a particular job. The conversation could be embarrassing. As a simple courtesy, you should ask the person's permission to use them as a reference. This will alert them that someone may call, and it gives you the opportunity to brief them about the position and how your skills best fit the employer's needs. Surprisingly, many employers don't follow through by contacting references.

> ***Never*** *put your references on a resume.* ***You*** *want to control your references for the interview.*

Producing the Resume

MYTH 14: **You should try to get as much information as possible on each page of your resume.**

REALITY: Each page of your resume should be appealing to the eye. It should make an immediate favorable impression, be inviting and easy to read, and look professional. You achieve these qualities by using a variety of layout, type style, highlighting, and emphasizing techniques. When formatting each section of your resume, be sure to make generous use of white space. Bullet and underline items for emphasis. If you try to cram a great deal on each page, your resume will look cluttered and uninviting to the reader. However, make sure you do not over-use such emphasizing techniques.

MYTH 15: **You should have your resume produced by a graphic designer and professionally printed.**

REALITY: You may want to go to the expense of hiring a graphic designer and printing, depending on your audience. However, for most positions, it is not necessary to go to such an extreme in order to impress your reader. Just make sure your resume looks first-class and professional. Employers are more interested in the content of your resume – documented work history, accomplishments, education, and objective related to their specific hiring needs – than in the "dress for success" visual elements. In some cases a resume produced by a graphic designer may look too professional for the type of position you are applying for and thus may communicate that you had someone else do your resume. Most word processing programs (i.e., Word or WordPerfect) using laser printers produce good quality documents, and many copy machines will give you original quality copies. If you use a word processing program, make sure you use a letter quality or laser printer. Dot matrix printers and many near letter quality printers do not produce professional copy. They look mass produced. Also, avoid creating multi-colored resumes just because you have a color printer. Such resumes often look amateurish and are distracting, if not irritating, to the reader.

MYTH 16: **The weight and color of the resume's paper and ink is unimportant to employers.**

REALTY: Weight, paper color, and ink do count, but how much they count in comparison to resume content is difficult to say. These are the very first things the employer sees and feels when receiving your resume. They make an important initial impression. If your resume doesn't look and feel right during the first five seconds, the reader may not be interested in reading the contents of your resume. Make a good initial impression by selecting a good weight and color of paper. Your resume should have a substantive feel to the touch – use nothing less than 20-pound paper that also has some texture. But

Weight, paper color, and ink do count. They make an important initial impression.

don't go to extremes with a very heavy and roughly textured paper. Stay with conservative paper colors: white, off-white, ivory, light tan, or light grey. Your choice of ink colors should also be conservative – black, navy, or dark brown. If, on the other hand, you are applying for a less conventional position, especially one in graphic design, fine arts, film, interior design, or advertising, where creativity is encouraged on resumes, you may decide to go with more daring paper and ink colors. We still like resumes printed on good quality white paper with black ink.

MYTH 17: **You should make at least 100 copies of your resume.**

REALITY: Make only as many as you need – which may be only one. Since most copy machines produce excellent quality copies, you have the flexibility to produce as many as you need. If you word process your resume, you can customize each resume for each position for which you apply. Your production needs should be largely determined by your strategy for distributing your resume.

Writing Letters

MYTH 18: **It's okay to send your resume to an employer without an accompanying cover letter.**

REALITY: Only if you want the employer to think his or her position and employment opportunity are not important. This myth is propagated by those who believe employers are too busy to read but not too busy to be pestered by cold telephone calls and networkers who invite themselves to interviews. Employers initially prefer succinct written communications. It enables them to screen candidates in and out for the next stage of the hiring process – a telephone screening interview. Sending a resume without a cover letter is like going to a job interview barefoot – your application is incomplete and your resume is not being properly communicated for action. Cover letters should **always** accompany resumes that are sent through the mail. They help position your interests and qualifications in relation to the employer's needs as well as indicate what action will be taken next. Above all, they give employers signals of your personality, style, and likability – important elements in the hiring decision.

> *Sending a resume without a cover letter is like going to a job interview barefoot.*

MYTH 19:   **The purpose of a cover letter is to introduce your resume to an employer.**

REALITY: A cover letter should be much more than mere cover for a resume. Indeed, it may be a misnomer to call these letters "cover letters." It's best to think of them as "interview generating" communications – a form of written communication that goes beyond the resume. Unlike a resume, which tends to follow a standard, conventional format, in a cover letter you can be more creative and unconventional. If written properly, the cover letter format enables you to express important qualities sought by employers in the job interview – your personality, style, energy, and enthusiasm. Like good advertising copy, your cover letter should be the "sizzle" or headline accompanying your high impact resume. After all, the purpose of a cover letter should be to get the employer to **take action** on your resume. Consequently, the whole structure of your cover letter should focus on persuading the employer to invite you for a job interview. Make your cover letter grab the attention of the reader and spur him or her to read your resume in depth and call you for an interview.

MYTH 20:   **End your letter indicating that you expect to hear from the employer: "*I look forward to hearing from you.*"**

REALITY: What do you expect will happen when you close your letter in this manner? Probably nothing. While this is a polite and acceptable way of closing such a letter, it is a rather empty statement of hope – not one of action. Remember, you always want specific **actions** to result from your written communication. Any type of action – positive or negative – should help you move on to the next stage of your job search with this or other potential employers. This standard closing is likely to result in no action on the part of the employer, who is by definition a busy person. It's better to indicate that **you** will take initiative in contacting the employer in response to your letter and resume. End your letter with an action statement similar to this one:

> I'll give you a call Thursday afternoon to answer any questions you may have regarding my interests and qualifications.

Such an action statement, in effect, invites you to a telephone interview – the first step to getting a face-to-face job interview. While some employers may avoid your telephone call, at least you will get some action in reference to your letter and resume. If, for example, you call on Thursday afternoon and the employer is not available to take your call, leave a message that you called in reference to your letter. Chances are the employer is expecting your call and will remember you because you are taking this initiative. In some cases, the employer will tell you frankly that you are no longer under consideration. While disappointing, this rejection has a positive side – it clarifies your status so you no longer need to waste your time nor engage in wishful thinking about the status of your application with this employer. Go on to others who may prove more responsive. In other cases, your phone call may result in getting a face-to-face interview early in the application process with this employer. Taking action in this manner will at least give you useful information that will bring your application nearer to closure. But make sure you call at the time you say you will call. If the employer expects your call on Thursday afternoon and you forget to do so, you prematurely communicate a negative message to the employer – you lack follow-through. Always do what you say you will do and in a timely fashion.

> *In a cover letter you can express important qualities often looked for by employers in the job interview – your personality, style, energy, and enthusiasm.*

MYTH 21: **The cover letter should attempt to sell the employer on your qualifications.**

REALITY: The cover letter should command attention and nicely provide an introduction to your resume. This letter should be professional, polite, personable, and to the point. The letter affords you an opportunity to demonstrate your personality and writing skills in a letter format. Remember, your resume is supposed to sell the employer on you. Your letter should be the sizzle accompanying the sale. The letter should mention your interest in the position, highlight your major strengths in relation to the position, and ask the employer for an opportunity to interview for the position. Avoid repeating in this letter what the reader will find in your resume. Keep the letter to one page.

MYTH 22: **Handwritten cover letters have a greater impact on employers than typed cover letters.**

REALITY: Handwritten cover letters are inappropriate as are scribbled notes on or attached to a resume. They are **too** personal and look unprofessional when applying for a job. If you are a professional, you want to demonstrate that you can present yourself to others in the most professional manner possible. Confine your handwriting activities to your signature only. The letter should be typed on a good quality machine – preferably a letter quality printer. When using a word processing program, it's best to justify the left margin only. Fully justified margins look too formal.

MYTH 23: **Letters are not very important in a job search. The only letter you need to write is a formal cover letter.**

REALITY: Your letters actually may be more important than your resume. In fact, cover letters are only one of several types of letters you should write during your job search. The other letters are some of the best kept secrets of effective job seekers. They may become your most powerful marketing tools:

- Resume letters
- Approach letters
- Thank-you letters

Different types of thank-you letters should be written on various job search occasions:

- Post-job interview
- After an informational interview
- Responding to a rejection
- Withdrawing from consideration
- Accepting a job offer
- Terminating employment

These are some of the most neglected yet most important forms of written communications in any job search. If you write these letters, your job search may take you much further than you expected!

MYTH 24: **A cover letter should be only one paragraph in length.**

REALITY: Cover letters should say something about you to the employer. While you should try to keep your letter short and to the point, don't limit it to a few lines. Remember what you are trying to do – get the employer to take action in reference to your interests and qualifications as outlined in your resume. A well constructed cover letter should be organized like advertising copy:

- catch the reader's attention
- persuade the reader about you (you are the product)
- convince the reader with more evidence
- move the reader to acquire your service or you

Since you need to accomplish a great deal in your letter, this letter will probably run three paragraphs and be confined to one page.

Distributing Resumes and Letters

MYTH 25: **It is best to send out numerous resumes and letters to prospective employers in the hope that a few will invite you to an interview.**

REALITY: Yes, if you play the odds, someone might call you. In fact, if you broadcast resumes and letters to 1,000 employers, you may have two or three invite you to an interview. However, this broadcast approach is most appropriate for people who are in desperate need of a job or who don't know what they want to do. Some inexpensive executive resume e-mail blasting services ($59+ to e-mail your resume to 10,000 ostensibly interested parties – see www.blastmyresume.com, www.resumeblaster.com, www.executiveagent. com), which primarily e-mail resumes to headhunters, claim remarkable results. In general, however, such distributed resumes and letters tend to communicate a "give-me-a-job" mentality. This non-focused approach will initially give you a false sense of making progress with your job search because it involves a major expenditure of time and money. But it will most likely increase your level of frustration when you receive few replies, with most of those being rejections. You should avoid this approach. Instead, concentrate on targeting your resume on particular organizations, employers, and positions that would best fit into your particular mix of skills and objectives. This approach will require you to network for information and job leads. As such, you will seldom send a resume and cover letter through the mail. Instead, you will write numerous approach and thank-you letters for the purpose of inviting yourself to interviews. Your resume never accompanies these letters.

> *The broadcast approach is most appropriate for people who are in desperate need of a job.*

MYTH 26: **When conducting an informational interview, you should present your resume at the beginning of the meeting.**

REALITY: In this type of interview, never ever introduce yourself with your resume. Instead, your resume should be presented at the very **end** of the informational interview. Keep in mind that the purpose of an informational interview is to get information, advice, and referrals. You are **not** asking for a job. If you present your resume at the beginning of such an interview, you give the impression that you are looking for a job. Near the end of the interview you want to ask the interviewer to review your resume and give you advice on how to strengthen it and to whom to send it.

Following Up Your Communication

MYTH 27:   **Once you distribute your resume and letters, there is little you can do other than wait to be called for an interview.**

REALITY: If you do nothing, you are likely to get nothing. There are many things you can do. First, you can write more letters to inquire about your application status. Second, you can telephone the employer for more information on

> *If you do nothing, you are likely to get nothing.*

when the interview and hiring decisions will take place. Third, you can telephone to request an interview at a convenient time. The first approach will likely result in no response. The second approach will probably give you an inconclusive answer. The third approach will give you a *"yes"* or *"no."* We prefer the third approach.

MYTH 28:   **The best way to follow up on your application and resume is to write a letter of inquiry.**

REALITY: Employers are busy people who do not have time to read all their e-mail and snail mail, much less sit down to write letters. Use the telephone instead. It's much more efficient and effective. Most important of all, you should monitor your resumes and letters by keeping records and regularly following up on your job search initiatives. Be sure to keep good records of all correspondence, telephone conversations, and meetings. Keep a separate paper or electronic file on each prospective employer. Record your contact information and dates for all employers on a master record form so you can quickly evaluate the present status of your contacts as well as use it as a handy reference.

Using New Resume Approaches

MYTH 29:   **Electronic resumes are the wave of the future. You must write and distribute them in order to get a good job.**

REALITY: During the past 10 years electronic resumes (scannable, e-mailable, HTML, video, and multimedia) have played an important role in the job search and recruitment processes. Since large employers increasingly used Optical Character Recognition (OCR) software to scan resumes as well as requested applicants to e-mail their resumes, job seekers were well advised to write both scannable and ASCII versions of their resumes in response to the technological requirements of such employers.

However, numerous changes have taken place during the past few years due to rapid advances in resume screening and processing technology. For example, scannable resumes have become obsolete, as have resumes sent in ASCII format. Software advances now allow employers to receive resumes in other formats. Ugly duckling ASCII resumes are disappearing as employers increasingly receive resumes via the Internet with all the "dress for success" elements that usually come with nicely crafted paper resumes. Many employers now require applicants to complete an online form that produces a "profile" in lieu of a regular resume. Therefore, given this transition period in resume technology, it is in your interests to understand the particular resume requirements of individual employers by asking what type of resume they prefer receiving, especially their technology requirements. At present no single electronic resume fits all employers.

If you are still writing only paper resumes, you should educate yourself on writing "computer friendly" and e-mail versions of your resume based on the principles of electronic resumes. These principles, along with examples, are outlined in several resume books: Fred Jandt and Mary Nemnich, *Cyberspace Resume Kit*, Rebecca Smith, *Electronic Resumes and Online Networking*, Pat Criscito, *e-Resumes*, and Susan Britton Whitcomb and Pat Kendall, *e-Resumes*. However, some of these books may be obsolete given recent changes in electronic resumes and online applicant systems. Rebecca Smith also provides useful advice on electronic resumes through her website: www.eresumes.com.

Electronic resumes differ from conventional resumes. Most are structured around "keywords" or nouns which stress capabilities. While such resumes may be excellent candidates for searchable resume databases and online applicant systems, they may be weak documents for human readers. Keep in mind that electronic resumes are primarily written for high-tech distribution systems (employment databases) rather than for human beings. Since humans interview and hire, you should first create a resume that follows the principles of human communication. For now, we also recommend developing a separate resume designed for e-mail transmission. We're less enthusiastic about HTML, video, and multimedia resumes.

> *Develop separate resumes designed for the different applicant screening requirements of employers.*

For the most recent update on the changing technology of employers for receiving, screening, and processing resumes, see Joyce Lain Kennedy's latest version of *Resumes for Dummies* (John Wiley & Sons), where she focuses on the return of the "beautiful resume" with the new technology.

At the same time, keep in mind that the resume requirements of employers differ given the size of the company. A company with 50,000 employees and an over-worked HR department will more likely be on the technological cutting edge for receiving, screening, and processing resumes than a company with only 25 employees. A large company must automate many aspects of the initial application process, whereas a small company can still handle applicants the old-fashioned way – paper and telephone. Your job is to understand the needs of different employers and craft different versions of your resume that respond to different technological requirements.

MYTH 30: **Individuals who include their resumes in resume banks or post them online in resume databases are more likely to get high paying jobs than those that don't.**

REALITY: During the past 15 years most electronic resume banks have become victims of the "free" Internet. They have either gone out of business or have transformed their operations by becoming resume databases on the Internet. While some resume banks and databases still charge users monthly or yearly membership fees, most are now supported by employers who advertise on the sites and/or pay fees to access resumes online through particular Internet employment sites. Essentially a high-tech approach for broadcasting resumes, inclusion of your resume in these resume banks and databases means your resume literally works 24 hours a day.

Major employers increasingly use these resume banks and databases for locating qualified candidates, especially for screening individuals with technical skills. And we know some individuals who join these resume banks do get jobs. However, there is no evidence that most people belonging to these groups ever get interviews or jobs through such membership. Nor is there any evidence that membership results in higher paying jobs than nonmembership.

The real advantage of such groups is this: they open new channels for contacting employers whom you might not otherwise come into contact with. Indeed, some employers only use these resume banks and databases for locating certain types of candidates rather than use more traditional channels, such as newspapers and employment offices, for advertising positions and recruiting candidates. Employers find the Internet to be a much cheaper way of recruiting personnel than through the more traditional approach of purchasing classified ads or hiring employment firms or headhunters.

MYTH 31: **The video resume is the wave of the future. You need to develop a video resume and send it to prospective employers.**

REALITY: The video resume is a novel approach to the employment process. However, since it is video-based, it's really a misnomer to call these videos a form of "resume." The so-called video resume functions more as a screening interview than a resume. Remember, the purpose of a resume is to get an interview. A video includes key elements that are best presented in a face-to-face interview – verbal and nonverbal communication. Unless requested by an employer in lieu of a traditional resume, we recommend avoiding the use of a video resume. However, if you are applying for a position that requires good presentation skills best demonstrated in the video format, such as in sales, broadcasting, and entertainment, a video resume may be the perfect approach to employers. But make sure you do a first-class job in developing the video. Avoid amateur productions that will probably reflect badly on your skills.

MYTH 32: **You should develop your own home page on the Internet and direct employers to your site.**

REALITY: Do this only if you are a real professional and can customize your site to particular employers. Like the video resume, home pages can be double-edged swords. Some employers may like them, but others may dislike them. Your particular site may reflect poorly on your qualifications, especially if it is not designed like a resume, i.e., stresses your accomplishments and goals. Furthermore, since most employers are too busy trying to get through paper resumes and letters and handling resumes submitted online, few have the time or desire to spend time accessing your Internet site – unless your paper and/or e-mailed resume sufficiently motivate them to do so. Like viewing videos, accessing sites on the Internet takes time. Remember, employers can still screen a paper resume and letter within 30 seconds! Why would they want to spend 15 minutes trying to access and review your site when they could be dispensing with another 30 resumes and letters during that time? If you decide to go this route, you'll need to give employers a good reason why they should invest such time looking for you on the Internet!

> *Like the video resume, home pages can be double-edged swords. Some employers may like them, but others don't.*

But these myths and realities only touch the surface of understanding how to create high impact resumes and letters. You also need to know something about common resume errors. Employers report observing numerous resume errors, from writing to follow-up, that candidates should avoid.

27 Writing Mistakes to Avoid

A resume must first get written – and written well. And it is at the initial writing stage that many deadly errors are made. The most common mistakes occur when writers fail to keep the purpose of their resume in mind – to clearly communicate your qualifications to employers whom you want to motivate to invite you to a job interview.

Most writing errors kill a resume even before it gets fully read. At best these errors leave negative impressions which are difficult to overcome at this or any other point in the hiring process. Remember, hiring officials have two major inclusion/exclusion concerns in mind when reading your resume:

- They are looking for excuses to eliminate you from further consideration.

- They are looking for evidence to consider you for a job interview – do you match their requirements and how much value will you give them?

When you make an error, you provide supports for being eliminated from further consideration. Concentrate, instead, on providing supports for being **considered** for a job.

Make sure your resume is not "dead on arrival." To ensure against this, avoid these most 27 common writing errors reported by employers:

1. Not related to the reader's interests or needs.
2. Fails to represent the real candidate.
3. Unrelated to the position in question.
4. Too long, short, or condensed.
5. Unattractive with a poorly designed format, small type style, and crowded copy.
6. Misspellings, bad grammar, wordiness, and repetition.
7. Punctuation errors.
8. Lengthy phrases, long sentences, and awkward paragraphs.
9. Slick, amateurish, or "gimmicky" – appears over-produced.
10. Boastful, egocentric, and aggressive.
11. Dishonest, untrustworthy, or suspicious information.
12. Missing critical categories, such as experience, skills, and education.
13. Unexplained time gaps between jobs.
14. Difficult to interpret because of poor organization and lack of focus – uncertain what the person has done or can do.
15. Too many jobs in a short period of time – a job hopper with little evidence of career advancement.
16. No evidence of past accomplishments or a pattern of performance from which to predict future performance; primarily focuses on formal duties and responsibilities that come with previous jobs.
17. Lacks credibility and content – includes much fluff and "canned" resume language.
18. States a strange, unclear, or vague objective.
19. Appears over-qualified or under-qualified for the position.
20. Includes distracting personal information (photo, height, weight, age) that does not enhance the resume nor the candidate.
21. Fails to include critical contact information (telephone number and e-mail address) and uses an anonymous address (P.O. Box number).
22. Uses jargon and abbreviations unfamiliar to the reader.
23. Embellishes name with formal titles, middle names, and nicknames which makes the candidate seem odd or somewhat strange.
24. Repeatedly refers to "I" and appears self-centered.
25. Includes obvious self-serving references that raise credibility questions.
26. Sloppy, with handwritten corrections – crosses out "married" and writes "single"!
27. Includes red flag information such as being incarcerated, fired, lawsuits or claims, health or performance problems, or stating salary figures, including salary requirements, that may be too high or too low.

This listing of writing errors and possible reader responses emphasizes how important **both** form and content are when writing a resume with purpose. You must select an important form, arrange each element in an attractive manner, and provide the necessary substance to grab the attention of the reader and move him or her to action. And all these elements of good resume writing must be related to the needs of your audience. If not, you may quickly kill your resume by committing some of these deadly errors.

Remember, hiring officials are busy people who only devote a few seconds to reading a resume. They quickly identify errors that will effectively remove you from consideration.

They want to see you error-free in writing and on paper so they can concentrate on what they most need to do – evaluate your qualifications prior to exchanging e-mails, speaking with you over the telephone, and meeting you in person.

21 Production, Distribution, and Follow-Up Errors

While writing errors are the most common reasons for eliminating candidates from consideration, several other errors relate to the production, distribution, and follow-up of resumes. Committing any of these 21 additional errors also can quickly eliminate you from consideration:

28. Poorly typed and reproduced – hard to read.
29. Produced on odd-sized paper.
30. Printed on poor quality paper or on extremely thin or thick paper.
31. Includes handwritten corrections or changes (crosses out "married" and writes in "single"!).
32. Soiled with coffee stains, hand prints, or ink marks.
33. Sent to the wrong person or department.
34. Sent to "To Whom It May Concern," "Dear Sir," or "info@."
35. E-mailed as an attachment which could have a virus if opened.
36. Enclosed in a tiny envelope that requires the resume to be unfolded and flattened several times.
37. Arrived without proper postage – the employer gets to pay the extra!
38. Sent the resume and letter by the slowest postage rate possible.
39. Envelope double-sealed with tape and is indestructible – nearly impossible to open by conventional means!
40. Back of envelope included a handwritten note indicating something is missing on the enclosed resume, such as your telephone number or e-mail address.
41. Resume taped to the inside of the envelope, an old European habit practiced by paranoid letter writers. Need to destroy the envelope and perhaps also the resume to get it out of the envelope.
42. Accompanied by extraneous or inappropriate enclosures which were not requested, such as copies of self-serving letters of recommendations, transcripts, or samples of work.
43. Arrived too late for consideration.
44. Came without a cover letter.
45. Cover letter repeats what's on the resume – does not command attention nor move the reader to action.
46. Sent the same or different versions of the resume to the same person as a seemingly clever follow-up method.
47. Follow-up call made too soon – before the resume and letter arrive!
48. Follow-up call is too aggressive or the candidate appears too "hungry" for the position – appeared needy or greedy.

Serious Business for Serious People

Writing and distributing resumes and letters is a serious business. To do resumes and letters properly and with impact requires specific writing, production, distribution, and follow-up skills centered around clearly defined strategies for getting a job interview. The chapters that follow convert each of these myths and realities into a set of **action steps** for producing your own high impact resumes and letters. If you follow these chapters carefully, you will indeed write and distribute your own resume and letters with sufficient impact to get interviews that should eventually lead to job offers for jobs you really want and will enjoy doing. We will revisit several of these myths and mistakes in a different format when we review 110 key resume and letter questions, with corresponding answers, in Chapter 14.

4

Resume Power, Process, and Ethical Behavior

WHAT EXACTLY IS A RESUME? How do resumes and letters relate to other important job search activities? How honest should you be on your resume? Answers to these questions tell us a great deal about what you should and should not include on your resume or in your letters. They tell us what you plan to do with your resume and indicate how effective you might be in conducting your job search.

Knowledge and Power

The old adage that *"knowledge is power"* is especially true when conducting a job search. But in and of itself, knowledge is neutral. When applied, it can cut two ways – for positive or negative outcomes. Let's make sure your knowledge of resumes and letters produces powerful outcomes for you.

Not surprisingly, many job seekers write resumes and letters based upon a little knowledge and advice they receive from well-meaning friends, relatives, and acquaintances, who tell several different stories about what and what not to include on a resume and letter and how to distribute them:

- *You should put _____ on your resume.*
- *Here's my resume – why don't you use it as a model?*
- *Keep it to one page. More than two pages and you're "dead upon arrival"!*
- *Try this letter – I bet it will work for you, too.*
- *If I were you, I'd send out 300 copies – and print it on colored paper.*
- *Good luck – I had to do that, too, a few years ago!*

With help like this, you would think you were making progress with your resume. After all, what are friends for?

When conducting a job search, friends may give you comfort and share bits and pieces of street-wise knowledge. But they seldom impart a **system** for making your job search as effective as it should and can be.

If, for example, your car had a flat tire, would you take it to McDonald's for service or would you push it through a carwash in the hope it would somehow revive? Of course not – that would be stupid. But that's exactly what many job seekers do when they are faced with writing resumes and letters. They go to the wrong sources and apply faulty principles for making an important process work in their favor. No wonder the whole job search looks like a big game of chance. Using such an approach, you have to believe that luck will come your way if you are to keep your sanity in persisting with your job search!

Often following bad advice, many job seekers confirm another old adage: *"A little knowledge can be a dangerous thing!"* Follow the advice of well-meaning yet uninformed friends, and you may find yourself taking a long, long journey down numerous dead-end roads. As we will see shortly, writing and distributing resumes and letters is serious business involving important writing and marketing principles centered around specific goals. You can and should do much better than borrowing the "expert" knowledge and well-meaning advice of friends, relatives, and acquaintances.

Mysticism, Misunderstanding, and Sabotage

Resumes are one of the most imitated, plagiarized, and misunderstood documents produced and used in today's job market. They also result in lots of bad behaviors on the part of ill-informed and thoughtless job seekers who literally sabotage their job search, and possibly their career, with their ostensibly job-winning resumes.

> *Resumes are one of the most imitated, plagiarized, and misunderstood documents produced.*

For many job seekers, resumes appear simple to create. Turn on your computer, type your name and address near the top of the screen, and begin listing your vital statistics – just like others do. All you need to do is change the names, titles, and dates. This shouldn't take you more than two hours to complete. And while you are at it, don't forget to do a cover letter. Once the resume and letter are finished, make hundreds of copies, get a list of names, type envelopes, stuff them, affix stamps, and send them out to prospective employers in the hope that someone will have a job for you. Alternatively, create an electronic resume and accompanying cover letter, and e-mail them to numerous employers you encounter online or for whom you have e-mail addresses. Next, wait for all the replies to hit home. Your biggest problem will probably be trying to select which employer's offer you should accept!

Congratulations on joining the wonderful, magical, costly, and annoying worlds of direct mail and spam! The U.S. Postal Service, envelope makers, and printers may love you, but few employers enjoy receiving such junk mail. We know of none who hires employees based upon a survey of their junk mail or spam. Most will appropriately file your resume and letter where it belongs – in the wastebasket. If you send it as an e-mail attachment, they will probably automatically delete it without opening the file.

Faith, hope, and ego continue to guide many people who produce and distribute resumes in this manner. The typical product is fit for the trash – which is exactly where most resumes find a quick and final resting place with employers, who are bombarded with hundreds of ineffective resumes and letters each week. Nonetheless, producing a resume in this manner is quick, easy, and "personalized." It gives you a false sense of making progress in what is an inherently confusing and chaotic job market. It also communicates the wrong message to prospective employers: you lack goals, appear unfocused, and may be uninformed, unprofessional, naive, or just plain lazy or stupid. You're probably a loser!

Even more interesting is to probe why people write resumes. Not surprisingly, they write resumes because everyone else does and, after all, employers expect to receive them. So they send many resumes to many employers as if employers don't have enough resumes to fill their files. Others monitor classified ads and send cover letters and resumes to total strangers in anticipation of getting jobs through the mail. Still others just hold onto their resume in the hope of eventually using it to hook an ideal job.

For the individual who has never written or used a resume, writing a resume seems to be an unnatural act. It's a foreign, confusing, bewildering, and exasperating experience, shrouded in mysticism and mysterious movement toward different types of jobs one may or may not be interested in doing.

> *Few employers enjoy receiving such junk mail . . . The typical product is fit for the trash.*

Doing Better

Assuming we can do better, let's take a little time to understand the job market, your goals, employers' needs, and effective strategies for penetrating today's job market. With a little bit of this knowledge, you will acquire power to effect positive job search outcomes. You will know exactly what you should be doing when writing and distributing resumes and letters. Acquiring this knowledge takes a few hours. It's a good investment of time, because the results can be dramatic for both your self-esteem and your job search.

Doing better means identifying goals and translating them into specific desired outcomes. In the job search, these goals must be employer-oriented while also satisfying your own objectives.

Know What You're Doing and Where You're Going

If not mysticism, resumes and letters are at least surrounded by plenty of myths, misunderstanding, misinformation, and wishful thinking. These are largely based upon one very simple problem – the failure to understand what a resume is (**definition**) and what it is expected to do (**outcomes**). In other words, we must define a resume and examine its expected outcomes for both you and employers. In the simplest form, a resume is defined as follows:

Definition:	A resume is an **advertisement** of who you are in terms of your competencies, accomplishments, patterns of performance, and predictable future capabilities. It is your chief marketing tool or calling card for opening the doors of prospective employers.
Your Expected Outcome:	From the job applicant's perspective, a resume is supposed to help get an **interview** which, in turn, leads to a job offer.

Employers'   From the employers' perspective, resumes are supposed to
Expected   communicate **value**, i.e., what applicants will do for them.
Outcomes: In addition, resumes are mechanisms for **screening** candi-
                          dates for interviews. They should ultimately result in inter-
                          viewing and hiring the best candidate.

To be most effective you must understand resumes from the perspective of employers
– the ones who must read and respond to them. Employers are not seeking to hire your
history – they want to know your capabilities in order to predict your future performance
in their organization. Based upon a cursory reading of resumes and letters, they seek to
screen a limited number of candidates. Screening
simplifies what they want to do the most – hire a
capable individual, do it soon, and take as little time
as possible from their busy schedule.

Employers are not seeking to hire your history – they want to know your capabilities in order to predict your future performance.

When writing resumes and letters, always remember **your purpose**: you are advertising yourself for an
interview – and not for a job. Job offers seldom come
until **after** interviews. Effective resumes and letters
should make prospective employers want to meet you
in person to discuss your qualifications and possible
contributions to their organization. These documents
should clearly and factually communicate to employers what it is you can do **for them**.
Most important, your resumes and letters should be honest, positive, concise, easy to read
– and **represent you and your major strengths**.

Knowing what resumes and letters are and what they are supposed to do makes their
production and distribution both easy and time-consuming. They are **easier** to write
because you can develop resume and letter content around the purpose of these
documents. They become **time-consuming** to produce because you must write your own
rather than imitate or plagiarize someone else's examples. You must begin from your own
ground of experience in developing a resume and letters which clearly communicate:

- What you want to do in terms of your job and career goals.

- Who you are in terms of specific skills and capabilities.

- What you are most likely to do in the future for an employer.

Since you must project your **past and present** into the employer's **future**, such
documents take time, effort, care, and professionalism on your part to produce and
distribute. You can get advice from others, but you must produce resumes and letters by
yourself based upon a thorough inventory of your past and present as well as projections
into the future.

Multi-Functional Documents

Resumes and letters play several roles in the overall career planning and job search
processes. While they advertise you for job interviews, a resume also performs other
important communication functions relating to the larger job search process:

- Reviews your experience and communicates your potential value to employers.

- Provides file information in any placement service you use.

- Accompanies your letters in response to vacancy announcements.

- Becomes an important element in the informational interview process.

- Focuses and communicates your job objective and qualifications around your major strengths.

- Serves as supplemental information to employment applications and letters of inquiry about possible job openings.

- Informs your personal and professional contacts – friends, relatives, colleagues, alumni, former employers, etc., and those writing letters of recommendation and providing reference information for you – about your job objective and qualifications.

You should keep these functions in mind as you develop each section of your resume. They will help focus the content of your writing. They also will help determine what types of job search letters you will need to write.

Career Development and Job Search Process

Resumes and letters play a central role in the larger career development and job search processes. If you understand how resumes and letters relate to these processes, you will know how, when, and where to effectively target them for your advantage.

Career development is a process involving the movement from one set of career activities to another. In the most comprehensive and integrated form, this process involves four major steps, each with specific characteristics and activities. Our model of this process is diagramed on page 42.

If you want to fully benefit from this process, you should develop a systematic plan of action. This plan involves assessing your abilities, skills, motivations, and interests (Stage 1); exploring career alternatives and options (Stage 2); developing job search competencies (Stage 3); and using your newly acquired competencies and knowledge for getting a job and advancing your career (Stage 4).

Writing effective resumes and letters is an important job search competency within the career development stages. These writing activities, in turn, are related to several other job search activities which are illustrated on page 43.

The **job search process** consists of seven separate yet closely related steps involving three distinct stages. Resume and letter writing (Step 4), the critical **transformation step**, lie at the very heart of this process. As illustrated on page 43, these products should not be written in isolation of the other steps. For example, prior to writing your resume, you should know your motivated abilities and skills (Step 1) and work objective (Step 2). At the same time, conducting research (Step 3) and networking (Step 5) should come prior to, during, and after writing the resume. These are mutually reinforcing steps which pro-

Career Development Process

STEP 1
Assessing Your . . .

- skills and abilities
- motivations
- interests
- values
- temperment
- experience
- accomplishments

STEP 2
Exploring Career . . .

- information
- objectives
- targets (individuals, organizations, and communities)
- alternatives

STEP 4
Implementing Job Search Steps . . .

- research
- prospecting
- networking
- informational interviews
- job interviews

STEP 3
Developing Skills to . . .

- conduct research
- write resumes and letters
- prospect
- network
- conduct informational interviews

Job Search Steps and Stages

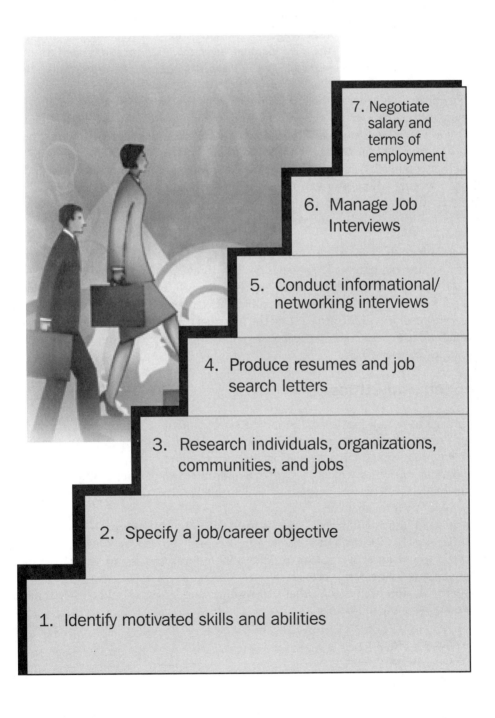

7. Negotiate salary and terms of employment

6. Manage Job Interviews

5. Conduct informational/ networking interviews

4. Produce resumes and job search letters

3. Research individuals, organizations, communities, and jobs

2. Specify a job/career objective

1. Identify motivated skills and abilities

vide useful feedback for improving the overall job search process. After completing these steps, you should be well prepared to interview and negotiate the job offer (Step 6) as well as start your new job or career (Step 7).

Each job search step represents important **communication skills** involving you in contact with others. But the critical resume and letter writing step (4) becomes the major communication challenge for most job seekers. Without strong writing skills, your job search is likely to founder. Indeed, your ability to write high impact resumes and letters largely determines how quickly you will transform your job search from the investigative stage (research) to employer contact stages (networking, interviewing, salary negotiations). Your writing skills become the key element in moving your job search from the investigative stage to the final job offer stage. You writing becomes an important indicator of your competence.

In the job search, paper in the form of resumes and letters is the great equalizer. Most employers want to first see you on paper before speaking with you on the telephone or meeting you in person. You, along with many others, must pass the written test **before** you can be considered for the face-to-face oral test.

Whether you like it or not, you must put your professionalism, competence, and personality in writing before you can be taken seriously for a job interview. Thus, your writing activities may well become the most critical **transformation step** in your job search. Your writing skills become your ticket to job interviews that lead to job offers and employment.

The following chapters relate Steps 1, 2, and 3 of the job search process to developing effective resumes and letters. These steps consist of several self-directed exercises which clarify and specify your abilities and objectives as well as generate a comprehensive database for writing your resume – the subject of Chapter 7. Step 5 is important for refining your resume and for penetrating the informal or hidden job market. We discuss this specialized use of resumes for prospecting, networking, and conducting informational interviews in Chapter 10.

Approach and Ethics

Our approach to resume and letter writing differs from many standard manuals on these subjects. Over-emphasizing **form**, many books neglect the important **substance** that needs to go into resumes and letters. They attempt to simplify resume and letter writing with numerous examples which you are encouraged to copy. Such an approach often results in ineffective resumes and letters which quickly find their way into employers' "circular files" – wastepaper cans.

We, instead, use an inductive, contingency approach. This approach emphasizes the need to develop both form and substance in resumes and letters. Our approach also stresses the importance of relating resume and letter activities to the larger career development and job search processes.

Basic to this approach is the belief that resumes and letters should clearly communicate to employers the following:

- What you **want** to do.
- What you **have** done.
- What you **can** do.
- What you **will** do.

You can develop such resumes and letters by first creating a comprehensive database which outlines your abilities and experience in relation to your objective (see Chapter 7). If you use this database for developing each section of your resumes and letters, you will be able to communicate your **strengths** in relationship to employers' needs.

Since employers' needs and expectations differ, so too should your resumes and letters. We see no "one best" resume and letter for all employers. Using our targeted approach, your resumes and letters become unique, personalized documents which stand out from the crowd of typical dull and copycat resumes and letters. You clearly communicate to prospective employers your goals, accomplishments, and predictable pattern of performance along with your intelligence, personality, and enthusiasm in response to the employer's specific hiring needs.

Our approach also stresses a particular **ethical position**. Some people, after learning how to develop and use positive resume and letter language, get carried away and exaggerate facts. Hyping a resume or letter is deceptive and unethical. As with most advertising, a fine line exists between ethical and unethical

> *A fine line exists between ethical and unethical sales techniques. Our rule is simple: Be honest, but don't be stupid!*

sales techniques. However you decide to communicate your strengths to employers, it is essential that you always demonstrate your honesty, integrity, and forthrightness. We have yet to see any value in developing a rip-off mentality or becoming a con artist in getting a job.

You must be professional at all times in your job search, and especially in your written communication. You can do this by (1) generating the facts about your strengths (self-assessment) and (2) using positive language to communicate those facts to others.

Never create a situation that would raise a question about your honesty and integrity. If you do, you may be asked during the interview to explain what you "hyped" in your letter or resume. This could result in embarrassment as well as a different outcome than you intended – no job offer.

At the same time, honesty and forthrightness should not create new liabilities for you. Honest people sometimes say the dumbest things about themselves: they confess their negatives, undersell themselves, or fail to communicate their strengths. Being ethical doesn't mean you must talk about what is wrong with you. Our rule for job search ethics is simple: Be honest, but don't be stupid!

5

Organize Your Time, Implement Your Campaign

OW MUCH TIME DO YOU PLAN to devote to your job search during the next three months? Ten hours a week? What about 20, 40, or 60 hours a week? What will you do during those hours to achieve success?

One of the most difficult tasks in any job search is organizing sufficient time to find a job. Each activity, be it self-assessment or writing a resume, takes hours of precious time. But time is not easy to find if you are already committed to other daily and weekly routines. If you work full time, allocating time to search for a new job can become a real challenge.

Let's see if we can find sufficient time to develop an effective job search, but especially time to write, produce, distribute, and follow up your high impact resumes and letters.

Failure to Find Time and Implement Properly

We and others consistently find one important reason for job search failure – the inability of individuals to devote the necessary **time and effort** to complete and sustain each job search step. They create a similar self-fulfilling prophesy. Initially high on motivation and knowledge, they soon demonstrate a very low level of time, effort, and overall commitment to achieving success. They simply don't **implement** the process properly. They get sound advice on how to make the process work for them, but they cut corners. They quickly become time, organization, and implementation cheaters. Rather than spend 30 hours on writing their resume, they cheat by devoting only four hours to this exercise. Instead of making 15 new job contacts (networking) each week, they cheat by only making two. Then they complain with the often-heard laments of frustrated job seekers – *"There are no jobs out there for me!"* and *"No one will hire me!"* Within a few weeks, they not only don't get a job, they also lose their enthusiasm, motivation, self-esteem, and sense of self-worth in the face of a few rejections. Frustrated and depressed, many of these job seekers start presenting an image of failure to potential employers.

These time cheaters often come back after a few frustrating weeks and complain that the job search process doesn't work for them. Our most nonjudgmental responses are:

*"How many new job contacts did you **really** make this week? May I please see your networking records?"*

*"How many hours did you **really** spend putting this resume together? Let's see the database you generated."*

*"How many job search letters did you **really** write to whom this week? Could I see copies of your correspondence?"*

Guess what their responses are to these questions? Yes, they devoted a little time and a little effort in the hope they would get a big payoff. They thought they could shortcut the process. Not that they are lazy; they just didn't seriously manage their time. In fact, some even confess, *"I'm so busy, I just don't have that much time. What can I do?"* Our sobering responses and advice are these:

"Are you really serious about finding a job? What exactly are your priorities at this stage in your life? So far you haven't made enough time to do this properly. It looks as if your job search is not a priority. Am I right?"

*"If finding a job is one of your priorities, then let's **make** it a priority by better using your time. Let's start over again. However, this time let's make some changes in your daily routine. First, examine your time. Second, reorganize and reserve sufficient time for each job search activity. Third, start over with the very first job search activity – self-assessment. When you get to the resume stage, follow our step-by-step procedures for putting it together with impact. If you spend two to three hours each day completing these steps, you should be able to complete your resume within one week."*

"Let's speak the truth about the possibility of going nowhere with your job search. If you can't find enough time to do this right, don't come back and waste my time with rationalizations. Yes, no one will hire you if you don't work at getting hired."

The first rule for conducting an effective job search is this: You must find the time to properly organize and implement each step of your job search. A second rule automatically follows: Organize, organize, organize in the process of implementing each step. You can't organize and implement unless you set aside sufficient time to do so.

But how do you find more time when you don't have extra time? One of the best ways is to examine several "tried and tested" time management practices that have worked well for others. These practices will help you find new time to organize your resume and letter writing activities. More importantly, time management practices are designed to relate activities to goals within specific time frameworks – a perfect methodology for your job search.

While you can complete a resume in a few hours by creatively plagiarizing examples, you should be able to produce a first-class resume on your own within a few days if you follow certain time management practices. If not, your job search may become confusing, frustrating, and ineffective.

Better Manage Your Time

You can easily begin your job search from your office, filing cabinet, or desk drawer. Your immediate needs are paper, pens, a computer, printer, envelopes, stamps, a telephone, index cards, file folders, Internet access, a nearby library, a copy machine, and this book.

As you begin organizing your job search, you may wish to examine a few "time management" books to help you better use your time. Such classics as Alan Lakein's *How to Get Control of Your Time and Life*, R. Alex Mac-Kenzie's *The Time Trap* and *Time for Success*, or Michael LeBoeuf's *Working Smart* are filled with practical time management advice. You will find numerous other time management books in your local library and bookstore delivering the same basic messages. Taken together, they stress the need to follow this checklist of time management practices:

> *You must find the time to properly organize and implement each step of your job search.*

- Evaluate how you normally use your time each day; identify time wasters; keep a "time log" to monitor your time patterns.
- Set objectives and priorities.
- Plan daily activities by listing and prioritizing things "to do."
- Create some flexibility in your daily schedule – do not over-schedule.
- Organize two- to three-hour blocks of time for concentrated work.
- Avoid interruptions.
- Organize your work space.
- Process your paperwork faster by responding to it immediately and according to priorities.
- Learn to say "no" and to shut your door.
- Do one thing at a time.
- Improve your ability and speed to remember, comprehend, and read.
- Continue to evaluate how you best use your time.

Time management follows a rational process involving the setting of goals and relating results-oriented activities to those goals. Four key questions help organize the steps in this process:

1. What am I trying to accomplish?
2. How am I organizing to achieve my goals?
3. What results am I achieving?
4. Have I evaluated my progress and with what outcomes?

Your most important time management goals should be to prioritize and reserve time for specific job search activities. Otherwise, such activities may get lost in the shuffle of daily personal and work routines or become victim to crisis management. Indeed, some time management experts estimate that most people waste 80 percent of their time on trivia, because they fail to organize, set goals, and prioritize their activities.

Inventory Your Time Management Behavior

Before re-organizing your time, you should inventory how you use your time. You can do this by addressing the statements in the exercise on pages 57 and 58. Although some of these statements in this exercise may not relate to your particular situation, complete those that do.

Your Time Management Inventory

1.	I have a written set of long-, immediate-, and short-range goals for myself (and my family).	Yes	No
2.	I have a clear idea of what I will do today at work (if student, at school) and at home.	Yes	No
3.	I have a clear idea of what I want to accomplish at work (or at school) this coming week and month.	Yes	No
4.	I set priorities and follow through on the most important tasks first.	Yes	No
5.	I judge my success by the results I produce in relation to my goals.	Yes	No
6.	I use a daily, weekly, and monthly calendar for scheduling appointments and setting work targets.	Yes	No
7.	I delegate as much work as possible.	Yes	No
8.	I get my subordinates to organize their time in relation to mine.	Yes	No
9.	I file only those things which are essential to my work. When in doubt, I throw it out.	Yes	No
10.	I immediately throw away junk mail.	Yes	No
11.	My briefcase, laptop, and/or electronic organizer are uncluttered and well organized, including only essential materials; they serve as my office away from the office.	Yes	No
12.	I minimize the number of meetings and concentrate on making decisions rather than discussing aimlessly.	Yes	No
13.	I make frequent use of the telephone and face-to-face encounters rather than written communication.	Yes	No
14.	I make minor decisions quickly.	Yes	No
15.	I concentrate on accomplishing one thing at a time.	Yes	No
16.	I handle each piece of paper once and only once.	Yes	No

17.	I answer most letters on the letter I receive with either a handwritten or typed message.	Yes	No
18.	I set deadlines for myself and others and follow through in meeting them.	Yes	No
19.	I reserve time each week to plan.	Yes	No
20.	My desk and work area are well organized and clear.	Yes	No
21.	I know how to say "no" and do so.	Yes	No
22.	I first skim books, articles, and other forms of written communication for ideas before reading further.	Yes	No
23.	I monitor my time use during the day by asking myself "How can I best use my time at present?"	Yes	No
24.	I deal with the present by getting things done that need to be done.	Yes	No
25.	I maintain a time log to monitor the best use of my time.	Yes	No
26.	I place a dollar value on my time and behave accordingly.	Yes	No
27.	I – not others – control my time.	Yes	No
28.	My briefcase, computer, and/or electronic organizer include items I can work on during spare time in waiting rooms, lines, airports, etc.	Yes	No
29.	I keep my door shut when I'm working.	Yes	No
30.	I regularly evaluate to what degree I am achieving my stated goals.	Yes	No

Effective time managers respond *"yes"* to most of these statements. If your *"no's"* outnumber your *"yeses,"* you should seriously consider acquiring some useful time management practices.

One way to begin reorganizing your time is to analyze how you use time by keeping a detailed activities log. Develop a time log, beginning at 7am and ending at 11pm. Use our form on page 51 for this purpose. Carry this log with you. After analyzing how you actually used your time for a week, you should begin improving your time use by completing the goal-setting exercise on page 52.

If you have a tendency to procrastinate – put off the most important but least desirable tasks – be sure to read Brian Tracy's ***Eat That Frog! 21 Great Ways to Stop Procrastinating and Get More Done in Less Time*** (Berrett-Koehler) on how to prioritize prioritize tasks. The book is available through Impact Publications (see the order form at the end of this book or visit www.impactpublications.com).

The final way to improve your time use is to keep a card in your pocket and on your desk which asks you: *"How can I better use my time at present?"* After two weeks of new time management effort, respond again to our 30 time management statements. Continue to review these statements at the end of each week until your *"yeses"* overwhelm your *"no's"*!

Time Management Log

Starting Time	Ending Time	Total Minutes	Activity Type	Who Initiated	Individual/Groups	Results/Outcomes/Notes
8:30	9:00	30	W	S	Self	Complete revisions on report
8:30	9:15	15	TP	O	Mr. Oats	Resolved problem with prepaid order
8:30	9:15	15	M	S	Ms. Siets	Planned meeting with department heads

Codes

Activity Type: **W** = writing **TP** = telephone **M** = meeting **C** = conference **P** = planning **D** = dictating **I** = inspecting

Who Initiated: **S** = self **O** = other

Goal Setting

Objective	Specific Tasks	Who does it?	Completion Date	Resource Needs: time, personnel, materials, etc.

Organize Your Campaign

As you incorporate our job search activities into your daily time schedule, always keep in mind what you are trying to accomplish. Your goal is to get a job that is right for you. This requires organizing specific activities within a definite time period. Since the activities are closely related to each other, they must be internally organized in reference to your final goal. We suggest that you treat your job search campaign as if it were a $1,000,000 investment. In fact, your job search effort may well yield $1,000,000 or more in additional income over the next 20 years – if you do it right.

> *Your goal is to get a job that is right for you.*

Your major job search activities should include those identified as key steps in the job search:

1. Identifying abilities and skills – your strengths.
2. Setting a job/career objective.
3. Writing a resume and job search letters.
4. Conducting research on individuals, organizations, and communities.
5. Prospecting, networking, and conducting informational interviews.
6. Interviewing for a specific position.
7. Negotiating the job offer and terms of employment.

These activities can be conducted on a full-time or part-time basis, depending on your goals and your time schedule. However, there are certain activities you should conduct regularly. These involve questioning, listening, evaluating, critiquing, adjusting, and thinking about what you are doing and where you are going (see the "Job Search Steps and Stages" illustration on page 43). Many people tend to become too involved in the urgencies of daily living and thus neglect to stand back and **think** about what is important to them. This tendency toward tunnel vision needs to be corrected with broader and more integrative thinking. Do reflective thinking by occasionally sitting down for an hour or two to **evaluate** your situation.

Depending on your personal situation, you may wish to initiate a one-, three-, six-, or 12-month job search campaign. Obviously, the shorter your campaign period, the more hours per week you must devote to each job search activity. In our model job search campaign on page 54, we illustrate what can and should happen in a job search conducted over a six-month period. Your monthly activities could be further divided into weekly and daily targets. We strongly suggest that you plan job activities in advance; set aside time each week, preferably each day, to accomplish specific tasks.

While most job searches should be completed – i.e., result in accepting a job offer – within three months, some are completed within one week; others may take as long as six months or more. We use the six-month period to illustrate the full range of activities and likely outcomes.

Remember, our model is hypothetical. While you may wish to vary how you organize your time for conducting a job search, to get the desired outcomes you should engage in each of the job search activities outlined in our model. If you front-load your job search by devoting more time to such preliminaries as self-assessment, research, and resume and letter writing, as well as accelerate your networking activities, you can expect interviews and job offers to come much sooner than illustrated in our model.

Organization of Job Search Activities

Activity	Weeks (1–24)
Thinking, questioning, listening, evaluating, adjusting	(weeks 1–24)
Identifying abilities and skills	(week 3–4)
Setting objectives	(week 4–5)
Writing resume	(week 5–6)
Conducting research	(weeks 6–24)
Prospecting, referrals, networking	(weeks 6–24)
Interviewing	(weeks 12–24)
Receiving and negotiating job offers	(weeks 13–24)

One word of caution before you head off to organize your time and plan your job search. Please do not fall victim to **too much planning** by slavishly following such a detailed plan of action. Planning may make you feel rational, but it does not guarantee competence or positive outcomes. Unfortunately, planning has one major downside: it can blind you to that wonderful experience called **serendipity** – chance occurrences that lead to unexpected opportunities and success. Indeed, planning is fine, but flexibility and receptivity to opportunities are even better. Being in the right place at the right time is even more important than planning.

Luck plays a role in the job search. Closely related to planning, luck is where preparation and opportunity meet. You get lucky when you plan.

Your most important planning goal should be to reserve specific time periods for activities related to your job search. In so doing, you designate the job search as a top priority activity and routinize it within your daily schedule. The tendency – especially when you see no immediate results, such as a job interview and offer next week – is to procrastinate by saying you can do this work tomorrow or next week. Your job search should have a central place in your overall time management scheme.

> *Luck is where preparation and opportunity meet.*

Complete the Resume

You can complete your resume in two to three hours if you imitate our examples or those of others. However, we don't recommend this quick and easy method. Instead, do this task properly and with impact by incorporating the larger job search process into your writing activities. You should be able to complete an outstanding resume within a week if you devote two to three hours each day to developing the database and producing drafts of the resume, as we outline in Chapter 7.

According to our time scheme for organizing the various job search activities (page 51), approximately three weeks are reserved for resume development. This, however, assumes that the resume is a direct by-product of the two previous job search activities – identifying abilities and skills and setting objectives. Once you complete these activities, you should be able to produce your resume within one day.

Chapter 7 includes the necessary worksheets and self-directed exercises for creating your resume database. While these are designed to help you generate a large amount of quality data, you may want to conduct a more in-depth analysis using our seven-step job search plan. By doing this, you will take advantage of the most advanced and effective job search techniques available.

Follow Key Success Principles

While we have no quick and easy formulas for success, we have found 22 principles for conducting a successful job search. Most are particular attitudes, orientations, and styles of behavior that will serve you well in most professional settings. These principles have proved effective for many job seekers; they should work well for you throughout your job search as well as on the job and into your next job and career transition. Rather than being facts, truths, or scientific findings, these principles emerge from research, theory, experience, and common sense.

22 Principles for Job Search Success

1. **You should work hard at finding a job:** Make this a daily endeavor and involve your family. Expect to spend 40 to 80 hours a week on organizing and implementing an effective job search. Focus on routinizing specific high-payoff job search activities, such as research and networking.

2. **You should not be discouraged by setbacks:** You are playing the odds, so expect disappointments and handle them in stride. You will have many *"no's"* before uncovering the one *"yes"* which is right for you.

3. **You should be patient and persevere:** Expect three months of hard work before you connect with the job that's right for you. Keep focused and active throughout this period.

4. **You should be honest with yourself and others – but not stupid:** Honesty is always the best policy. But don't confuse honesty with frankness and the confessional. Indeed, many people say the stupidest things about themselves in the name of honesty. Naive job seekers often volunteer their negatives and short-comings to potential employers. They present an unfortunate image of someone who lacks street smarts and who potentially will say the darnest things – both frank and honest – to clients and customers even about the inner workings of the business!

5. **You should develop a positive attitude toward yourself**: Nobody wants to employ guilt-ridden people with inferiority complexes and low self-esteem. Focus on your positive characteristics with enthusiasm. Sell your positive self – those things you do well and enjoy doing.

6. **You should associate with positive and successful people:** Finding a job largely depends on how well you relate to others. Avoid associating with negative and depressing people who complain and have a "you-can't-do-it" attitude. Run with winners who have a positive "can-do" outlook on life.

7. **You should set goals:** You should have a clear idea of what you want and where you're going. Without these, you will present a confusing and indecisive image to others. Clear goals help direct your job search into productive channels. Moreover, setting high goals will help you work hard to get what you want.

8. **You should plan and implement for success:** Convert your goals into realistic action steps that are organized as short-, intermediate-, and long-range plans. Then put these plans into action by taking the necessary actions that should lead to success. Unfortunately, many people are good at planning their job search but they fail to implement it properly. Planning without implementation is a waste of time.

9. **You should manage your time and get organized:** Translate your plans into activities, targets, names, addresses, telephone numbers, and materials. Develop

an efficient and effective filing system and use a large calendar for setting time targets and recording appointments and useful information.

10. **You should be a good communicator:** Take stock of your oral, written, and nonverbal communication skills. How well do you communicate? Since most aspects of your job search involves communicating with others, and communication skills are one of the most sought-after skills, always present yourself well both verbally and nonverbally.

11. **You should be energetic and enthusiastic:** Employers are attracted to positive people who appear to be energetic and demonstrate that magical quality called **drive**. They don't like negative and depressing people who toil at their work. Generate enthusiasm both verbally and nonverbally. Check on your telephone voice – it may be more unenthusiastic than your voice in face-to-face situations. After all, your first interview is likely to take place over the telephone.

12. **You should ask questions:** Your best information comes from asking questions. Asking questions also communicates interest and intelligence. Learn to develop questions that are non-aggressive, probing, polite, and interesting to others. But don't ask too many questions and thereby dominate conversations and become an annoying inquisitor.

13. **You should be a good listener:** Being a good listener is often more important than being a good questioner and talker. Learn to improve your face-to-face listening behavior (nonverbal cues) as well as remember and use information gained from others. Make others feel they enjoyed talking with you, i.e., you are one of the few people who actually **listens** to what they say.

14. **You should be polite, courteous, and thoughtful:** Treat gate keepers, especially receptionists, like human beings. Avoid being aggressive or too assertive. Try to be polite, courteous, and gracious. Your social graces are being observed. Remember to send thank-you letters – a very thoughtful thing to do in a job search. Even if you are rejected, thank employers for the "opportunity" given to you. After all, they may later have additional opportunities, and they will remember you.

15. **You should be inclusive, give credit to others, and help others look good:** Avoid the egocentrism associated with taking credit for everything by constantly referring to "I." Give credit to others by frequently referring to "we" when discussing your accomplishments and "us" or the "company" when speculating about your future role. Employers love to work with competent employees who make them look good even though the credit belongs to others.

16. **You should be tactful:** Watch what you say about other people as well as yourself. Be very careful how you talk about previous employers and co-workers, especially anything negative about your relationships and their competence. Don't be a gossip, back-stabber, or confessor.

17. **You should demonstrate your intelligence and competence:** Present yourself as someone who gets things done and achieves results – a **producer**. Talk about your accomplishments by including examples of what you did and with what consequences. Employers want to see proof of performance. They generally seek people who are bright, hard-working, responsible, energetic, have drive, can communicate well, have positive personalities, maintain good interpersonal relations, are likable, observe dress and social codes, take initiative, are talented, possess expertise in particular areas, use good judgment, are cooperative, trustworthy, and loyal, generate confidence and credibility, and are conventional. In other words, they like people who can score in the "excellent" to "outstanding" categories of a performance evaluation.

> *You should modify, adapt, innovate, and experiment throughout your job search.*

18. **You should maintain a professional stance:** Be neat in what you do and wear, and speak with the confidence, authority, and maturity of a professional.

19. **You should not overdo your job search:** Don't engage in overkill and bore everyone with your "job search" stories. Achieve balance in everything you do. Occasionally take a few days off to do nothing related to your job search. Develop a system of incentives and rewards – such as two non-job search days a week, if you accomplish targets A, B, C, and D.

20. **You should be open-minded and keep an eye open for "luck":** Too much planning can blind you to unexpected and fruitful opportunities. You should welcome serendipity. Learn to re-evaluate your goals and strategies. Seize new opportunities if appropriate.

21. **You should evaluate your progress and adjust:** Take two hours once every two weeks and evaluate your accomplishments. If necessary, tinker with your plans and reorganize your activities and priorities. Don't become too routinized and thereby kill creativity and innovation.

22. **You should focus on what's really important in conducting a successful job search:** If you spend most of your job search time sending your resume in response to job ads or submitting your resume in response to online job listings, you're not conducting a smart job search. Instead, focus most of your job search activities on research, networking, and making direct contacts with employers. Above all, use the Internet wisely for acquiring information and advice rather than for responding to job listings.

Let's also be realistic. You should not assume you must follow every principle or piece of advice we and others give you. Develop a healthy sense of skepticism and initiative. Since individual circumstances and situations differ, you should modify, adapt, innovate, and experiment throughout your job search. At the very least, our guidelines and principles should help you channel your energies into fruitful directions.

Work With Others

Writing a resume, like writing letters, basically is a pencil, paper, and typing exercise – relatively passive activities. Other job search activities, such as networking and interviewing, mainly involve interacting with individuals over the telephone, in face-to-face situations, or over the Internet. Therefore, the guidelines for writing an effective resume will differ somewhat from the principles for conducting an effective job search.

A good resume can be completed in the solitude of one's office or study. Just complete the worksheets and self-directed exercises, write drafts, and type the final product. But remember, the resume ultimately plays an important role in the most critical interpersonal encounter with employers – the interview.

Because resumes have this important interpersonal dimension, we strongly urge you to **field test** your resume by talking to others about it and your job search. Involve your spouse, family, friends, or acquaintances. Why not, for instance, form a job search or resume writing group? Such a group should meet regularly to share information, pool resources, critique each other's progress, and provide support. By doing this, you should greatly improve your chances of finding a job. Indeed, according to some career counselors, you may cut your job search time in half if you join such a group. Through these activities you will also form lasting and rewarding personal relationships; lessen your frustrations by sharing them with others who understand; and find the job search process to be more enjoyable. Most important, such a group provides both structure and motivation for implementing an effective job search.

The support and encouragement you receive from others will keep your motivation and self-esteem high, as well as help you handle the psychological bumps and bruises associated with the job search. By all means get out from behind your desk and computer and **talk** with people about your job search. If you ask them for advice, you'll be surprised how concerned and helpful they will be. In so doing, the quality of your resume and letters will improve accordingly!

6

Create High Impact Form, Content, and Structure

WRITING A RESUME IS MORE THAN just putting information about your work history on paper. Like any effective piece of advertising, your resume must have good form **and** content. It should look and read like good advertising copy or an effective press release – grab attention and motivate the reader to take action.

The form and content principles outlined in this chapter are valid for 95 percent of all resumes written today. These are **conventional resumes** that get mailed or faxed to employers who actually read them. The major exception to our discussion relate to various types of electronic resumes. These resumes follow a different set of form and content principles since they are designed to be either transmitted electronically, and thus lose important design elements, or they are initially read by computers rather than by human beings. We outline alternative form and content principles when we discuss electronic resumes in Chapter 12.

Make Form and Content Work Together

You can create good advertising copy by paying particular attention to how well you combine both the form and content of your resume. While most writers concentrate only on the content of their resume *("What should I include on it?")*, you must be equally concerned about its form *("What type of resume should I write and how should the elements visually relate?")*. Questions relating to specific categories of information to be included must be related to questions concerning resume type and appearance.

Our concern with form versus content is central to writing an effective resume. **Form** – how you communicate your message – is the very first thing communicated to the reader. **Content** – what's in your message – follows after the reader has been sufficiently motivated by the form to read your message.

Form is indeed important in communicating your message to employers. Consider the fact that many employers receive hundreds of resumes each week.

Not surprisingly, some resumes receive less than 15 seconds of consideration while others may be read all the way through. Why the difference? Form is the first thing noticed by a reader. The form may or may not motivate the reader to explore the document further. Thus, the form of your resume should be pleasing to the eye and easy to read.

One word of caution before you tackle form and content questions. While you should not neglect form, neither should you over-emphasize it at the expense of content. A resume may be strong in content but weak in form, and vice versa. For example, you may have ten years of increasingly responsible management experience, but you will greatly weaken your application if your resume has an inappropriate format, stresses unrelated information categories, uses awkward language, presents information in a crowded and sloppy manner, and is produced on cheap quality paper. Indeed, poor resume presentation may communicate an unanticipated and disastrous message – that you are an unprofessional and careless individual. On the other hand, your resume may be written in the most professionally appearing manner, with strong headings and clear language, and be produced on high quality paper. But if it fails to communicate the substance of your objective, abilities, and experience, it will primarily demonstrate proper form and an absence of content.

> *It should look and read like good advertising copy or an effective press release – grab attention and motivate the reader to take action.*

Effective resumes successfully communicate **both** form and content. The remainder of this chapter deals with how to best communicate through resume form and structure. Chapter 7 continues this theme by examining how to develop and communicate content within the various forms.

Be Aware of Resume Positives and Negatives

Since resumes play many roles, no single resume format or style is the "best." Resume formats are more or less effective, depending on your goals, experience, style, and audience. Ideally, high impact resumes should:

- Immediately **impress and motivate the reader** to read on and take action – a real attention-grabber (an "aha" resume) requiring further investigation.

- Be visually **appealing** and easy to read.

- Be **concise** – ideally one to two pages that can be consumed in 30 seconds.

- Summarize your **work history – what you have done**, where, when, and with whom.

- Indicate your **career aspirations and goals** – what you **want to do**.

- Focus on the **employer's needs** – what you **can and will do**.

- Address the specific **requirements of a position** under consideration – your **related** skills, qualifications, and accomplishments.

- Emphasize your job-related **abilities** rather than past or present job duties.

- Stress your **value and productivity** in terms of your potential to solve employers' problems.

- Communicate that you are a **responsible, purposeful, energetic, and enthusiastic** person who gets things done.

- Appear **likable** – you're someone who should be interviewed and possibly hired because you will probably "fit in."

Employers try to quickly dispense with hundreds of resumes. In fact, we have timed employers at hiring conferences spending an average of 10 to 15 seconds reading each resume. Other observers report 30 to 40 seconds per resume as an average screening time. Many employers now use computers to sort hundreds of resumes in only a few minutes. Indeed, if your resume gets scanned, the computer may screen your resume in less than one second!

Since most resumes do not catch the reader's interest, you should try to make your resume stand out from the rest. At the very least, you should avoid the resume pitfalls frequently identified by employers and placement specialists as ones that can effectively kill your chances of being further considered for a position. As we noted in our more expanded discussion in Chapter 2, employers frequently encounter resumes exhibiting these negative characteristics:

- Too long, short, or condensed.
- Poor layout and physical appearance.
- Misspellings, bad grammar, and wordiness.
- Poor punctuation.
- Lengthy phrases, sentences, and paragraphs.
- Too slick, amateurish, and "gimmicky."
- Too boastful or dishonest.
- Poorly typed and reproduced.
- Irrelevant information.
- Critical categories missing (i.e., *Where's the work experience?*).
- Hard to understand or requires too much interpretation.
- Unexplained time gaps.
- Does not convey accomplishments nor give evidence of performance.
- Text does not support objective.
- Unclear objective.
- Lacks credibility and content.

The majority of these pitfalls relate to the form rather than the substance of the resume. They further substantiate the importance of developing an effective resume format **before** dealing with questions of resume substance or content.

Make the Right Choices

Resume development follows a three-stage process: preparation, writing, and production. Equally important, each stage has a set of sound principles you can learn and apply. The preparation stage, for example, involves creating a solid database from which to initiate the writing stage. Unfortunately, wanting to go directly into the writing and production stages, most people neglect to devote sufficient time and effort to the preparation stage. A thorough preparation means conducting a comprehensive self-inventory based upon a complete review of your work history, education, and related experiences as well as a clear understanding of your accomplishments and skills. Chapter 7 is designed to help you generate this database.

You should initially try to write your own resume for one simple reason: the final product should reflect **your** goals, abilities, and style. Alternatively, for a minimum of $100, a commercial resume writing service will be happy to quickly produce a resume for you. Others may charge $600 or more for an executive-level resume. Many of these services follow a standard format which may or may not incorporate your unique qualities and abilities. You will save money and retain quality control over your resume by doing it yourself. The process will be both enlightening and ultimately more effective. However, should you be unwilling or unable to do this yourself – you lack the necessary writing and analytical skills to create a first-class resume – at least use this book to shop around for a resume writing service that incorporates our principles of effective resume writing. At the end of this book we identify several professional resume writers who contributed resume examples to this book. These are exceptionally talented professionals who are experienced in writing high impact resumes as well as offering related job search services.

Select the Proper Format

You will find many books and guides on how to write effective resumes. We recommend consulting some of these for examples of different types of resumes and corresponding formats. But do so with a critical eye. The easiest thing to do is to copy someone else's work. Our strategy is different. We help you create your own by outlining useful strategies for developing and targeting your resume. Then, and only then, do we present examples to illustrate important resume writing principles.

You should write your resume based on a solid understanding of yourself as well as your audience. You do this by first analyzing yourself and your audience as you begin to link your aspirations to employers' needs. Remember, you are not writing the resume to your mother, spouse, yourself, or the newspaper obituary column.

There are many different types of resumes from which you can select an appropriate format to communicate your qualifications to employers. The most common types include

- Chronological resume
- Functional resume
- Combination resume
- Resume letter

Each type and corresponding format has advantages and disadvantages, depending on your purpose and audience. We include examples of these resume types in Appendix A.

Chronological Resumes

The chronological resume seems to be everyone's favorite, from job seekers to employers. It is the standard format used by a high percentage of resume writers today. The $100-plus resume writing services and the typical resume writing books, for example, most frequently use this format. It is the easiest type of resume to produce.

Chronological resumes also are known in some quarters as "obituary resumes." In other words, if you died today and we looked at your chronological resume, your resume would be excellent copy for writing a standard three-inch column obituary about what you did in the past. Furthermore, some people feel this resume literally "kills" your chances of getting an interview – particularly if you are changing careers – because it locks you into your past as well as fails to communicate your strengths.

Chronological resumes force readers to interpret candidates' backgrounds and qualifications.

The typical chronological resume has several standard characteristics, many of which constitute major resume weaknesses:

- Lacks a purposeful job objective and thus lacks internal coherence.

- Lists work experience in reverse chronological order and describes it as formal job duties and responsibilities rather than in terms of individual abilities, skills, and accomplishments.

- Puts dates first, followed by job titles and the names and addresses of former employers.

- Emphasizes work history rather than one's capabilities or patterns of performance in reference to employers' performance needs. Says a lot about what you did in the past but little about what you can and will do in the future.

While chronological resumes are the easiest to write in this traditional form, they are the least exciting and effective resumes for individuals beginning professional careers or making career changes – unless they have direct and progressive work experience related to a position in question. They force readers to interpret candidates' backgrounds and qualifications. If, for example, you have little work experience, a chronological resume clearly communicates this fact to potential employers.

If you choose a chronological resume, try to minimize the amount of interpretation required by the reader. Control the interpretations yourself by including an objective, relating your experience to the objective, emphasizing major strengths, and using a more appropriate language to express your strengths in relationship to both your objective and employers' needs. For example, describe your job activities and talk in functional terms which highlight your transferable skills. Leave out extraneous information which usually clutters this type of resume, such as height, weight, hobbies, and references.

Chronological resumes have several advantages and disadvantages. While they are much maligned by "expert" resume writers, they do have one major **advantage**: most employers are familiar with them and expect to receive them. Sending a functional or combination resume to an employer accustomed to traditional resumes may upset him or her because these other types of resumes violate the traditional norm of chronology. After all, a chronological resume has one major advantage for employers: it helps them screen in and screen out applicants based upon job titles and work history. On the other hand, functional and combination resumes enable **you** to structure the thinking of your audience around your strengths. You take the initiative in interpreting your qualifications throughout the resume rather than force the prospective employer to draw conclusions about your future performance based upon a reading of historical information.

Chronological resumes have other advantages too. They are relatively easy to write. If you have a stable employment history, you can effectively highlight your experience using this format. Employers find these resumes useful outlines for discussing your past employment record during the interview.

The **disadvantages** of the chronological resume are particularly evident for individuals first entering or re-entering the job market or changing careers. Employment gaps stand out sharply. The format may emphasize too many unrelated job experiences – you're an unfocused job hopper. Your strongest competencies are not emphasized to your advantage. Overall, this format does not provide the best presentation of your background and abilities if you are trying to enter a new occupation.

Since the majority of job applicants use this format, you can make your chronological resume stand out from the rest by writing it well and designing it tastefully. You can do this by doing the following:

- State a functional work objective.

- Include a summary of your qualifications which emphasizes your major skills, accomplishments, and patterns of performance.

- Write functional descriptions of your work experience immediately following your position titles and places of employment.

We illustrate these principles in the chronological resume examples in Appendix A.

Functional Resumes

The functional resume (Appendix A) tends to be the logical opposite of the chronological resume. De-emphasizing dates, positions, and responsibilities while emphasizing qualifications, skills, and related accomplishments, this resume begins with a functional job objective and organizes skills into functional categories. The functional resume is internally coherent because all elements focus on an objective and an audience. This resume essentially outlines abilities and transferable skills and tells employers what you will most likely do for them.

Functional resumes are especially useful for individuals lacking work experience or for those trying to enter a new occupation where they lack direct job-related experience. While this is one of the most difficult resumes to compose, it is much easier once you develop the database defining your objective, skills, and accomplishments as outlined in Chapter 7.

Functional resumes do have certain weaknesses if not done properly. For example, this type of resume can communicate "fluff" if not expertly structured around concrete experience and a clear objective. Some writers have a tendency to make generous use of a functional language which appears "canned" and says little about the specifics employers look for in candidates. Rather than grabbing the attention of employers, some of these resumes may turn off employers because they appear cleverly designed to cover over the lack of experience or hide a history of job hopping. Reading this type of resume, employers may wonder, *"Where's the beef?"* Lacking content, these resumes may raise more questions than you want to answer. Therefore, your functional resume must be a delicate balance between the employer's need to know the "details" and your desire to motivate the employer to invite you to the interview where you will talk about the "details." Nonetheless, a well structured functional resume can be an outstanding document for presenting your skills.

Combination Resumes

The combination resume (Appendix A), which is also known as the hybrid resume, combines the best elements of the chronological and functional formats. Although similar to the functional resume in describing and explaining experience, this format includes a brief employment history section. For many individuals, this is the ideal type of resume – bridging both the chronological and functional resume formats and language as well as drawing on the strengths of each.

The combination resume combines the best elements of the chronological and functional formats.

Combination resumes stress skills and competencies, yet include names and dates. These resumes enable you to stress your qualifications in both chronological and functional terms as well as handle employment history easily. As such, this is a unique and complete resume for many employment situations.

Combination resumes have one major problem: they are usually difficult to write. In addition, their functional and chronological sections may overlap and create annoying redundancy.

Resume Letters

Resume letters (Appendix A) should be used if a resume is not available or if a situation is not appropriate for sending a resume. This is basically a letter that summarizes your employment goals and qualifications. When using this letter, your goal should be to communicate directly to a specific person in an organization your skills and qualifications. This letter should follow the same rules for writing a good resume: be concise, use action verbs, identify the needs of the employer, talk about your accomplishments, and show how your abilities and skills can meet the employer's needs.

Know Your Situation

The format you choose should reflect your personal situation and goals. Consider your qualifications, your objective, your work history, and the kind of employer you seek before you select a style. The functional and combination resumes are conceptually superior to chronological resumes – especially if your audience understands the superior quality of such resumes and knows what type of person they want to hire. Therefore, you should try to learn as much as possible about your audience.

Functional and combination resumes can be very effective in getting interviews that result in job offers. These resumes communicate four important things about you that employers want to know:

1. What you **want to do** (your objective).

2. What you **have done** (your work history).

3. What you **can do** (your pattern of skills and accomplishments – your strengths).

4. What you **will most likely do** in the future (best prediction of your future performance based upon how you answered questions 1, 2, and 3).

Above all, these resumes address the **needs of employers**. You **must** respond to employers' needs if you are serious about getting job interviews based on your resumes and letters.

But none of these resumes are inherently superior – they only offer advantages and disadvantages for job seekers with varying work-related experience and for different audiences with varied expectations, likes, and dislikes. If, for example, you want to advance within a particular occupational area and have a strong job-related background, by all means use a chronological resume. Use functional language which will further strengthen the objective and work experience sections of this resume.

> *None of these resumes have inherent superiority – only advantages and disadvantages.*

On the other hand, if you are changing careers, we recommend a combination resume which emphasizes functional categories more than chronological ones. In this situation, it's important to communicate your transferable skills. This resume best bridges the gap between traditional and functional thinking. It should satisfy all audiences without alienating any particular one.

Finally, if you are entering the workforce for the first time or re-entering it after a lengthy absence, the functional format may be best suited to your situation. This is especially true for students who may be entering the job market without a history of formal job titles. Use the criteria in the chart at the top of page 68 for selecting a resume format appropriate for your career situation.

Whichever format you choose, remember: **we** are not your audience; **we** will not be interviewing you; and **we** will not be offering you a job. You must use **your** own judgment based upon **your** work experience and your information on **your** audience. If you are uncertain about which format to use, experiment with the chronological, functional, and combination styles to see which one best communicates your qualifications to employers. The best resume format for you will be the one that sufficiently grabs the attention of employers to call you for an interview.

Format	Your Goal/Experience Base
Chronological	Advance within your present occupational area or field. Demonstrate strong job-related background.
Combination	Change careers but have substantial work experience directly or indirectly related to the occupational area.
Functional	Lack work experience in an occupational area, wish to change careers, or re-enter the job market after lengthy absence.
Resume Letter	Use at appropriate time as a substitute for any of the other resume formats.

Organize It Right

After choosing a format, you should be ready to organize pertinent information for producing an effective resume. Your organization and production activities should follow these five distinct steps:

1. Creating a database (Chapter 7)
2. Producing a first draft (Chapter 8)
3. Critiquing and evaluating (Chapter 8)
4. Producing and distributing (Chapter 10)
5. Following up (Chapter 11)

As you develop your database in Chapter 7 for writing your first draft, you should keep in mind these **general guidelines** for organizing your resume:

Format and Organization

The internal organization of your resume should include several items. The following are **recommended** for **all** resumes:

- Contact information: name, address, telephone and/or fax number, e-mail address
- Objective
- Summary of qualifications
- Qualifications or functional experience
- Education

In addition, you should consider including some of the following **optional** elements:

- Work history or professional experience
- Publications, presentations, and research
- Memberships and affiliations

- Reference section
- Personal summary statement
- Miscellaneous information: hobbies, licenses, special skills **supporting your objective**

A very effective resume would combine several recommended and optional elements within a one- or two-page format. The format should be enticing to the reader's eyes. Avoid cluttering, by providing ample spacing and margins so the reader does not strain. Knowing that our eyes tend to focus on the middle and move from left to right and up and down when reading, we suggest using the format on page 70. Do this:

- Center your name, address, and telephone number at the top. Capitalize your name.
- Capitalize all headings and run them along the left side of the paper.
- Place all descriptive material to the right of the headings.

You should examine other formats. However, we believe this one is kindest to your audience, because it is easy to read.

Length

We agree with most resume advisors that the one-page resume is the most appropriate. We prefer it because it focuses the reader's attention on a single field of vision. This is a definite asset considering the fact that many employers must review hundreds of resumes each week. Research clearly demonstrates that retention rates decrease as one's eyes move down the page and nearly vanish on a second or third page! At first the thought of writing a one-page resume may pose problems for you, especially if you think your resume should be a presentation of your life history. However, many executives with 25 years of experience, who make $100,000 or more a year, manage to get all their major qualifications onto a one-page resume. If they can do it, so can you.

Sequencing of Elements

The sequence of elements will vary depending on the type of resume you decide to use. The **chronological resume**, for example, should have the following order of elements:

- Contact information
- Objective
- Summary of qualifications
- Work experience (or education, depending on your objective and audience)
- Education
- Optional personal statement

Resume Format

Contact
Information

Summary of
Qualifications

descriptive material   descriptive material

We recommend using the following order of elements for a **functional resume**:

- Contact information
- Objective
- Summary of qualifications
- Presentation of transferable skills supported by achievements ("Areas of Effectiveness")
- Education
- Optional personal statement

The **combination resume** should include the following sequence of elements:

- Contact information
- Objective
- Summary of qualifications
- Presentation of transferable skills supported by achievements
- Brief outline of work history
- Education
- Optional personal statement

In each resume **always place the most important information first**. For example, if your work experience is your strongest qualification, place it immediately following the objective. However, if your education is most relevant, place it ahead of work experience.

Details and Balance

Lengthy, detailed descriptions are inappropriate on a resume. They become liabilities rather than assets. Readers prefer a writing style which uses short succinct statements that get to the point quickly. Be sure to emphasize specific areas of expertise beneficial to the employer. Keep each section neat, organized, and balanced.

Abbreviations

Do not use abbreviations except for your middle initial. Avoid the use of "etc.", "i.e.", "e.g."

Documentation

You should view each section of your resume as providing **supports** for your objective. Each section should document your supports.

Consistency

Format should be consistent, especially verb tense, order of information, and layout.

Language   Use crisp, succinct, expressive, and direct language. Avoid poetic, bureaucratic, vernacular, and academic terms. For example, instead of stating your objective as:

> *"I would like to work with a consulting firm where I can develop new programs and utilize my decision making and systems engineering experience. I hope to improve your organization's profits."*

Re-word the objective so it reads like this:

> *"An increasingly responsible research and development position, where proven decision-making and systems engineering abilities will be used to improve productivity."*

Use the first person, but do not refer to yourself as "I" or "the author." Always use active verbs and parallel sentence structure. Avoid introductory and wind-up phrases like *"My duties included..."* or *"Position description reads as follows."* Do not use jargon unless it is appropriate to the situation – for example, *"proficient in C++ and Java."*

Appearance   Use various visual techniques to emphasize important aspects of your resume – spacing, marginal descriptions, centered headlines, underlining, boldface, different type sizes and styles, uppercase letters. Develop an attractive, uncrowded format. Remember, "less is often more" when deciding what to include in your layout.

The exact structure of each information category within your resume will vary depending on your objective and choice of resume format. Chapter 7 examines each resume category and provides worksheets and exercises for developing the necessary database for writing your first draft. We have included these worksheets and exercises because you need to generate a large database so you will have enough information to develop each resume section. At the minimum, your database should include the following:

Contact Information   Full name, address (office and home), telephone/fax numbers, e-mail address.

Career or Job Objective   A one-sentence statement of what you intend to do for the employer. Immediately follows the contact information at the top of the resume.

Education	Degree(s), school(s), highlights, and/or special training/ courses.
Work Experience	Paid and non-paid experiences – employment, internships, volunteer work.
Military Experience	Rank, service, assignments, achievements, demonstrated skills and abilities.
Community Involvement	Offices held, organizations, dates, contributions, projects, demonstrated skills.
Professional Affiliations	Memberships, offices held, projects, certifications, licenses.
Special Skills	Foreign languages, computers, special equipment, artistic talent, etc.
Interests and Activities	Avocations, hobbies, and special interests that relate to your objective.
Miscellaneous	<ul><li>Salary requirements</li><li>Extent of job-related travel acceptable</li><li>Are you willing to relocate? To where?</li><li>When can you start work?</li><li>References: May they be contacted?</li><li>Anything else you think is important</li></ul>

Selecting what should go on a resume also involves making judgments concerning what **not** to include. We find several items to be inappropriate for most resumes, although some of these will be included in your database:

Present Date	Include it in a cover letter, if necessary.
Photograph	Provide only if it is essential for a job, such as in modeling or theater.
Ethnicity, Religion, or Politics	Include only if it is part of the main thrust of your resume or a bona fide occupational qualification.
Salary	Salary usually is negotiable, but it should only arise at the end of the interview or during the job offer – not given prematurely on a resume.
References	Always make your references "available upon request." You want to control the selection of references as well as alert them that you are applying for a specific position and ask to use their name as a reference.

| **Personal Information** | Height, weight, age, sex, marital status, and health – few, if any, of these characteristics strengthen or relate to your objective. Some may, for example, if you are a model or karate instructor. |
| **Any Negative Information** | Employment gaps, medical problems, criminal record, divorced, fired. There is absolutely no reason for you to volunteer potential negatives on your resume. |

Remember What's Really Important

When deciding what to include or exclude on your resume, always remember these important writing guidelines for creating high impact communications:

1. Your resume is your personal **advertisement**.

2. The purpose of the resume is to get an **interview**. How well you present your skills and accomplishments in the interview determines whether or not you will get the job.

3. Take the offensive by developing a resume that **structures the reader's thinking** around your objective, qualifications, strengths, and projections of future performance.

4. Your resume should **generate positive thinking** rather than raise negative questions or confuse readers.

5. Your resume should **focus on your audience** and should communicate clearly what it is you can do for them.

6. Always be **honest** without being stupid. Stress your positives; never volunteer or confess your negatives.

If you keep these purposes and principles in mind, you should produce a resume as well as conduct a job search that is both purposeful and positive. Your resume should stand out above the crowd as you communicate your qualifications to employers with impact!

7

Develop Powerful
Resume Content

S O WHAT ARE YOU PLANNING TO PUT on your resume? Should you include an objective? What about your references, hobbies, and salary expectations? Better still, what should you leave off? What are the sources for this information? How should each section be developed and related to other sections? Do you have a clear plan for putting each section of your resume together? Let's find some good, practical answers to these questions by examining the structure of your resume.

Present Your Best Self

Communicating your qualifications to employers via resumes and job search letters requires that you produce particular types of documents that will have an impact on employers. Your resume should represent your best self – the best of what you have done, can do, and will do in the future. Your best self includes your strengths and achievements reformulated and targeted around your career goals. This document must communicate both your goals and strengths in direct relation to employers' needs. You do this through a process of self-discovery that flushes out this key information on yourself:

1. What you do well.
2. What you enjoy doing.
3. What you plan to do for the employer.

After doing this, you take this information and reformulate it so that it becomes the basis for structuring each section of your resume and letters.

Create a Powerful Database for Analysis

Our approach to producing high impact resumes requires that you follow this four-step procedure:

1. Create a large database on yourself.
2. Distill the database into concise one- or two-page resume drafts.
3. Evaluate each draft.
4. Revise the final draft for production.

You need to begin with the database so you will have sufficient information to complete each section of your resume. This step involves recalling and classifying your past into proper information categories. When generating your database, always go for volume. It's best to begin with more and selectively distill it to less. You can always select and condense information if you begin with a large enough pool of data.

The remaining three steps primarily involve your analytical and creative writing skills. You must analyze and synthesize the information in your database as well as distill it into short yet powerful sentences and paragraphs. This is the most challenging aspect of developing a high impact resume.

We've designed exercises and forms in this chapter to guide you through the first step. They will help sharpen your recall, analysis, synthesis, and creative writing skills. Chapter 8 organizes the data generated in this chapter for completing the remaining three resume production steps.

As you put together your resume, keep in mind that your resume is not your life history. It is supposed to communicate your purpose and abilities to others. It advertises your **future** – not your past. At the same time, you must show how your past is relevant to your future performance.

Specify Contact Information

The first item appearing on your resume should be your contact information. Make it both attractive and functional. It always appears at the top of the resume, preferably centered, and includes the following information categories and writing rules:

Category	Writing Rules
Name	State your full professional name. Avoid the coldness of abbreviations, such as "I. T. Snell." Do not use more than one abbreviated initial. If you use titles such as Mr., Mrs., Ms., Dr., or Ph.D., you may appear pompous and distant. It is best to capitalize all letters in your name.
Address	Use your home mailing address – avoid P.O. Box numbers. Do not forget to include your zip code. If you are at a temporary location, include both permanent and temporary addresses. The purpose of your address is to get the mail to you as quickly as possible – and not to indicate where you are "from."
Contact Numbers	List telephone, cell phone, fax, and pager numbers where you can be reached during the day and evening or a number where a message can be left for you. The long distance area code should be included. If you are highly mobile, use a pager, enlist a telephone answering service, or use a telephone answering machine. Be sure

you record a message that sounds professional – no humorous greetings or lots of bells and whistles. If you have e-mail, include your e-mail address.

Formats   Your contact information can appear in several alternative forms. Take for example the following resume headings – all of which are acceptable:

JOHN C. TALBORT
_____

2261 Gateway Dr.   Richmond, VA 23612   823-467-9042

JOHN C. TALBORT
823-467-9042 (home)
823-467-2148 (office)
E-mail: talbortj@aol.com

2261 Gateway Drive   Richmond, VA 23612

JOHN C. TALBORT

2261 Gateway Drive   Richmond, VA 23612   823-467-9042

JOHN C. TALBORT
2261 Gateway Drive   Home: 823-467-9042
Richmond, VA 23512   Office: 823-467-2148
                                      E-mail: talbortj@aol.com

---

JOHN C. TALBORT
_____

2261 Gateway Drive   Richmond, VA 23612   823-467-9042
_____

Make sure your contact information is uncluttered and pleasing to the eye. Since it will be the very first piece of information the reader sees on your resume, it should invite him to read further.

State an Employer-Oriented Objective

The job objective normally appears immediately following your contact information. However, some resume advisers recommend starting with a "Summary," "Summary of Qualifications," "Career Highlights," "Career Profile," or "Career Focus" section in lieu of an objective statement. Many of them consider an objective statement to be an unnecessary, pretentious, and optional item. Nonetheless, we see an objective statement to be necessary, professional, and thoughtful. Following it with these other types of summary statements is an excellent idea.

You have two options here: (1) place an objective on the resume or (2) leave it off but include it in your accompanying cover letter. The reason many people prefer putting an objective in a cover letter rather than on the resume is that they don't want to re-type their resume every time they want to reword their objective for a particular position. Since most people word-process their resume, changing the objective on the resume is relatively easy. In so doing, you can literally custom design your resume around specific jobs.

> *The objective should be the central focal point around which all other elements in the resume relate.*

However, changing your objective for each employer is a sign of trying to fit into a job rather than finding a job fit for yourself. It indicates a lack of clear purpose and direction – you don't know what you really want to do other than land a job.

We still prefer the objective at the top of the resume, because it should be the central focal point around which all other elements in the resume relate. If you know what you want to do and can state your objective in general terms, it can be used repeatedly for different positions and audiences. An objective appearing at the top of your resume makes your resume more complete and balanced.

The relative impact of these different strategies may be the old proverbial *"Six one way, half a dozen another."* It may not make much difference in the end. But be sure you communicate, in some manner, your career direction. Otherwise, you may conduct a traditionally disorganized search with a weak chronological resume. Our resume examples in Appendices A and B include resumes with and without objectives

Using Objectives

Your objective should be a concise statement of what you want to do and what you have to offer to an employer. The position you seek is *"what you want to do"*; your qualifications are *"what you have to offer."* Your objective should state your strongest qualifications for meeting employers' needs. It should communicate what you have to offer an employer without emphasizing what you expect the employer to do for you. In other words, your objective should be **work-centered**, not self-centered; it should not contain trite terms which emphasize what you want, such as give me a(n) *"opportunity for advancement," "position working with people," "progressive company,"* or *"creative position."* Such terms are viewed by employers as "canned" resume language saying little of value about you. Above all, your objective should reflect your honesty and integrity; it should not be "hyped."

Identifying what it is you want to do can be one of the most difficult job search tasks. Indeed, most job hunters lack clear objectives. Many engage in a random and somewhat mindless search for jobs by identifying available job opportunities and then adjusting their skills and objectives to "fit" specific job openings. While you will get a job using this approach, you may be misplaced and unhappy with what you find. You will fit into a job rather than find a job that is fit for you.

Knowing what you want to do can have numerous benefits. First, you define the job market rather than let it define you. The inherent fragmentation and chaos of the job market should be advantageous for you because it enables you to systematically organize job opportunities around your specific objectives and skills. Second, since your resume will focus on an objective, you will communicate professionalism to prospective employers. They will receive a precise indication of your interests, qualifications, and purposes, which places you ahead of most other applicants. Third, being purposeful means being able to communicate to employers what you want to do. Employers are not interested in hiring indecisive and confused individuals. They want to

> *Your objective should be **work-centered**, not self-centered.*

know what it is you can do for them. With a clear objective – based on a thorough understanding of your abilities and skills – you can take control of the situation and demonstrate your value to employers.

Finally, many employers don't really know what they want in a candidate. Like most job seekers, employers often lack clear employment objectives and knowledge about how the job market operates. Thus, if you know what you want and can help the employer define his or her "needs" as your objective, you will have achieved a tremendously advantageous position in the job market.

Transferable Skills

The first step in developing your objective is to understand your transferable skills. Some writers also refer to these as "functional skills." Transferable skills are skills which can be used in different job settings. Most people possess hundreds of such skills. Once you become aware of them, you will be better able to use a functional skills vocabulary throughout your resume.

Take, for example, the case of educators seeking career changes. While educators tend to view their qualifications as mastery of specific disciplines and subject matters, they also possess functional skills which are transferable to jobs and careers in business, industry, and government. These skills first develop in childhood and subsequently expand through other life experiences, such as schools, universities, and community organizations. In the case of graduate students in the humanities, studies show that the most important transferable skills acquired in graduate training, in order of importance, are:

1. critical thinking	7. general knowledge
2. research techniques	8. cultural perspective
3. perseverance	9. teaching ability
4. self-discipline	10. self-confidence
5. insight	11. imagination
6. writing	12. leadership ability

Educators possess many of these and other transferable skills, acquired while performing the role of educator. **Teaching**, for example, involves skills other than instructing:

__ organizing	__ problem solving	__ coordinating
__ making decisions	__ public speaking	__ managing
__ counseling	__ advising	__ reporting
__ motivating	__ coaching	__ administering
__ leading	__ evaluating	__ persuading
__ selling	__ training	__ encouraging
__ assessing	__ supervising	__ improving

Research and publication activities of academicians involve many additional transferable skills:

__ initiating	__ interpreting	__ analyzing
__ updating	__ planning	__ designing
__ communicating	__ estimating	__ implementing
__ performing	__ achieving	__ reviewing
__ attaining	__ negotiating	__ synthesizing

Interacting with students, faculty, administrators, and staff requires using several skill-related personality qualities:

__ dynamic	__ unique	__ challenging
__ imaginative	__ versatile	__ sophisticated
__ innovative	__ responsible	__ diplomatic
__ perceptive	__ concerned	__ discreet
__ outstanding	__ successful	__ creative
__ tactful	__ easygoing	__ effective
__ reliable	__ humanistic	__ adept
__ vigorous	__ competent	__ efficient
__ sensitive	__ warm	__ aware
__ accurate	__ objective	__ honest
__ trained	__ broad	__ self-starter
__ expert	__ outgoing	__ strong
__ astute	__ experienced	__ talented
__ calm	__ democratic	__ empathic

Such transferable skills are generic to other occupational areas. You may wish to identify and prioritize those which relate to your experiences. In addition, most individuals are capable of working with different elements in the workplace which are related to transferable skills:

__ data	__ reports	__ designs
__ recommendations	__ systems	__ unusual conditions
__ inefficiencies	__ programs	__ communication systems
__ facts	__ conclusions	__ research projects
__ feelings	__ groups	__ training programs

__ procedures	__ art	__ journals
__ techniques	__ methods	__ growth
__ project planning	__ objectives	__ approaches
__ relations	__ individuals	__ presentations
__ events	__ information	__ problems
__ goals	__ theories	__ statistical analyses
__ processes	__ records	__ human resources
__ statistics	__ handbooks	__ costs
__ equipment	__ inputs	__ duties
__ living things	__ investigations	__ plants
__ tools	__ outputs	__ surveys
__ charts	__ surveys	__ energy
__ points of view	__ strategy	__ senior executives
__ prima donnas		

Identifying your transferable skills may be simple or complex, depending on how much time and effort you wish to invest. Career counselors have developed numerous inductive approaches – mostly self-directed exercises – for helping you identify your skills. Since you may want options, we outline alternative "skills" approaches, point out their strengths and weaknesses, and explain the importance of using redundancy to your benefit. We advise you to try several approaches and assess which ones give you the most useful information.

Intensive Skills Identification

Intensive Skills Identification is widely used by career counselors. This technique helps you identify which skills you **enjoy** using. Since you will need six to eight hours to properly complete this exercise, divide your time into two or three work sessions. The exercise consists of six steps:

1. **Identify 15-20 achievements.** These consist of anything you enjoyed doing, believe you did well, and felt a sense of satisfaction, pride, or accomplishment in doing. You can see yourself performing at your best and enjoying your experiences when you analyze your achievements. This information reveals your motivations, since it deals entirely with your voluntary behavior. In addition, it identifies what is right with you, by focusing on your positives and strengths. Identify achievements throughout your life, beginning with your childhood. Your achievements should relate to specific experiences – not general ones – and may be drawn from work, leisure, education, military experience, or home life. Put each achievement at the top of a separate sheet of paper. For example, your achievements might appear as follows:

    "When I was 10 years old, I started a small paper route and built it up to the largest in my district."

    _____

    "I started playing chess in ninth grade and earned the right to play first board on my high school chess team in my junior year."

    _____

"Learned to play the piano and often played for church services while in high school."

_____

"Designed and constructed a dress for a 4-H demonstration project."

_____

"Although I was small compared to other guys, I made the first string on my high school football team."

_____

"I graduated from high school with honors even though I was very active in school clubs and had to work part-time."

_____

"I was the first in my family to go to college and one of the few from my high school. Worked part-time and summers. A real struggle, but I made it."

_____

"Earned an 'A' grade on my senior psychology project from a real tough professor."

_____

"Finished my master's degree while working full-time and attending to my family responsibilities."

_____

"Proposed a chef's course for junior high boys. Got it approved. Developed it into a very popular elective."

_____

"Designed the plans for our house and had it constructed within budget."

_____

2. Prioritize your seven most significant achievements.

1. _____

2. _____

3. _____

4. _____

5. _____

6. _____

7. _____

3. **Write a full page on each of your prioritized achievements.** Describe:

   - How you initially became involved.
   - The details of **what you did** and **how you did it.**
   - What was especially enjoyable or satisfying to you.

   Use copies of the "Detailing Your Achievements" form on page 84 to outline your achievements.

4. **Elaborate on your achievements.** Have one or two other people interview you. For each achievement have them note on a separate sheet of paper any terms used to reveal your skills, abilities, and personal qualities. To elaborate on details, the interviewer(s) may ask:

   - What was involved in the achievement?
   - What was your part?
   - What did you actually do?
   - How did you go about that?

   Clarify any vague areas by providing an example or illustration of what you actually did. This interview should clarify the details of your activities by asking only "what" and "how" questions. Reproduce the "Strength Identification Interview" form on page 85 to guide you through this interview.

5. **Identify patterns by examining the interviewer's notes.** Together, identify the recurring skills, abilities, and personal qualities **demonstrated** in your achievements. Search for patterns. Your skills pattern should be clear at this point, and you should feel comfortable with it. If you have questions, review the data. If you disagree with a conclusion, disregard it. The results must accurately and honestly reflect how you operate.

6. **Synthesize the information by clustering similar skills into clusters.** For example, your skills might be grouped in the following manner:

Synthesized Skill Clusters

Investigate/Survey/Read	Teach/Train/Drill
Inquire/Probe/Question	Perform/Show/Demonstrate
Learn/Memorize/Practice	Construct/Assemble/Put together
Evaluate/Appraise/Assess	
Compare	Organize/Structure/Provide
	definition/Plan/Chart course/
Influence/Involve/Get	Strategize/Coordinate
participation/Publicize	
Promote	Create/Design/Adapt/Modify

Detailing Your Achievements

ACHIEVEMENT # __: _____

_____

1. How did I initially become involved? _____

   _____

   _____

   _____

   _____

   _____

2. What did I do? _____

   _____

   _____

   _____

   _____

3. How did I do it? _____

   _____

   _____

   _____

   _____

4. What was especially enjoyable about doing it? _____

   _____

   _____

   _____

   _____

Strength Identification Interview

Interviewee _____   Interviewer _____

INSTRUCTIONS: For each achievement experience, identify the **skills** and abilities which the achiever actually demonstrated. To obtain details of the experience, ask **what** was involved with the achievement and **how** the individual made the achievement happen. Avoid "why" questions which tend to mislead. Ask for examples or illustrations.

Achievement # ____

Achievement # ____

Achievement # ____

Recurring Skills and Abilities:

This exercise yields a comprehensive inventory of your skills. The information will better enable you to use a **skills vocabulary** when identifying your objective, writing your resume and letters, and interviewing. Your self-confidence and self-esteem should increase accordingly.

Checklist Method

One of the most popular approaches to skills identification is Richard Bolles's "Quick Job Hunting Map." It is found in the resource section of his book, *What Color Is Your Parachute?*, or it can be purchased as a separate workbook: *What Color Is Your Parachute Workbook* (Ten Speed Press, Berkeley, CA). It's included in the order form at the end of this book.

The "Map" contains a comprehensive skills checklist for helping you build your skills vocabulary. You simply identify your most satisfying accomplishments, jobs, or roles in life and relate these to a listing of skills. Depending on how thoroughly and detailed you treat each experience, this exercise may take six hours to complete. While the "Map" is a rather laborious exercise, it's easy to use and yields an enormous amount of interrelated information on things you both do well and enjoy doing. The exercise gives you a fairly comprehensive snapshot of your past skills and motivational patterns. Like most such self-assessment devices based upon examining past patterns of behavior, the "Map" may or may not be a good predictor of your future. It does have one major advantage – it helps you build your "skills vocabulary" for developing a useful resume language.

Other Alternatives

Alternative techniques are available for identifying transferable skills. Most are inductive self-directed exercises which identify skills based upon analyzing past experiences. Any of the following exercises can be used interchangeably to inventory your skills:

1. Write your autobiography with special emphasis on your pleasures and accomplishments. This may run from 30 to 200 pages or more. Analyze this document by identifying those things you most enjoyed doing and wish to continue doing in the future. Identify which set of skills best cluster with your favorite experiences.

2. List all your hobbies and analyze what you do in each, which ones you like the most, what skills you use, and your accomplishments.

3. Acquire a copy of Arthur F. Miller and Ralph T. Mattson's *The Truth About You* (Ten Speed Press) and work through the exercises found in the Appendix. This is an abbreviated version of the authors' SIMA (System for Identifying Motivated Abilities) technique used by their career counseling firm, People Management, Inc. (www.jobfit-pmi.com).

4. Get a copy of Nella Barkley's and Eric Sandburg's *The Crystal-Barkley Guide to Taking Charge of Your Career* (Workman) and complete its various chapters. This book is based on the pioneering self-assessment work of John Crystal, which is the basis for Richard Bolles's work.

5. Complete John Holland's *"The Self-Directed Search."* You'll find it in his book, *Making Vocational Choices: A Theory of Careers*, or in a separate publication entitled *The Self-Directed Search – A Guide to Educational and Vocational Planning* (Psychological Assessment Resources, self-directed-search.com).

6. Conduct a job analysis by writing about your past jobs and identifying which skills you used in each job. Cluster the skills into related categories and prioritize them according to your preferences.

Benefiting From Redundancy

The self-directed "skills" exercises generate similar information. They identify transferable skills you already possess. While aptitude and achievement tests may yield similar information, the self-directed exercises have three major advantages over the standardized tests: less expensive, self-monitored and evaluated, and measure motivation **and** ability.

Completing each exercise demands a different investment of your time. Writing your life history and completing the Intensive Skills Identification exercise as well as Bolles's "Map" are the most time-consuming. On the other hand, Holland's self-directed search can be completed in a few minutes. But the more time you invest with each technique, the more useful information you will generate. We recommend creating redundancy by using two or three different techniques. This will help reinforce and confirm the validity of your observations and interpretations. If you are making a mid-career change and/or have a considerable amount of experience, we recommend using the more thorough exercises. The more you put into these techniques and exercises, the more your resume and other stages of the job search will benefit.

Understanding and Realism

Your objective should communicate that you are a **purposeful individual who achieves results**. It can be stated over different time periods as well as at various levels of abstraction and specificity. You can identify short-, intermediate-, and long-range objectives and very general to very specific objectives. Whatever the case, it is best to know your prospective audience before deciding on the type of objective. Your objective should reflect your career interests as well as employers' needs.

> *Your objective should communicate that you are a purposeful individual who achieves results.*

Objectives also should be **realistic**. You may want to become president of the United States or solve all the world's problems. However, these objectives are probably unrealistic. While they may represent your ideals and fantasies, you need to be more realistic in terms of what you can personally accomplish in the immediate future. What, for example, are you prepared to deliver to prospective employers over the next few months? While it is good to set challenging objectives, you can overdo it. Refine your objective by thinking about the next major step or two you would like to make in your career advancement – not some grandiose leap outside reality!

Projecting Into the Future

Even after identifying your abilities and skills, specifying an objective can be the most difficult and tedious step in the job search process; it can stall the resume writing process indefinitely. This simple one-sentence, approximately 25-word statement can take days or weeks to formulate and clearly define. Yet, it must be specified prior to writing the resume and engaging in other job search steps. An objective gives meaning and direction to all other activities.

Your objective should be viewed as a function of several influences. Since you want to build upon your strengths and you want to be realistic, your abilities and skills will play a central role in formulating your work objective. At the same time, you do not want your objective to become a function solely of your past accomplishments and skills. You may be very skilled in certain areas, but you may not want to use these skills in the future. As a result, your values and interests filter which skills you will or will not incorporate into your work objective.

Overcoming the problem of historical determinism – your future merely reflecting your past – requires incorporating additional components into defining your objective. One of the most important is your ideals, fantasies, or dreams. Everyone engages in these, and sometimes they come true. Your ideals, fantasies, or dreams may include making $1,000,000 by age 45; owning a Mercedes-Benz and a Porsche; taking trips to Rio, Hong Kong, and Rome; owning your own business; developing financial independence; writing a bestselling novel; solving major social problems; or winning the Nobel Peace Prize. If your fantasies require more money than you are now making, you will need to incorporate monetary considerations into your work objective.

You can develop realistic objectives many different ways. We don't claim to have a new or magical formula, only one which has worked for many individuals. We assume you are capable of making intelligent career decisions if given sufficient data. Using redundancy once again, our approach is designed to provide you with sufficient corroborating data from several sources and perspectives so that you can make preliminary decisions. If you follow our steps in setting a realistic objective, you should be able to give your job search clear direction and create a well-integrated resume.

Four major steps are involved in developing a work objective. Each step can be implemented in a variety of ways:

STEP 1

Develop or obtain basic data on your functional/transferable skills, which we discussed earlier in this chapter.

STEP 2

Acquire corroborating data about yourself from others, tests, and yourself. Several resources are available for this purpose:

A. From others: Ask three to five individuals who know you well to evaluate you according to the questions in the "Strength Evaluation" form on page 89. Explain to these people that you believe their candid appraisal will help you gain a better understanding of your strengths and weaknesses from the perspectives of others. Make copies of this form and ask your evaluators to

Strength Evaluation

TO: _____

FROM: _____

I am going through a career assessment process and thought you would be an appropriate person to ask for assistance. Would you please candidly respond to the questions below? Your comments will be given to me by the individual designated below; s/he will not reveal your name. Your comments will be used for advising purposes only. Thank you.

What are my strengths?

What weak areas might I need to improve?

In your opinion, what do I need in a job or career to make me satisfied?

Please return to: _____

complete and return it to a designated third party who will share the information – but not the respondent's name – with you.

B. From vocational tests: Although we prefer that you use self-generated data, vocationally oriented tests can help clarify, confirm, and translate your understanding of yourself into occupational directions. If you decide to use vocational tests, contact a professional career counselor who can administer and interpret the tests. We recommend several of the following tests:

- *Myers-Briggs Type Indicator ™*
- *Strong Interest Inventory ™*
- *The Self-Directed Search (SDS)*
- *Campbell Interest and Skill Survey*
- *Keirsey Character Sorter*
- *Birkman Method*
- *Enneagram*
- *FIRO-B*
- *California Psychological Inventory (CPI)*
- *16 Personality Factors Profile*
- *Edwards Personal Preference Schedule*
- *Kuder Occupational Interest Survey*
- *APTICOM*
- *Jackson Vocational Interest Survey*
- *Vocational Interest Inventory*
- *Temperament and Values Inventory*
- *Career Assessment Inventory*

C. From yourself: Numerous alternatives are available for you to practice redundancy:

1. Identify your work values or "satisfiers" by checking the items which pertain to you in this "Identifying Your Work Values" exercise:

I prefer employment which enables me to:

__ contribute to society	__ be creative
__ have contact with people	__ supervise others
__ work alone	__ work with details
__ work with a team	__ gain recognition
__ compete with others	__ acquire security
__ make decisions	__ make lots of money
__ work under pressure	__ help others
__ use power and authority	__ solve problems
__ acquire new knowledge	__ take risks
__ be a recognized expert	__ work at own pace

Select four work values from the above list which are the most important to you and list them in the space below. List any other work values (desired satisfactions) which were not listed above but which are important to you:

1. _____

2. _____

3. _____

4. _____

   _____

   _____

   _____

   _____

2. Develop a comprehensive list of your past and present **job frustrations and dissatisfactions**. This should help you identify negative factors which should be avoided in future jobs:

My Job Frustrations and Dissatisfactions

List as many past and present things that frustrate or make you dissatisfied and unhappy in job situations:

Rank

1. _____ ____

2. _____ ____

3. _____ ____

4. _____ ____

5. _____ ____

6. _____ ____

7. _____ ____

8. _____ ____

9. _____ ____

10. _____ ____

3. Brainstorm a list of "Ten or More Things I Love to Do." Identify which ones could be incorporated into what kinds of work environments:

Ten or More Things I Love To Do

To the right of each item you list, indicate what work environment best relates to the particular item:

Item	Related Environment
1. _____	_____
2. _____	_____
3. _____	_____
4. _____	_____
5. _____	_____
6. _____	_____
7. _____	_____
8. _____	_____
9. _____	_____
10. _____	_____

4. List "Ten Things I Enjoy the Most About Work" and rank each item accordingly:

Ten Things I Enjoy the Most About Work

Rank

1. _____ ____
2. _____ ____
3. _____ ____
4. _____ ____
5. _____ ____
6. _____ ____

7. _____ ____

8. _____ ____

9. _____ ____

10. _____ ____

5. Your "Interpersonal Environments" of work are extremely important. Identify the types of people you like and dislike associating with:

Interpersonal Environments

Characteristics of people I like working with:	Characteristics of people I dislike working with:
_____	_____
_____	_____
_____	_____
_____	_____
_____	_____
_____	_____
_____	_____
_____	_____
_____	_____
_____	_____
_____	_____

STEP 3

Project your values and preferences into the future by completing simulation and creative thinking exercises:

A. Ten Million Dollar Exercise: First, assume that you are given a $10,000,000 gift; now you don't have to work. Since the gift is restricted to your use only, you cannot give any part of it away. What will you do with your time? At first? Later on? Second, assume that you are given another $10,000,000, but this time you are required to give it all away. What kinds of causes, organizations, charities, etc. would you support?

What Will I Do With Two $10,000,000 Gifts?

First gift is restricted to my use only:

_____

_____

_____

_____

Second gift must be given away:

_____

_____

_____

_____

B. **Obituary Exercise:** Make a list of the most important things you would like to do or accomplish before you die. Two alternatives are available for doing this. First, make the list in response to this lead-in statement: *"Before I die, I want to . . ."*

Before I Die, I Want To . . .

1. _____

2. _____

3. _____

4. _____

5. _____

6. _____

7. _____

8. _____

9. _____

10. _____

Second, write a newspaper article which is actually your obituary for ten years from now. Stress your accomplishments over the coming ten-year period.

My Obituary

Obituary for Mr./Ms. _____ to appear in the _____
_____ Newspaper in the year 20___.

_____

_____

_____

_____

_____

_____

_____

_____

_____

_____

_____

_____

_____

C. **My Ideal Work Week:** Starting with Monday, place each day of the week on the headings of seven sheets of paper. Develop a daily calendar with 30-minute intervals, beginning at 7am and ending at midnight. Your calendar should consist of a 119-hour week. Next, beginning at 7am on Monday (sheet one), identify the **ideal activities** you would enjoy doing, prefer doing, or need to do for each 30-minute segment during the day. Assume you are capable of doing anything; you have no constraints except those you impose on yourself. Furthermore, assume that your work schedule consists of 40 hours per week. How will you fill your time? Be specific.

My Ideal Work Week

Monday
am   pm

7:00 _____   4:00 _____

7:30 _____   4:30 _____

8:00 _____   5:00 _____

8:30 _____   5:30 _____

9:00 _____   6:00 _____

9:30 _____	6:30 _____
10:00 _____	7:00 _____
10:30 _____	7:30 _____
11:00 _____	8:00 _____
11:30 _____	8:30 _____
12:00 p.m. _____	9:00 _____
12:30 _____	9:30 _____
1:00 _____	10:00 _____
1:30 _____	10:30 _____
2:00 _____	11:00 _____
2:30 _____	11:30 _____
3:00 _____	12:00 _____
3:30 _____	Continue for Tuesday, Wednesday, Thursday, and Friday

D. My Ideal Job Description: Develop your ideal future job. Include:

- Specific interests you want to build into your job
- Work responsibilities
- Working conditions
- Earnings and benefits
- Interpersonal environment
- Working circumstances, opportunities, and goals

Use "My Ideal Job Specifications" on page 97 to outline your ideal job. After completing this exercise, synthesize the job and write a detailed paragraph which describes the kind of job you would most enjoy:

Description of My Ideal Job

_____

_____

_____

_____

_____

_____

_____

My Ideal Job Specifications

Job Interests	Work Responsibilities	Working Conditions	Earnings/Benefits	Circumstances/Opportunities/Goals

STEP 4

Test your objective against reality. Evaluate and refine it by conducting market research, a force field analysis, library research, and informational interviews.

A. Market Research: Four steps are involved in conducting this research:

1. **Products or services:** Based upon all other assessment activities, make a list of what you **do** or **make**:

Products/Services I Do or Make

1. _____
2. _____
3. _____
4. _____
5. _____
6. _____
7. _____
8. _____
9. _____
10. _____

2. **Market:** Identify who needs, wants, or buys what you do or make. Be specific. Include individuals, groups, and organizations. Then, identify **what** specific **needs** your products or services fill. Next, assess the **results** you achieve with your products or services.

The Market for My Products/Services

Individuals, groups, organizations needing me:

1. _____
2. _____
3. _____
4. _____
5. _____

Needs I fulfill:

1. _____

2. _____

3. _____

4. _____

5. _____

Results/outcomes/impacts of my products/services:

1. _____

2. _____

3. _____

4. _____

5. _____

3. **New Markets:** Brainstorm a list of **who else** needs your products or services. Think about ways of expanding your market. Next, list any new needs your current or new market has which you might be able to fill:

Developing New Needs

Who else needs my products/services?

1. _____

2. _____

3. _____

4. _____

5. _____

New ways to expand my market:

1. _____

2. _____

3. _____

4. _____

5. _____

New needs I should fulfill:

1. _____

2. _____

3. _____

4. _____

5. _____

4. **New products and/or services:** List any new products or services you can offer and any new needs you can satisfy:

New Products/Services I Can Offer

1. _____

2. _____

3. _____

4. _____

5. _____

New Needs I Can Meet

1. _____

2. _____

3. _____

4. _____

5. _____

B. **Force Field Analysis:** Once you have developed a tentative or firm objective, force field analysis can help you understand the various internal and external forces affecting the achievement of your objective.

Force field analysis follows a specific sequence of activities:

- **Clearly state your objective** or course of action.

- **List the positive and negative forces affecting your objective.** Specify the internal and external forces working **for** and **against** you in terms of who, what, where, when, and how much. Estimate the impact of each force upon your objective.

- **Analyze the forces.** Assess the importance of each force for your objective and its probable effect on you. Some forces may be irrelevant to your goal. You may need additional information to make a thorough analysis.

- **Maximize positive forces and minimize negative ones.** Identify actions you can take to strengthen positive forces and to neutralize, overcome, or reverse negative forces. Focus on the key forces which are real, important, and probable.

- **Assess the feasibility of attaining your objective** and, if necessary, modifying it in light of new information.

C. **Conduct Online and Library Research:** This research should strengthen and clarify your objective. Consult various reference materials on alternative jobs and careers. Most of these resources are available in print form at your local library or bookstore. Some are available in electronic versions online. If you explore the numerous company profiles and career sites available on the Internet, you should be able to tap into a wealth of information on alternative jobs and careers. Two good resources for initiating online research are Margaret Riley Dikel's *The Guide to Internet Job Search* (McGraw-Hill) and Pam Dixon's *Job Searching Online for Dummies* (IDG Books). For directories to key employment websites, see Ron and Caryl Krannich, *America's Top Internet Job Sites* and *The Directory of Websites for International Jobs* (Impact Publications); and Bernard Haldane Associates, *Haldane's Best Employment Websites for Professionals* (Impact Publications). Many of the resources traditionally found in libraries are available online. The following websites function as excellent gateway sites, online databases, and research tools:

■ CEO Express	www.ceoexpress.com
■ Hoover's Online	www.hoovers.com
■ Dun and Bradstreet's Million Dollar Databases	www.dnbmdd.com/mddi
■ Corporate Information	www.corporateinformation.com
■ BizTech Network	www.brint.com
■ AllBusiness	www.allbusiness.com
■ BizWeb	www.bizweb.com

▪ Business.com	www.business.com
▪ America's CareerInfoNet	www.acinet.org
▪ Newspapers USA	www.newspapers.com
▪ Salary.com	www.salary.com
▪ Annual Report Service	www.annualreportservice.com
▪ Bloomberg	www.bloomberg.com
▪ Chamber of Commerce	www.chamberofcommerce.com
▪ CNN Money	http//money.cnn.com
▪ Daily Stocks	www.dailystocks.com
▪ The Corporate Library	www.thecorporatelibrary.com
▪ Forbes Lists	www.forbes.com/lists
▪ Fortune 500	www.fortune.com
▪ Harris InfoSource	www.harrisinfo.com
▪ Inc. 500	www.inc.com/500
▪ Moodys	www.moodys.com
▪ Motley Fool	www.fool.com
▪ NASDAQ	www.nasdaq.com
▪ One Source Corp Tech	www.onesource.com
▪ Standard & Poors	www.standardandpoors.com
▪ The Street	www.thestreet.com
▪ Thomas Regional	www.thomasregional.com
▪ Thomas Register	www.thomasregister.com

Career and Job Alternatives

- *25 Jobs That Have It All*
- *50 Cutting Edge Jobs*
- *Almanac of American Employers*
- *Almanac of American Employers Mid-Size Firms*
- *America's Top 100 Jobs for People Without a Four-Year Degree*
- *America's Top Jobs for People Re-Entering the Workforce*
- *Enhanced Guide for Occupational Exploration*
- *Guide to Occupational Exploration*
- *Quick Prep Careers*
- *Occupational Outlook Handbook*
- *Occupational Outlook Quarterly*
- *O*NET Dictionary of Occupational Titles*

Industrial Directories

- *Dun and Bradstreet's Middle Market Directory*
- *Dun and Bradstreet's Million Dollar Directory*
- *Encyclopedia of Business Information Sources*
- *Geography Index*
- *Poor's Register of Corporations, Directors, and Executives*
- *Standard Directory of Advertisers*
- *The Standard Periodical Directory*

- *Standard and Poor's Industrial Index*
- *Standard Rate & Data Business Publications Directory*
- *Thomas' Register of American Manufacturers*

Associations

- *Associations USA*
- *Encyclopedia of Associations*
- *National Trade and Professional Associations*
- Access thousands of associations online through: www.ipl.org/ref/AON and www.asaenet.org.

Government Sources

- *The Book of the States*
- *Congressional Directory*
- *Congressional Staff Directory*
- *Congressional Yellow Book*
- *Federal Directory*
- *Federal Yellow Book*
- *Municipal Yearbook*
- *Taylor's Encyclopedia of Government Officials*
- *United Nations Yearbook*
- *United States Government Manual*
- *Washington Information Directory*

Newspapers

- Major city newspapers and trade newspapers. Many are available online through these gateway sites: www.ipl.org/reading/news, http://.newsdirectory.com, www.newspaperlinks.com, and www. newspapers.com.
- Your targeted city newspaper – the Sunday edition.

Business Publications

- *Business 2.0, Business Week, The Economist, Fast Company, Inc., Forbes, Fortune, Harvard Business Review, Newsweek, Smart Money, Time, U.S. News and World Report, Wired.* These and other business-oriented publications can be viewed online through this terrific website: www.CEOExpress.com.

- Annual issues of publications surveying the best jobs and employers for the year: *Money, Fortune, Forbes,* and *U.S. News and World Report.* Several of these reports and publications are available online: www.money.com, www.fortune.com, and www.forbes.com/lists.

Other Library Resources

- Trade journals
- Publications of Chambers of Commerce; state manufacturing associations; and federal, state, and local government agencies
- Telephone books – The Yellow Pages
- Books on "how to get a job" (see order form at the end of this book and www.impactpublications.com)

D.   Conduct Informational Interviews: This may be the most useful way to clarify and refine your objective. See Chapter 10 for details.

After completing these steps, you will have identified what it is you **can** do (abilities and skills), enlarged your thinking to include what it is you would **like** to do (aspirations), and probed the realities of implementing your objective. Thus, setting a realistic work objective is a function of the diverse considerations outlined on page 105.

Your work objective is a function of both subjective and objective information as well as idealism and realism. The strongest emphasis should be placed on your competencies and should include a broad database. Your work objective is realistic in that it is tempered by your past experiences, accomplishments, skills, and current research. An objective formulated in this manner permits you to think beyond your past experiences.

Stating a Functional Objective

We agree with Germann and Arnold (***Bernard Haldane Associates Job and Career Building***) that your job objective should be oriented toward skills and outcomes. You can begin by stating a functional job objective at two different levels: a general objective and a specific one for your resume. For the general objective, begin with the statement:

"I would like a job where I can use my ability to _____ *which will result in* _____.*"*

The objective in this statement is both a **skill** and an **outcome**. For example, you might state:

"I would like a job where my experience in program development, supported by innovative decision-making and systems engineering abilities, will result in an expanded clientele and a more profitable organization."

At a second level you may wish to re-write this objective in order to target it at various consulting firms. For example, on your resume it becomes:

"An increasingly responsible research position in consulting, where proven decision-making and systems engineering abilities will be used for improving organizational productivity."

Examples of weak and strong objective statements are given on page 106. Various styles are also presented.

Objective Setting Process

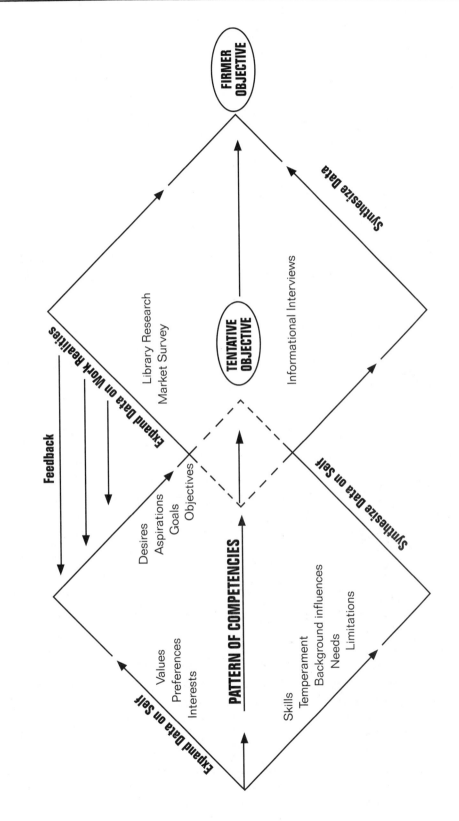

Weak Objectives

"Management position which will utilize business administration degree and will provide opportunities for rapid advancement."

"A position in social services which will allow me to work with people in a helping capacity."

"Sales Representative with opportunity for advancement."

Strong Objectives

"A position in data analysis where skills in mathematics, computer programming, and deductive reasoning will contribute to new systems development."

"Retail Management position which will use sales/customer service experience and creative abilities for product display and merchandising. Long term goal: Progression to merchandise manager with corporate-wide responsibilities for product line. Willing to travel and relocate."

"A public relations position which will maximize opportunities to develop and implement programs, to organize people and events, and to communicate positive ideas and images. Effective in public speaking and in managing a publicity/promotional campaign."

"General Sales Representative position with a pharmaceutical house which will use chemistry background and ability to work on a self-directed basis in managing a marketing territory."

---

*"To use computer science training in **software development** for designing and implementing operating systems."*

"Responsible position in investment research and analysis. Interests and skills include securities analysis, financial planning, and portfolio management. Long range goal: to become a Chartered Financial Analyst. Willing to travel and relocate."

It is important to relate your objective to your audience. While you definitely want a good job, prospective employers wants to know what you can do for them. Remember, your objective should be work-centered, not self-centered.

Summarize Qualifications

The previous exercises for specifying an objective also generate a great deal of information for summarizing your qualifications. A "Summary of Qualifications," "Qualifications Profile," "Executive Qualifications," or "Professional Qualifications" section should appear immediately following your objective. This section can provide a powerful summary of your key skills and accomplishments for focusing the reader's attention. It usually consists of three to five bulleted items or a two- or three-sentence paragraph summarizing your key qualifications. It might appear as follows:

Summary of Qualifications

- Fifteen years experience in office supervision and personnel management
- Highly motivated self-starter with aptitude for solving system problems
- Proficient in the use of major software programs, including Microsoft Word, PowerPoint, Excel, and Access
- Skilled in linking performance evaluation systems to career development programs

Alternatively, you might want to summarize your major experience and qualifications as an expert in a particular position relevant to the employer:

Senior Personnel Manager
Turn-around Specialist and Senior Manager

Dynamic, creative, and results-oriented professional successful in developing model supervisory and personnel management systems for small businesses involved in restructuring their core manufacturing operations. Talented in custom-designing performance evaluation systems that dramatically increase employee satisfaction and retention as well as minimize recruitment and training costs.

Describe Experience

Begin compiling information on your past experiences by using the forms on pages 108-110. Include paid employment; full-time, part-time, and summer employment; internships; and significant volunteer work. Refer to the database you generated previously for identifying your abilities and skills and stating your objectives. Make multiple copies of these forms.

When transforming this data to "experience" statements on your resume, avoid listing formal duties and responsibilities. Describe your experience in functional terms as outlined in our section on transferable skills and objectives. Always stress your accomplishments. Use action verbs to emphasize the skill-oriented nature of your experience and qualifications, such as "managed," "created," "supervised," "coordinated," "planned," "analyzed," and "initiated." Be sure everything you outline relates to your objective.

Your experience statements will vary depending on the type of resume format you use. For example, in a chronological resume, your experience may be stated as follows (page 111):

Employment Experience Worksheet

1. Name of employer:_____

2. Address: _____

   _____

3. Inclusive dates of employment: from _____ to _____.
   month/year   month/year

4. Type of organization: _____

5. Size of organization/approximate number of employees: _____

6. Approximate annual sales volume or annual budget: _____

7. Position held: _____

8. Earnings per month/year: _____

9. Responsibilities/duties: _____

   _____

   _____

   _____

10. Achievements or significant contributions: _____

    _____

    _____

11. Demonstrated skills and abilities: _____

    _____

    _____

12. Reason(s) for leaving: _____

    _____

Military Experience Worksheet

1. Service: _____

2. Rank: _____

3. Inclusive dates: from _____ to _____.
   $\qquad\qquad\qquad$ month/year $\qquad\qquad$ month/year

4. Responsibilities/duties: _____

   _____

   _____

   _____

   _____

5. Significant contributions/achievements: _____

   _____

   _____

   _____

   _____

   _____

6. Demonstrated skills and abilities: _____

   _____

   _____

   _____

   _____

   _____

7. Reserve status: _____

Community/Civic/Volunteer Experience

1. Name and address of organization/group: _____

    _____

    _____

    _____

2. Inclusive dates: from _____ to _____.
                          month/year   month/year

3. Offices held/nature of involvement: _____

    _____

    _____

    _____

4. Significant contributions/achievements/projects: _____

    _____

    _____

    _____

    _____

    _____

5. Demonstrated skills and abilities: _____

    _____

    _____

    _____

    _____

    _____

EMPLOYMENT: **Engineering Draftsman.** Naval Electronics Systems Engineering Command, San Diego, California. Worked with engineers and technicians in developing electrical diagrams and schematics (2003 to present).

Draftsman with Dominion Sheetmetal Corporation, Washington, DC. Became familiar with manufacture of HVAC systems. Designed prototype of equipment for employer. Twenty hours per week (2002).

In a functional resume you may choose to use the terms "EXPERIENCE" or "AREAS OF EFFECTIVENESS" instead of "EMPLOYMENT" or "WORK HISTORY." In this case you will describe your transferable skills in functional terms without mentioning formal titles and dates. Notice that the discussion focuses on specific skills and accomplishments rather than on duties and responsibilities related to any particular jobs that would normally be listed by employer name, job title, and inclusive employment dates on a chronological resume. This section may appear on your resume as follows:

Experience Statement – Functional Resume

AREAS OF EFFECTIVENESS

Planning/ organizing	Planned, organized, and delegated responsibility for several successful fund raising projects. Established objectives and planned yearly budget, which involved balancing club objectives and community needs. Coordinated and planned summer camps for handicapped children, which gained favorable recognition.
Managing/ directing	Coordinated and scheduled individuals for activities such as the Bloodmobile and the Community Health Center. Solicited and evaluated applicants for club scholarship award.
Interpersonal/ communication	Developed liaison relationship between city officials and people in the community. Established support of the local business community for club projects.

The combination resume will include both functional categories and work history. However, "EXPERIENCE" or "AREAS OF EFFECTIVENESS" should appear first and "EMPLOYMENT HISTORY" last, as in the example on page 112.

Present Educational Background

A statement in reference to your educational background can appear anywhere after your objective, depending on how much you wish to emphasize it in relationship to your objective and experience. If you appear over- or under-educated for a job, you may wish to de-emphasize your training by placing the education category near the end. Again, where you place this item depends on your purpose.

The same is true for deciding what to include in the education statement. If you are a recent graduate with little work-related experience, you may want to highlight those educational achievements which indicate your ability to achieve results, such as *"edited conference papers," "financed 80% of personal expenses," "held leadership positions in*

Combination Resume Format

NAME
address
telephone number
e-mail

_____

OBJECTIVE   _____

                         _____

                         _____

AREAS OF EFFECTIVENESS

   Planning/
   organizing   _____

                         _____

   Managing/
   directing   _____

                         _____

   Interpersonal/
   communication   _____

                         _____

                         _____

EMPLOYMENT   Mathematics Teacher, Peoria Junior High School, Peoria,
HISTORY   Illinois, 2003 to present.

                         Administrative Assistant, U.S. Government, Fort Monroe,
                         Virginia, 1998-2002.

EDUCATION   _____

                         _____

various organizations," and *"maintained a 3.5 GPA on a 4.0 index."* Whatever you choose to include, begin by compiling as much information on your education and training as possible and then condense it in relationship to your objective. Complete copies of the "Educational Data" form on page 114 for this purpose.

The education statement can appear in different forms. But, remember, you are trying to get everything on one page. Unless you are a recent graduate, your objective and experience categories will be more important to readers than your education statement. So, plan accordingly by not making this category excessively large. Examples of education statements appear as follows:

EDUCATION:	**B.S. in Business Administration** – Accounting, 2003. University of North Carolina, Chapel Hill.
	Highlights: G.P.A.: 3.6 (4.0 index) Earned 75% of education and personal expenses. Member, Accounting Club.
EDUCATION:	M.A., Journalism, Columbia University, 2004. B.A., English Literature, Barnard College, 1999.

If you have training and certification other than formal degrees and diplomas, and it is pertinent to your objective, you may wish to include it in a section immediately following "EDUCATION" and label it "ADDITIONAL TRAINING" or "CERTIFICATION":

Education and Additional Training/Certification Statement

EDUCATION:	**B.S. in Business Administration** – Accounting, 2004. University of North Carolina, Chapel Hill.
ADDITIONAL TRAINING:	Zero-Base Budgeting, Army Budgeting I, Commercial Accounts, Introduction to Data Processing, Personnel Management.

Consider Personal Statements

You may want to disregard this section altogether since it remains one of the most tradition-bound and non-functional sections on resumes. If you include it, keep it brief and to the point. Avoid extraneous information, such as your height, weight, hair color, and other personal characteristics, unless they are essential to your job objective. In some cases this information merely raises negative questions. If you are single, divorced, or separated, so what? Your sex and marital life are not your employer's business – unless you or they make it so. However, if you are single, and you are applying for a job requiring considerable travel, identifying your marital status can be a plus in your favor. On the other hand, if a job requires stability, and you are married and have children, you may include your marital status – but don't include the names of your children, even though you are proud of them! As for age, if it will help, put it down. Leave your age off altogether if it serves no useful purposes, particularly if you are middle-aged or over.

Educational Data

1. Institution: _____

2. Address: _____

   _____

3. Inclusive dates: from _____ to _____.
                          month/year   month/year

4. Degree or years completed: _____

5. Major: _____ Minor(s): _____

6. Education highlights: _____

   _____

   _____

7. Student activities: _____

   _____

   _____

8. Demonstrated abilities and skills: _____

   _____

   _____

9. Significant contributions/achievements: _____

   _____

   _____

   _____

   _____

10. Special training courses: _____

    _____

11. G.P.A.: _____ (on _____ index)
                     point

You may wish to include some other personal information for strengthening your objective, such as in the following example:

Personal Statement

PERSONAL: Excellent health . . . married . . . children . . . enjoy challenges . . . interested in productivity.

Alternatively, you could write a personal statement about yourself so that the reader might remember you in particular. For example,

Special Interests Statement

SPECIAL Love the challenge of solving problems, taking initiative, and
INTERESTS: achieving results . . . be it in developing new marketing strategies, programming a computer, climbing a mountain, white water rafting, or modifying a motorcycle.

Such statements can give hobbies and special talents and interests new meaning in relationship to the resume objective. Whatever you do, avoid trite statements.

Assess and Screen References

Never list your references on your resume. Always control these yourself. Be sure to inform your references of your job search activities. Give them a copy of your resume so they understand your objective and qualifications.

When deciding whether to include a reference section on your resume, you essentially have two choices: leave this section off altogether, since it is an empty category without names, or use the following statement:

REFERENCES: Available upon request

We see no useful purpose served by stating this. It merely takes up valuable space that can be allocated to a more thorough presentation of your qualifications. If you drop this category completely, most readers will assume you will make your references available upon request. Employers will ask you for references when the time is right – which usually is during the interview. Sometimes they don't ask for references or don't contact the individuals on your list. However, it is good practice to list the names of your professional references on a separate sheet of paper, and carry the list with you to interviews. The list should be typed and include the full name, title, business, address, telephone number, and e-mail address of each person.

Decide on Miscellaneous Information

You may wish to include other information on your resume: special skills, professional memberships and affiliations, and hobbies. If you have special licenses or special training and skills (can program a computer, invented the laser gun) relevant to your job objective, include this information on your resume. If you are actively involved in a professional organization – hold an office or organized a program – and it is relevant to your qualifications, include it on your resume with appropriate statements to emphasize your role. Membership alone is not particularly impressive. Most people understand the nature of professional memberships and affiliations: you do little other than write a check for your annual dues.

Hobbies, like your height and weight, seldom enhance your objective, and some simply distract by raising unnecessary questions about your sanity or "normality"! Nonetheless, you may engage in some hobbies or activities that will strengthen your professional and personal marketability, such as writing books, articles, and speeches – or composing music. Such hobbies stress your organizational, communication, and creative abilities. Other hobbies may leave a lasting positive impression on the reader and thus he or she will remember you in particular. But swimming, collecting stamps, and playing cards may communicate the wrong things – you're a jock, withdrawn, or a gambler.

Never, never, never put your salary expectations on your resume. Salary is the last thing you discuss in a job interview, and it is negotiable.

You should complete the "Additional Information" forms on pages 117-118 so you will at least have this information available for reference. After compiling information on these miscellaneous categories, include in the resume only those items which enhance your objective and qualifications. Again, your purpose is to produce as much information on your background and qualifications as possible and then condense it into a one- or two-page resume draft. It is much easier to condense than to expand such information.

Additional Information

1. Professional memberships and status:

   a. _____

   b. _____

   c. _____

   d. _____

2. Licenses/certifications:

   a. _____

   b. _____

   c. _____

3. Expected salary range: $ _____ to $ _____ (but do not include this on your resume)

4. Acceptable amount of on-the-job travel: _____ days per month.

5. Areas of acceptable relocation:

   a. _____   c. _____

   b. _____   d. _____

6. Date of availability: _____

7. Contacting present employer:

   a. Is he or she aware of your prospective job change? _____

   b. May he or she be contacted at this time? _____

8. References: (name, address, telephone number, e-mail address – not on resume)

   a. _____   c. _____

   b. _____   d. _____

9. Foreign languages and degree of competency:

   a. _____

   b. _____

10. **Interests and activities:** hobbies, avocations, pursuits

    a. _____

    b. _____

    c. _____

    d. _____

    Circle letter of ones which support your objective.

11. **Foreign travel:**

	Country	Purpose	Dates
a.			
b.			
c.			

12. **Special awards/recognition:**

    a. _____ _____ _____

    b. _____ _____ _____

    c. _____ _____ _____

13. **Special abilities/skills/talents/accomplishments:**

    a. _____

    b. _____

    c. _____

8

Draft, Evaluate, and Produce the Final Product

Armed with the information you compiled in Chapter 7, you should be well prepared to write first and second drafts of your resume. The drafting process involves producing each section of the resume in reference to specific evaluation criteria as well as re-working it until the finished product looks first-class.

Do First and Second Drafts

Your first resume draft will directly evolve from the information you put together on the data forms in Chapter 7. Take several sheets of paper and at the top of each write the title of one resume category: OBJECTIVE, SUMMARY OF EXPERIENCE, WORK EXPERIENCE, EDUCATION, PERSONAL. Refer to your master data forms in writing each category as you want them to appear on your resume. As you do this, keep in mind two questions:

- Does this information strengthen my objective as well as demonstrate my strengths?

- Is the language crisp, succinct, and expressive?

Your choice of language is important throughout this process. Be sure to use action verbs and keywords to enhance the readability of each section and to strengthen the presentation of your abilities and skills. Work and re-work each sentence until the statements are concise and meaningful in reference to your objective. Remember, less is often more when writing your resume. You want to edit, edit, edit, edit! If, for example, your objective statement is written in six or seven lines, keep editing until it is no more than three lines. You can say just as much – if not more – and say it better in three lines than in six. Resume writing gives you a license to rid yourself of useless language in order to communicate clearly and with impact.

Always keep in mind your objective **and** audience when deciding what to include in each section. A good rule to follow is: *When in doubt, throw it out.* Otherwise, you will have difficulty putting all the essential information on one or two pages.

After completing the individual sheets, arrange each category into a chronological, functional, or combination format, according to our advice in Chapter 7 and following our examples in Appendices A and B. At this stage your resume may be more than one page – but not more than two pages. If necessary, eliminate the less important categories, such as "PERSONAL" and "REFERENCES."

You should subject your initial draft to both internal and external evaluations. An **internal evaluation** examines the proper form and content of your resume. An **external evaluation** involves circulating your draft resume to at least three individuals who will critique it in terms of its strengths and weaknesses. Choose individuals who have hiring expertise. We examine both types of evaluations in the next section.

> *Less is often more when writing your resume. When in doubt, throw it out.*

Your second draft should incorporate the results of the internal and external evaluations. At this point you should subject your resume to major surgery to further condense it into a one- to two-page format. Keep editing until you eliminate extra pages. Again, follow our rule for condensing resume content – *"when in doubt, throw it out."*

After completing the second draft, conduct another external evaluation by circulating the new resume to the same individuals who critiqued your first draft. In addition, contact three other individuals with hiring experience; ask them also to critique this draft. If all goes well, your second draft will become the final resume. If not, revise again by incorporating this new audience feedback. Circulate it again and again until your final product receives high marks from your evaluators.

It is critical to field test your drafts in this manner. While you may need to further revise your resume in response to new advice and information on the job market, these preliminary trial runs should get you started in the right direction. Writing resumes is a skill or competency you develop through experience. The more extensive your experience, the better your final product.

Conduct Internal and External Evaluations

It is important to conduct both internal and external evaluations of your resume. The **internal evaluation** identifies the strengths and weaknesses of your resume in reference to principles of effective resume writing. Complete the first phase of this evaluation exercise on pages 121-123; the remainder of the exercise appears on pages 127-128. Be sure to follow up each weak rating with a note to yourself on how you might best improve that aspect of your resume. This activity enables you to evaluate **and** follow through in revising the resume. Refer to the following evaluation exercise to conduct your internal evaluation.

Internal Resume Evaluation

INSTRUCTIONS: Examine your resume writing skills in reference to the following evaluation criteria. Respond to each statement by circling the appropriate number to the right that most accurately describes your resume:

1 = Strongly agree	4 = Disagree
2 = Agree	5 = Strongly disagree
3 = So-so (neutral)	

1. Wrote the resume myself – no creative plagiarizing from others' resume examples.   1   2   3   4   5

2. Conducted a thorough self-assessment which became the basis for writing each resume section.   1   2   3   4   5

3. Have a plan of action that relates my resume to other job search activities.   1   2   3   4   5

4. Selected an appropriate resume format that best presents my interests, skills, and experience.   1   2   3   4   5

5. Included all essential information categories in the proper order.   1   2   3   4   5

6. Eliminated all extraneous information unrelated to my objective and employers' needs (date, picture, race, religion, political affiliation, age, sex, height, weight, marital status, health, hobbies) or better saved for discussion in the interview (salary history and references).   1   2   3   4   5

7. Put the most important information first.   1   2   3   4   5

8. Resume is oriented to the future rather than to the past.   1   2   3   4   5

9. Contact information is complete – name, address, phone and fax numbers, e-mail. No P.O. Box numbers or nicknames.   1   2   3   4   5

10. Limited abbreviations to accepted words.   1   2   3   4   5

11. Contact information attractively formatted to introduce the resume.   1   2   3   4   5

12. Included a thoughtful employer-oriented objective that incorporates both skills and benefits/outcomes.   1   2   3   4   5

13. Objective clearly communicates to employers what I want to do, can do, and will do for them.   1   2   3   4   5

14. Objective is neither too general nor too specific.   1   2   3   4   5

15. Objective serves as the central organizing
element for all other sections of the resume.   1   2   3   4   5

16. Included a powerful "Summary of Qualifications"
or "Professional Profile" section immediately
following the "Objective."   1   2   3   4   5

17. Elaborated work experience in detail, emphasizing
my skills, abilities, and achievements.   1   2   3   4   5

18. Each "Experience" section is short and to the point.   1   2   3   4   5

19. Consistently used action verbs and active voice.   1   2   3   4   5

20. Incorporated language appropriate for the keywords
of electronic resume scanners.   1   2   3   4   5

21. Did not refer to myself as "I."   1   2   3   4   5

22. Used specifics – numbers and percentages – to
highlight my performance.   1   2   3   4   5

23. Included positive quotations about my performance
from previous employers.   1   2   3   4   5

24. Eliminated any negative references, including
reasons for leaving.   1   2   3   4   5

25. Did not include names of supervisors or others
involved with my professional or personal life.   1   2   3   4   5

26. Summarized my most recent job and then
included other jobs in reverse chronological order.   1   2   3   4   5

27. Descriptions of "Experience" are consistent.   1   2   3   4   5

28. Put the most important information on my
skills first when summarizing my "Experience."   1   2   3   4   5

29. No time gaps nor "job hopping" apparent to reader.   1   2   3   4   5

30. Documented "other experience" that might
strengthen my objective and decided to either
include or exclude it on the resume.   1   2   3   4   5

31. Included complete information on my educational
background, including important highlights.   1   2   3   4   5

32. If a recent graduate with little relevant work
experience, emphasized educational background
more than work experience.   1   2   3   4   5

33. Put education in reverse chronological order and
eliminated high school if a college graduate.   1   2   3   4   5

34. Included special education and training relevant
to my major interests and skills.　　　　　　　1　2　3　4　5

35. Included professional affiliations and membership
relevant to my objective and skills; highlighted
any major contributions.　　　　　　　　　　1　2　3　4　5

36. Documented any special skills not included
elsewhere on resume and included those that
appear relevant to employers' needs.　　　　1　2　3　4　5

37. Included awards or special recognition that
further document my skills and achievements.　1　2　3　4　5

38. Weighed pros and cons of including a personal
statement on my resume.　　　　　　　　　　1　2　3　4　5

39. Did not mention salary history or expectations.　1　2　3　4　5

40. Did not include names, addresses, and phone
number of references.　　　　　　　　　　　1　2　3　4　5

41. Included additional information to enhance the
interest of employers.　　　　　　　　　　　1　2　3　4　5

42. Used a language appropriate for the employer,
including terms that associate me with the industry.　1　2　3　4　5

43. My language is crisp, succinct, expressive, and direct.　1　2　3　4　5

44. Used emphasizing techniques to make the resume
most readable.　　　　　　　　　　　　　　1　2　3　4　5

45. Selected language that is appropriate for being "read"
by today's resume scanning technology.　　　　1　2　3　4　5

46. Resume has an inviting, uncluttered look,
incorporating sufficient white space and using a
standard type style and size.　　　　　　　　1　2　3　4　5

47. Kept the design basic and conservative.　　　1　2　3　4　5

48. Kept sentences short and succinct.　　　　　1　2　3　4　5

49. Resume runs one or two pages.　　　　　　　1　2　3　4　5

TOTAL

Add the numbers you circled to the right of each statement to get a cumulative score. If your score is higher than 85, you need to work on improving your resume.

You conduct an **external evaluation** by circulating your resume to three or more individuals. For guidelines, give your evaluators the form on page 124. But most impor-

External Evaluation

INSTRUCTIONS: Circle the number that best characterizes various aspects of my resume. Please include any recommendations on how I could best improve the resume:

1 = Excellent   2 = Okay   3 = Weak

Recommendations for Improvement

1. Overall appearance	1 2 3	_____
2. Layout	1 2 3	_____
3. Clarity	1 2 3	_____
4. Consistency	1 2 3	_____
5. Readability	1 2 3	_____
6. Language	1 2 3	_____
7. Organization	1 2 3	_____
8. Content/completeness	1 2 3	_____
9. Length	1 2 3	_____
10. Contact information/header	1 2 3	_____
11. Objective	1 2 3	_____
12. Experience	1 2 3	_____
13. Skills	1 2 3	_____
14. Achievements	1 2 3	_____
15. Education	1 2 3	_____
16. Other information	1 2 3	_____

tant of all, choose people whose opinions are objective, frank, and thoughtful. Do not select friends and relatives who usually flatter you with positive comments. Professional acquaintances or people you don't know personally but whom you admire may be good evaluators. An ideal evaluator has experience in hiring people in your area of job interest. In addition to sharing their experience with you, they may refer you to other individuals who would be interested in your qualifications. If you choose such individuals to critique your resume, ask them for their frank reaction – not what they would politely say to a candidate presenting such a resume. You want the people to role play with you – a potential interview candidate. Ask your evaluators:

> _"If you don't mind, would you look over my resume? Perhaps you could comment on its clarity or make suggestions for improving it?"_

> _"How would you react to this resume if you received it from a candidate? Would it grab your attention and interest you enough to invite the person to an interview?"_

> _"If you were writing this resume, what changes would you make? Any additions, deletions, modifications?"_

Such an evaluation should especially take place in the process of networking and conducting informational interviews, the subjects of Chapter 10.

You will normally receive good cooperation and advice by approaching people in this manner. In addition, you will probably get valuable unsolicited advice on other job search matters, such as job leads, job market information, and employment strategies.

In contrast to the closed and deductive nature of the internal evaluation, the external evaluation should be open-ended and inductive. Avoid preconceived evaluation categories; let the evaluator react to you and your resume as if you were in a job interview situation.

Taken together, the internal and external evaluations should complement each other by providing you with maximum information for revising your draft resume.

Produce a First-Class Resume

When you are ready to produce the final resume, you must consider quality **and** cost. Both will influence the effectiveness of your resume. Do not cut quality because of costs, since differences in resume quality amount to only a few dollars. On the other hand, don't go to the extreme with a slick Madison Avenue advertising brochure. You may threaten some employers with your overkill approach; others may think you are lazy because they assume you hired a professional resume writing service to do your work; still others may suspect you are hiding weaknesses.

Production techniques will vary depending on your targeted audience. If you are competing with 500 applicants for a position, your resume must stand out from the crowd. This may mean producing a non-conventional resume. Hopefully you will not be competing with so many applicants. Indeed, if you seek non-publicized job opportunities, only **your** resume will stand between you and a prospective employer.

Let's assume you will apply for publicized and highly competitive positions as well as look for unpublicized job opportunities which have little competition. In both cases, your resume should respond to the type of position you are seeking. It should look professional, be eye appealing, and stand out from other resumes. You do this by following various guidelines and techniques for producing an outstanding resume.

Production Programs and Printers

You can home-produce your resume on a computer and print it on a letter quality printer. By using a letter quality printer, you can achieve a professional looking resume which also communicates your personal style.

You can produce an attractive resume using one of several standard word processing programs such as Word or WordPerfect. Good quality desktop publishing programs, such as PageMaker and QuarkXPress, are even better since they enable you to incorporate attractive graphic elements into your resume. At the same time, several companies have developed inexpensive software and CD-ROM packages specifically designed to produce resumes and letters. Two excellent quality off-the-shelf programs found in most computer stores include *Win-Way Resume* and *ResumeMaker*. However, many such programs force you to produce a resume using their templates and automated formats which may or may not be the best for you.

If you don't have a computer and/or a letter quality printer, find someone who does and have them put your resume on a disk. You can hire someone to word process your resume for $25-50. Many fast-copy businesses, such as FedEx Kinko's or Kwik Kopy Printing, can provide such resume word-processing and printing services.

Layout and Use of Space

Your resume should have a crisp and clear look which is visually pleasing to the reader. You achieve this by using white space frequently yet sparingly. Avoid the crammed and crowded look; the more blank space you leave around each section, the better. Section headings should be arranged to the left or above each section. Separate each section with at least one and a half spaces – preferably two. Use ellipses to break sentences and ideas on the same line (. . .). You may want to experiment with a variety of different layouts until you achieve the visual effects you desire. The use of single and double lines to accent sections and a full or partial border drawn along the edge of the resume can give it an unusual effect which also looks very professional.

Highlights and Emphasis

You can emphasize various elements in your resume by arranging space, using different lettering styles and symbols such as bullets (●), boxes (■), hyphens (—), or asterisks (*). You also can CAPITALIZE, underline, and use **bold print** for emphasizing words, phrases, and sentences. However, be careful not to over-emphasize these elements; many readers do not like having their reading flow broken so frequently, and emphasizing too much actually diminishes impact. If you do a good job at editing your resume, you will not need to highlight points so frequently by using such techniques.

Paper

Use high quality stock, preferably 20 to 50 lb. bond paper with 100 percent cotton fiber ("rag content"), which has a first-class look and feel. Bond paper costs 3-7¢ per sheet. It can be purchased through office supply stores and printers.

If you choose a poor quality paper, you may communicate the wrong message to employers. Paper quality, texture, and weight say something about your professional style.

Color

We prefer a conservative white, off-white, ivory, or light gray paper to other colors. Two decades ago, the best resumes were considered to be one-page, typeset documents printed on high quality off-white or beige paper. Since so many resumes were produced in these colors, they did not stand out as different or unique. Indeed, the standard black and white resume often stands out among the many off-white resumes! Some combinations of these colors, such as a gray paper framed with a half-inch white border, also work very well.

Although we used to prefer the off-white and beige colors, we now prefer the light grey with dark blue, navy, or black print. Whatever you choose, avoid extremes, such as bright red, pink, orange, or green. Conservative, light, muted color papers with dark inks are your best choices. However, if you are an artist or are in some other less conventional career, choose a color that best expresses your professional goals, personality, and style. Furthermore, if you are competing with hundreds of other applicants and wish to stand out from the crowd, you may prefer to take your chances with a less conservative paper color. Knowing your audience is your best guide to selection of colors and designs. But when in doubt, go with conservative colors.

> *Some combinations of colors, such as a gray paper framed with a half-inch white border, work well.*

When dealing with employers who do not know you, assume they will be conservative and cautious. They look for symbols of your personality, style, and performance **prior to** inviting you to an interview. Regardless of the content of your resume – experience, education, objective – your choice of resume colors and style gives employers nonverbal cues for screening you in or out of consideration for an interview.

Reproduction

If you computer-generate your resume and use a good letter quality printer, all of your resumes will be originals. Otherwise, reproduce your resume by using a high quality copying machine that gives you as good as, if not better than, original quality reproduction. Producing your resume in this manner will be relatively inexpensive and will look very professional. Whatever you do, please **do not** get cheap at this stage by (1) making copies of your resume on a chintzy copy machine, or (2) substitute 1¢ a sheet copy machine paper for 3¢ a sheet high quality, bond paper. At best you will probably save $5 on 100 copies. This is not the place to cut corners, since your resume is your calling card for getting interviews. Pay the extra pennies, nickels, and dimes required to produce a first-class professional resume. You will be more than rewarded in the end for incurring such limited additional costs.

Evaluate the Final Product

Similar to evaluating your first and second drafts, evaluate your final resume both internally and externally. Include in your internal evaluation (pages 121-123) the following additional evaluation criteria relevant to the **production** aspects of your resume:

50. Carefully proofread and produced two or three drafts which were subjected to both internal and external evaluations before producing the final copies.   1 2 3 4 5

51. Chose a standard color and quality of paper.   1 2 3 4 5

52. Used 8½" x 11" paper.   1 2 3 4 5

53. Printed resume on only one side of paper.   1   2   3   4   5

54. Used a good quality machine and an easy-to-read
    typeface.   1   2   3   4   5

Include in your external evaluation on page 124 four additional evaluation criteria as well as a summary statement:

17. Paper color   1   2   3   _____

18. Paper size and stock   1   2   3   _____

19. Overall production quality   1   2   3   _____

20. Potential effectiveness   1   2   3   _____

SUMMARY EVALUATION: _____

_____

_____

_____

_____

How can you produce a professional looking resume when the competition is doing the same? Simply don't compete with the same product. Make your resume look professional and **different**. Follow the guidelines in this chapter and vary the layout as well as the quality and color of paper.

Your final resume should approximate one or two of the resume examples found in Appendices A and B. While you should refer to these examples, under no circumstances should you copy their contents. Your resume must reflect **your** goals and strengths. Moreover, it should indicate the fact that **you** produced it. By all means avoid producing another "canned" resume.

9

Write Powerful Job Search Letters

YOU SHOULD WRITE SEVERAL TYPES of letters during your job search. The most common ones are resume, cover, approach, and thank-you letters. While this chapter mainly focuses on how to develop effective resume and cover letters, it also briefly examines other types of letters which are equally important to your job search. For a more extended discussion of this subject, see Ron and Caryl Krannich's *Nail the Cover Letter!, 201 Dynamite Job Search Letters*, and *Haldane's Best Cover Letters for Professionals*, all of which are available through Impact Publications (see order form at the end).

Letters are similar in purpose to resumes: your advertisement for interviews and job offers. High impact letters combine the principles of effective advertising copy with good business correspondence. Your letters, like good ads and business communication, should command attention and evoke positive responses from your audience. They should not repeat the contents of your resume. Instead, they should express some of the most important qualities employers look for during face-to-face interviews – your personality, enthusiasm, and intelligence.

Writing high impact job search letters follows similar principles to writing good advertising copy. While some English teachers and journalists may help you develop these letters, it is best to consult advertising books or freelance copywriters who are specialists on **how to write with impact**. They focus on developing high impact communication that **motivates** others to take action.

Having Impact in a Sea of Paper

Your letter writing should follow various principles of good advertising and effective business correspondence. This involves a simple three-step formula for writing well: **think, write**, and **edit**. Effective writers devote time to each step.

Successful ad writers stress several principles for writing with impact. Their writing:

- Uses an eye-catching headline to capture the reader's attention.

- Captures and sustains the reader's interest by persuasively describing and explaining the benefits of the product or service.

- Creates additional credibility and desire by presenting evidence, testimonials, or further explanations of the value of the product or service.

- Stimulates the reader to take action.

You can easily adapt these advertising principles to your letter writing if you first address these questions:

- Who is my audience?

- What are the objectives and needs of my audience?

- What is my objective?

- How can I best express an objective that relates to my audience's needs and goals?

- What specific benefits can I offer to my audience and how can I best express them?

- What opening sentence and paragraph will grab the attention of my audience in a positive manner and convince them to read further?

- How can I maintain and heighten the interest and desire of the reader throughout the letter?

- What evidence of my value can I present to my audience?

- If a resume is enclosed with the letter, how can I make the letter best advertise the resume?

- What closing sentence or paragraph will best assure the reader of my capabilities and persuade him/her to contact me for further information?

- Is the letter my **best** professional effort?

- Have I spent sufficient time drafting, revising, and proofreading the letter before sending it to the reader?

At the same time, your letter is more than an advertisement. It is your business communication. Therefore, you must present yourself in a professional, business-like manner by incorporating the principles of effective business correspondence in your resume. Eight rules generally define these principles:

1. Organize what you will say by outlining the content of your letter.

2. Know your purpose and plan the elements of the letter accordingly.

3. Communicate your message in a logical and sequential manner.

4. State your purpose immediately in the first sentence and paragraph; main ideas always go first.

5. Close your letter by stating what the reader can expect next from you.

6. Use short paragraphs and sentences; avoid long complex sentences.

7. Punctuate properly and use correct grammar and spelling.

8. Use simple and straightforward language; avoid jargon. Communicate your message as directly and briefly as possible.

The first five rules help you **organize** your letter. The final three rules stress how you should **communicate** your message. Underlying these rules is an advertising principle you should follow at all times: **know your audience's needs and keep your purpose in mind**.

You can achieve impact by using different writing styles or by communicating the unexpected. Some candidates use unorthodox ways to get attention. For example, career counselors often tell the story of the applicant who sent a shoe in a box to a company executive with this short accompanying letter:

> *"Now that I've got my shoe in the door, how about an interview?"*

John Molloy (*Live for Success*) recalls receiving a letter from a woman applying for a secretarial job with his company:

> *"You know I don't have a great deal of experience, and I know I've worked for several companies in the last few years and that may not look good. But I guarantee you one thing. If I do come to work for you I'll work like hell!"*

This letter definitely had impact. Molloy was initially turned off by her language, but it struck him as honest and powerful. He interviewed her and took a chance by hiring her. But all did not go well:

> *"She did work like hell. She spelled like the devil, showed up when she felt like it, and gave everyone around her a lot of heat. As a result I had to let her go in a few weeks. But she did know how to sell herself in a cover letter."*

We do not recommend such hard-sell, kinky, or unorthodox letters – unless the situation is appropriate for them. If, for example, you are applying for a sales position, your letter may be somewhat aggressive and unorthodox because of the nature of sales positions. In fact, many people in sales still use the old "shoe-in-the-box" letter – and it works! After all, employers expect a high turnover rate among sales people. Employers often are willing to take chances, because sales people tend to be low-cost employees who are paid on the basis of their performance (commissions). However, the hard-sell, aggressive, and unorthodox letter may get you in trouble for a non-sales position. For example, send your shoe with a letter to the head of an accounting department and see what happens. Or, apply for a management position by broadcasting how you work like hell and are the greatest thing since sliced bread! Job search letters should have impact, but they should not be overbearing or obnoxious.

Creating Resume Letters

As noted in Chapter 6, resume letters can substitute for chronological, functional, and combination resumes. Use this letter to communicate your specific skills and qualifications directly to someone in an organization. The letter should follow the same rules we outlined earlier for writing a good resume.

Resume letters have one major advantage over cover letters and resumes: you can easily customize them to target specific positions. These letters provide you with flexibility. This is especially true if you run multiple copies of a general resume but need to alter its contents for particular jobs.

A resume letter should be addressed to a name **and** title. Produce the letter on good quality bond paper – 20 to 50 lb. bond with 100 percent cotton fiber – and try to keep it to one page. A resume letter should not run more than two pages.

The internal organization of this letter should approximate the following format and rules:

Paragraph 1:	Clearly state your purpose for writing.
Paragraph 2:	Stress your objective, interests, and qualifications in reference to the employer's interests and possible needs. This paragraph substitutes for the "SUMMARY OF EXPERIENCE" or "AREAS OF EFFECTIVENESS" sections of your resume, and it should follow similar writing principles. If you are responding to a specific position, list your skills and experience in direct reference to the employer's required skills and experience.
Paragraph 3:	Request to meet with the individual to discuss your mutual interests. Indicate that you will call to arrange a meeting. This section sets the stage for follow-up activities that result in some form of action on your application.

We include several examples of these letters in Appendix C.

Your resume still plays an important role in the job search process even when you use a resume letter. While most job seekers send resumes with cover letters for getting interviews, the resume letter is designed to get the interview without an accompanying resume. In this case, the resume is presented at the **end** of the interview.

The resume letter may have greater impact on potential employers because it is targeted. Ho wever, since many emp loyers expect to see resumes prio r to inviting candidates to interviews, a resume letter may not be well received by employers who want more information. Again, use your own judgment as to when you should best use this letter in lieu of your resume.

Writing Cover Letters

Cover letters should do precisely what they are intended to do – provide cover for an enclosure. The enclosure is your resume. If you want your reader to examine your resume, your cover letter must have impact. This letter advertises your resume; it should neither regurgitate nor substitute for it.

Some career counselors recommend against writing and sending cover letters with resumes. They believe these letters distract from the resume; a cover letter, in effect, downgrades the resume. As an alternative, they recommend handwriting a personal note at the top of your resume which states you will telephone the employer at a particular time to make an appointment for an interview. If you do this many times – such as broadcast or "shotgun" 200 resumes – you will get results – perhaps three to five appointments and interviews. Indeed, in many cases this approach can work. The keys to making it work are (1) playing the probability game of sending many resumes in anticipation of only a few positive responses, and (2) following the resume and handwritten note with a telephone call. In this case, the **telephone call** substitutes for the cover letter. This approach has one major advantage: it saves you the trouble of writing and typing many cover letters. However, a disadvantage is also apparent: high costs of long-distance telephone calls.

> *A cover letter advertises your resume; it should neither regurgitate nor substitute for it.*

Nonetheless, at times you must write cover letters because they are expected in certain situations. If you are "shotgunning" resumes, it makes sense to eliminate the cover letter because it saves additional typing on your part and requires less reading for employers. But "shotgunning" is only one approach to uncovering job leads. As we note in Chapter 10, it is not the most effective way to find a job. More frequently you will respond to job listings or uncover unpublicized job opportunities by sending a resume accompanied by a cover letter. In these situations, a cover letter is necessary. Since you have written a high impact resume, your cover letter should give added impact to your resume.

The cover letter should be viewed as an advertisement to learn more about the "product," which is outlined in the resume. In other words, your cover letter advertises your advertisement. It should provide the initial sizzle. It captures the reader's attention, stresses the employer's needs and your value, and invites him or her to read the resume indepth. The resume, in turn, repeats the process of grabbing attention and stressing value. Moreover, the resume sustains and heightens the reader's interest. It provides additional credibility by detailing your value in relationship to your goals and the employer's needs.

Similar to other types of letters, your cover letters should follow certain general rules:

1. **Produce on good quality bond paper.** Use 20 to 50 lb. bond paper with a 100 percent cotton fiber ("rag") content. Avoid very light- or heavy-weight papers with overly coarse textures.

2. **Address to a specific name and title.** If you are uncertain whom to address, look in library reference materials, surf the Internet, or call the company and ask the receptionist for an appropriate name and title. For openers, use some variation of the following lines:

   "I am sending some important papers to the head of the _____ Department. However, I'm not sure I have the correct name and address. Could you please tell me to whom I should address these documents?"

3. **Writing style should be direct, powerful, and error free.** Edit to eliminate extraneous words and to check grammar, spelling, and punctuation. In addition to stating your purpose, the letter tells the reader how well you communicate.

4. **No more than one page.** Do not overwhelm the resume with a lengthy cover letter or excessive repetition of the resume content.

5. **Keep the letter short and to the point.** Three paragraphs will suffice:

   Paragraph 1:   State your interest and purpose. Try to link your interests to the employer's needs.

   Paragraph 2:   Highlight your enclosed resume by stressing what you will do for the employer in reference to the employer's specific needs.

   Paragraph 3:   Request an interview and indicate you will call for an appointment.

6. **Use appropriate language.** Repeat terms the employer uses. Avoid jargon and the passive voice. Use action verbs as well as the active voice. Don't try to be cute or too aggressive.

7. **Always be positive** by stressing your past accomplishments and skills as well as your future value.

Examine the cover letter on page 135. The letter is written in response to a specific job vacancy. It is purposeful without being overly aggressive or boastful. The writer's purpose is already known by the employer. The first paragraph should re-state the position listed as well as the source of information. It links the writer's interests to the employer's needs. The writer also indicates knowledge of the organization. Overall, the first paragraph is succinct, purposeful, and thoughtful. The writer invites the reader to learn more about him.

High Impact Cover Letter

931 Davis Street
Boston, MA 01931
January 18, 20 __

John F. Baird, Manager
Hopkins International Corporation
7532 Grand Avenue
Boston, MA 01937

Dear Mr. Baird:

Your listing in the January 17 issue of the *Daily News* for a managerial trainee interests me for several reasons. I possess the necessary experience and skills you outline in the ad. Your company has a fine reputation for quality products and a track record of innovation and growth. I seek a challenging position which will fully use my talents.

My experience and skills are summarized in the enclosed resume. You may be interested in several additional qualifications I would bring to this position:

- the ability to relate well to others
- a record of accomplishments and a desire to achieve better results
- a willingness to take on new responsibilities
- enthusiasm and initiative

I would appreciate more information concerning this position as well as an opportunity to meet with you to discuss our mutual interests. I will call you Thursday morning concerning any questions we both may have and to arrange an interview if we deem it is appropriate at that time.

I appreciate your consideration and look forward to meeting you.

Sincerely yours,

Steven Reeves

Steven Reeves

In the second paragraph the writer generates additional interest by referring to his enclosed resume and including additional information for emphasizing his qualifications vis-a-vis the employer's needs. The writer also attempts to re-write the employer's ad around his qualifications. In so doing, this writer should stand out from other candidates because he **raises** the expectations of the employer beyond the position description. The writer, in effect, suggests to the employer that they will be getting more for their money than anticipated. This paragraph does not appear hyped, boastful, or aggressive. It is low-keyed yet assertive.

In the third paragraph of this example, the writer makes an open-ended offer to the employer which is difficult to refuse. Linking his interest to the reader's, the writer softens the interview request without putting the employer on the spot of having to say "yes" or "no." Overall, the writer presents the employer with an opportunity to examine his **value**. Accompanied with an outstanding resume, this letter should make a positive impression on the employer. A phone call within 48 hours of receiving the letter will further enhance the writer's candidacy.

See Appendix C for additional examples of cover letters.

Producing Approach Letters

An approach letter is a letter designed to gain access to individuals who may or may not provide you with contacts, leads, and information on job opportunities. These letters are also used for building networks which may lead to informational interviews (Chapter 10).

Approach letters are associated with two major job search and distribution strategies. The first strategy involves conducting an indiscriminate mass mailing of hundreds of resumes and cover letters to specific individuals in your area of interest – the **broadcast or shotgun approach**. If you follow up your direct mailing with telephone calls, you will get results. However, the results will be more negative than positive.

While some individuals report impressive results with this version of the shotgun method, we do not endorse it with enthusiasm. Employers are being flooded with hundreds and thousands of such resumes and phone calls. The increased use of copy machines and word processors in the job search process has led to a tremendous increase in such mass mailings over the past decade. As employers become increasingly inundated with slick resumes and cover letters – many produced by professional job search firms – this strategy has become less effective.

The second strategy involves selectively writing letters to prospective employers or to individuals who might provide you with useful job search information and referrals – the **targeted approach**. Normally you should not include your resume with this letter. Instead, take your resume to the informational interview and discuss it near the end of the interview. This is done for two purposes:

- gathering **advice** on how to improve your resume.

- getting the interviewer to **read** your resume as well as **refer** it to others who might be interested in your qualifications.

With this second strategy you tailor the contents of the letter to your audience. However, certain common elements should appear in the letters. Make sure your approach letters incorporate these elements:

1. **Start with a personal statement which connects you to the reader.** If you lack a personal referral, you might open with: *"I am writing to you because of your position as..."* or *"Because of your experience in..."*, or *"We have a common interest in..."*, or *"Since we are both alumni of _____ I thought..."* If you have a referral, start with: *"Mr., Mrs., Dr., Professor _____ suggested that I contact you..."*

2. **Orient the reader to your purpose.** Explain that you do not expect the reader to know of any current job openings, but you would like his or her help, advice, suggestions, or guidance. Stress your purpose(s): to get his or her advice on your career plans, obtain occupational information, or discuss future work possibilities. Explain your current situation.

3. **Close your letter by requesting a brief meeting** at a mutually convenient time. Indicate that you will call in a few days to arrange a meeting.

4. **Be clear.** Have a specific purpose in mind before writing this letter.

5. **Always address the letter to a name**, never to a position or title.

6. **Make your letter brief**, unless there are special reasons for going into detail.

7. **Make your letters warm and personal.** Avoid officious, stereotyped, or jargonistic language.

8. **Carefully proofread** for grammatical, spelling, or typing errors.

9. **Type an eye-catching letter.** Leave wide margins, select an attractive type style and size, balance the text on the page, and use a letter quality printer.

10. **Type on good quality bond stationery.** Avoid using cheap looking copy machine paper, which will not enhance your professional image.

11. **Keep copies of all correspondence** in an efficient filing system for follow-up purposes (see Chapter 10).

See Appendix C for examples of approach letters. While you'll find additional examples of approach letters in other resume and letter writing books, never copy or edit such letters for your use. Follow our general rules, target your specific audience, and convey your message in your own way. Again, you want to express the "unique you" to potential employers and others who can assist you with your job search.

Adding Impact With Thank-You Letters

When was the last time you received a thank-you letter or note from someone you helped or who came to your party or dinner? Chances are you receive few such letters. Furthermore, you remember those you receive, and you tend to have a positive impression of the individuals who sent them. Why? Because they are **thoughtful** people.

Thoughtful people are **remembered**. When conducting a job search you should always strive to stand out from other candidates. A thank-you letter is one of the most effective letters you can write. You normally should write this letter within 48 hours following an interview. Thank-you letters also can be used in other types of situations, such as responding to advice over the telephone or a letter of rejection. Thank people for their advice, time, and consideration. Interestingly enough, some people report receiving job offers after being first rejected because they sent a nice thank-you letter.

We include examples of thank-you letters in Appendix C. A **standard** thank-you letter should immediately follow a formal job interview. This letter highlights your interview discussion and reiterates your qualifications and continuing interest.

> *Thoughtful people are remembered. You want to be **remembered** in a positive manner.*

Thank-you letters in reference to **telephone conversations and informational interviews** should follow a similar format. Keep the letters short, be concise, reiterate major points of the conversation, and express your gratitude for assistance.

The thank-you letter in response to a **rejection** should follow a similar format. Express your gratitude for being considered for the position as well as your continuing interest in working with the employer. Few employers receive this type of letter. Hence, it may leave a lasting impression on the employer, who will remember you for future openings.

Other types of thank-you letters also are appropriate to write at times. For example, if you **withdraw from consideration** for a position or turn down a job offer, send a polite and positive thank-you letter which leaves the door open for future consideration. Once you receive a **job offer**, send a thank-you letter to your new employer. This can be one of the most effective letters in getting you off to a good start and forming a positive and lasting relationship with your new employer. Since few employers receive such letters, you will stand out as a thoughtful and considerate new employee.

If you **terminate** employment for any reason, consider sending a thank-you letter to your former employer. Try to be as positive as possible, even though you may be parting under strained circumstances. A thank-you letter can clear the air, mend broken fences, generate positive references, and leave the door open for future reconsideration.

You should write these different types of thank-you letters because you want to be **remembered** in a positive manner. You communicate your thoughtful and considerate style. Coupled with your paper qualifications, as evidenced in your outstanding resume, you will achieve a degree of impact few candidates ever display in their job search. You will stand out in the crowd. Better yet, you may avoid the crowd altogether!

10

Distribute, Market, and Manage With Impact

YOUR RESUME AND LETTERS ARE only as effective as the quality of your distribution, marketing, and follow-up activities. If you neglect to wisely engage in these key implementation steps, your job search will most likely become ineffective. You need to take purposeful action with your resume and letters.

What Do You Do Next?

Now that you have your resume and letters in hand, what are you planning to do with them? Broadcast or "shotgun" them by mail or e-mail to 500 personnel offices or key executives? Send them one at a time in response to job listings. Enter your resume into several online resume databases? Wait for employers to request your resume? Pass your resume around to friends, relatives, and acquaintances? Regardless of how you distribute your resume and letters, how will you measure the effectiveness of your marketing campaign? What records do you need to keep, and how can you best organize your records in order to manage your marketing campaign?

These questions may seem minor compared to the importance of writing the resume and letters. However, if you neglect distribution, marketing, and follow-up activities, you may blame your failures on the quality of your resume and letters. More often than not, the problems lie in how you link your documents to your audience. Neglect marketing, distribution, and follow-up and you will effectively kill your job search campaign.

We've always been amazed by the fact that most resume and cover letter books only provide advice on how to write resumes and letters. Few ever address the critical issues of production, distribution, and follow-up. Preoccupied with trying to make your resumes and letters "look good," they neglect what needs to happen next if you are to connect with the right employers and get job interviews for which you've designed your resumes and letters.

This chapter fills a major gap in the job search literature on resumes and letters. It focuses on effective marketing and distribution techniques. The next chapter examines effective follow-up activities in relation to the techniques developed in this chapter.

Approach the Publicized Job Market With Caution

You can distribute your resumes and letters through several channels. The most apparent channel is the **publicized job market** of classified ads and vacancy announcements that appear in newspapers, magazines, and trade journals as well as on Internet employment sites and company websites. These channels tend to be controlled by personnel offices and employment agencies that screen applicants for hiring officials located elsewhere in the organization. While your chances of getting a job through these channels are not particularly good, they are not hopeless. If your timing is right and you have the right set of qualifications, you may get lucky and land a job through this highly visible job market.

> *Neglect marketing and distribution and you will effectively kill your job search campaign.*

While the publicized job market is the least effective channel through which to distribute your resumes and letters, it is still used by most people as their primary channel. This is unfortunate because it yields less than satisfactory results for most applicants. The publicized job market is characterized by **high competition**. It also gives you a **misleading picture** about employment opportunities. For example, when navigating this job market, you may get the impressions that *"there are few jobs available," "getting a job is really tough these days,"* and *"there are so many other well qualified candidates – I don't have enough experience."* Given such obvious limitations, you are well advised not to invest more than one-third of your marketing time responding to publicized listings. Your time is better spent on higher payoff activities involving more responsive channels.

Nonetheless, you should focus some of your job search efforts – maybe 15 percent – on this traditional publicized employment channel. Jobs do exist there, many applicants are successful there, and you, too, could get lucky applying for a publicized job. Read the classified ads and browse online job postings, but have realistic expectations about the odds of actually getting a job through these channels. Job listings may be the least accurate gauge of the number and types of jobs available for someone with your qualifications. Most vacancy announcements normally fall into one of four categories:

1. Jobs that are difficult to fill by informal means because they (a) offer low wages, (b) require a high level of technical expertise, or (c) face a labor shortage in a particular occupation or geographical area.

2. Jobs that go unfilled because employers are relatively ignorant about how to hire; instead, they are forced to use the publicized channels.

3. Jobs which are already filled or "wired" by informal means but are listed in order to fulfill affirmative action and equal opportunity requirements.

4. Non-existent jobs – the blind ad where someone tests the waters or is collecting resumes for future reference.

You may encounter one or more of these situations if you respond to publicized job listings. Since many others will be applying simultaneously, your chances of getting an interview for a legitimate job are very slim. After sending resumes and letters in response to 100 ads, you may get five interviews – if you are lucky!

If you're looking for job listings and vacancy announcements to respond to with your resume and letters, we highly recommend looking at Dan Lauber's four "Job Finders" on sources for job listings that go far beyond the newspapers. These key volumes include everything from trade journals and job hotlines to Internet sites with job postings: *The Professional's Job Finder, The Non-Profits and Education Job Finder, The Government Job Finder,* and *The International Job Finder* (Planning/Communications). Kenton Elderkin's *How to Get Interviews From Classified Job Ads* (Impact Publications) provides useful tips on how to best respond to classifieds.

> *You are well advised not to invest more than one-third of your marketing time responding to publicized listings.*

Respond Effectively to Vacancy Announcements

The best way to respond to classified ads is to target your resume and letter to the specifications of the ad or vacancy announcement. Make sure your qualifications and experience match those outlined in the ad. Underline **key words** in the ad and include these in your correspondence. The **language** in your resume and letter must fit the language used by the employer. One of the most effective letters to send in response to a classified ad or vacancy announcement is the classic "T" letter, which outlines your qualifications in direct reference to each qualification required for the position. We includes examples of powerful "T" letters in Appendix C.

Your resume and letter also should be addressed to a particular individual. If this is not possible because the ad lacks a name, address, or phone number, omit the salutation and write the body of the letter according to our suggestions in Chapter 9.

Wherever possible, get a phone number and call the individual about four to five days after sending your resume and cover letter. Restate your interest in the job and stress your value, request an interview at a mutually convenient time, project enthusiasm for the job and the company, and listen carefully for hiring clues.

Regardless of the outcome of this telephone conversation, send a thank-you letter immediately in which you (1) stress your gratitude for the individual's time, (2) highlight your qualifications, (3) re-emphasize important points discussed in your conversation, and (4) reaffirm your interest in and enthusiasm for the position.

By injecting the use of the telephone and thank-you letter as follow-ups to your resume and cover letter, you should increase your probability of getting an interview in response to publicized job listings. However, these actions may only increase your chances from 5 to 10 percent. The publicized job market remains a game of probability and chance. By all means do not become too ego-involved with this market. It is full of false hopes, dashed expectations, and disappearing job opportunities. This does not mean you should avoid or neglect this job market. Indeed, it offers numerous good jobs for those who are talented enough to get employers' interest in inviting them to a job interview. Do the best you can in the publicized job market, but concentrate your major efforts on other distribution and marketing channels which should prove more effective and fruitful.

Penetrate the Hidden Job Market

> *The publicized job market remains a game of probability and chance. It is full of false hopes, dashed expectations, and disappearing job opportunities. You should focus most of your efforts on the hidden job market.*

Anywhere from 60 to 80 percent of all jobs are found on the hidden job market. These jobs are not publicized in traditional channels and few job seekers know how to find them. They are found through networks of friends, acquaintances, or strangers who know of impending vacancies or hiring needs that go unpublicized. Many are with small companies employing fewer than 20 people. The hidden job market also encompasses nontraditional communication and distribution channels, such as executive search and employment firms. There is **less competition** for these jobs and the **rewards tend to be greater** than those for publicized jobs.

Being unpublicized, this job market requires creative job search strategies for effectiveness. You must use your resume and letters to open doors which may or may not produce useful information, job leads, interviews, and offers. The uncertainty and unpredictability of this chaotic job search channel may initially frustrate you because it is difficult to know when you are making progress. Instead, you invest your time in increasing the probabilities of uncovering job opportunities and interviews.

Broadcast for Dumb Luck and Lightning

You can market yourself several ways in the hidden job market. First, you can broadcast or "shotgun" resumes to organizations and individuals. This is the least effective way of penetrating the hidden job market, but it will yield results – if you play the numbers game and believe lightning will strike you. Send out 100 resumes and expect maybe one interview. Send out 500 resumes and expect perhaps three interviews. If you persist long enough – and can afford the mailing costs – you will get more and more interviews which may lead to job offers. But don't send out 50 resumes and expect results. You are playing the odds at their worst with this approach. Your normal response will be a polite "thank-you" letter:

> *"There are no openings at present for someone with your qualifications. We will keep your resume on file for future reference."*

This is a polite way of telling you that they may be throwing away your materials along with the many other unsolicited resumes and letters they regularly receive from job seekers who apparently believe employers want to interview candidates for nonexisting jobs!

However, you can improve your "shotgun" odds by immediately following your resume and letter with a **phone call** (see Chapter 11). In your telephone conversation stress, as you should in your letter, that you are seeking information and advice on opportunities for someone with your qualifications. Don't put the individual on the spot by asking for a job, since he or she may not be currently in a hiring mode for someone with your qualifications. Ask for information and hope you will get referred to others who have vacancies or impending hiring needs. Above all, you want to be **remembered** in case the employer would have, or would know of, an opening for you in the future.

Despite the poor odds of success, many people are broadcasting their resumes today and more and more employers are using automated resume management systems. As more resumes and letters descend on employers, the effectiveness rates may be even lower. This also can be an expensive marketing method. You would be much better off posting an electronic version of your resume on various online employment sites where your exposure rate will be much higher and more targeted to the needs of specific employers. Start by surveying job listings and posting your resume on these top Internet sites:

- www.directemployers.com
- www.monster.com
- www.careerbuilder.com
- www.jobs.com
- www.careerjournal.com
- http://hotjobs.yahoo.com
- www.nationjob.com
- www.careerflex.com
- www.employment911.com
- www.ajb.org

This electronic form of broadcasting is also the cheapest way to go – it's usually free to job seekers. We examine this approach to resume writing and distribution in Chapter 12.

The Case for High-Tech Resume Blasting

Resume distribution approaches have always been controversial, whether offline or online. Indeed, we, along with many other career counselors, usually caution job seekers about literally "throwing money to the wind" by shotgunning, or blasting, their resumes to hundreds of employers. This is usually the approach of unfocused, and often desperate and unrealistic, job seekers. The experience is usually the same: few if any worthwhile returns. Like direct-mail responses, one can expect less than a one-percent return rate. If you mail your resume to 10,000 potential employers, chances are you'll get fewer than 100 responses and even fewer than 10 positive responses. There's also a good chance you'll get zero responses for all the time, effort, and costs involved in this unfocused "wishful thinking" approach to finding a job.

> *The old adage that you usually get what you pay for is equally valid for the job search. . . . To be effective with this approach, you need to be the perfect ($$$) candidate.*

There's no reason to think that this direct-mail approach to the job search gets any better when you shift mediums – from snail mail to electronic mail – by blasting your resume to hundreds of employers and recruiters by e-mail. Nonetheless, numerous resume distribution companies would make you believe this is an effective way to market your resume. They operate resume blasting businesses that usually charge anywhere from $50 to $200 to e-mail your resume to hundreds of employers and recruiters; some may charge thousands of dollars for more specialized blasting services. Many of them post testimonials from satisfied clients who claim great success using this approach. But as any direct-mail specialist will tell you, response rates are largely determined by the quality of both the mailing list and the mailing piece. When the two come together, expect a good response rate. The problem is that you never know the quality of the e-mail lists of these companies until *after* you use them.

We still remain skeptical about using this approach to marketing your resume. In fact, we have yet to meet any employers who would subscribe to such a questionable service. While blasting your resume by e-mail may make you initially feel good – because you are doing something and have high hopes of reaching many potential employers and recruiters – motion does not equate momentum. In the end, it may be a waste of time and money, accompanied by dashed expectations. Indeed, if you want to quickly experience the highs and lows of conducting a job search, this approach will surely provide such an experience. Resume blasting largely violates a key principle of conducting an effective job search that leads to an excellent job "fit" – target specific employers around your specific career goals, skills, and experience. Shooting a resume en masse to hundreds of employers and recruiters is not a very targeted approach. It's a "pot luck" and sometime desperate approach to finding any job you think you might be able to fit into. We strongly recommend that you find a job that is fit for you. You do this with a more targeted approach.

Having read all of this as a cautionary note about taming your expectations, you may still want to blast your resume for under $100, just to see if you get any nibbles on this type of fishing expedition. At $19.95, you don't have much to lose and perhaps much to gain if you are an experienced professional who connects with the right job. But again, don't believe all the hype surrounding this approach, and have realistic expectations of what you are likely to get for only $19.95, or even $3,000. The old adage that you usually get what you pay for is equally valid for the job search.

Chances are your greatest success with this approach will come in having reached key recruiters or headhunters rather than specific employers – individuals who are primarily interested in marketing candidates who are skilled and experienced enough to make over $60,000, but preferably over $100,000, a year. These individuals are in constant need of new resumes to refresh their pool of fast-aging resumes and candidates who find jobs. Indeed, many recruiters and headhunters welcome the receipt of such blasted resumes which they, in turn, can "flip" to employers for hefty finder's fees, if and when one of the candidates gets a job through their "recruiting" efforts. Their sourcing "commission" is usually 20 to 30 percent of the candidate's first-year salary, which is paid by the employer. In other words, you need to be the perfect candidate for this approach.

If, for example, you are making under $50,000 a year, this approach is probably a waste of time and money. Most recruiters simply don't have time, nor a market, for such low-end candidates. This approach is one way to quickly reach hundreds of recruiters whom you might not reach by other means, such as putting your resume online with recruitersonline.com.

Indeed, if you are a near or over six-figure job seeker, you can quickly rachet up your job search, as well as go global, by using these services to contact thousands of headhunters or executive recruiters who are always looking for high quality resumes and candidates they can market to their high-paying clients. The approach does work, but it works best for only certain types of candidates who fit the needs of recruiters and headhunters.

If and when you decide to play this game – knowing full well the odds are probably against you – start by investigating the following fee-based resume distribution firms (your cyberspace "blasters"). Try to find out the relative mix in their database of recruiters versus actual employers who might be looking for someone with your qualifications. These sites know the "mix" since they require employers and recruiters to sign up or register to receive "free" resumes from these services. For example, one of the largest such firms, Resumezapper.com, tells you up front that they only work with third-party recruiters and search firms – no employers; they primarily appeal to candidates who prefer being marketed through an executive recruiter. The recipients of these free resumes usually specify filters, so they only receive resumes that meet their marketing criteria. Not surprisingly, most of these resume distribution sites will blast your resume to almost solely to recruiters or headhunters. Some sites, such as www.resumeagent.com and www.resume rabbit.com, will blast your resume to numerous sites that have resume databases, thus saving time in entering your resume into each unique resume database.

■ Allen and Associates	www.resumexpress.com
■ BlastMyResume	www.blastmyresume.com
■ CareerXpress.com	www.careerxpress.com
■ E-cv.com	www.e-cv.com
■ Executiveagent.com	www.executiveagent.com
■ HotResumes	www.hotresumes.com
■ Job Search Page	www.jobsearchpage.com (international focus)
■ Job Village	www.jobvillage.com
■ Resume Agent	www.resumeagent.com
■ ResumeBlaster	www.resumeblaster.com
■ Resume Booster	www.resumebooster.com
■ ResumeBroadcaster	www.resumebroadcaster.com
■ ResumeMachine.com	www.resumemachine.com
■ Resume Rabbit	www.resumerabbit.com
■ ResumeZapper	www.resumezapper.com
■ RocketResume	www.rocketresume.com
■ See Me Resumes	www.seemeresumes.com
■ WSACORP.com	www.wsacorp.com

If you want to try your luck, for anywhere from $19.95 to over $3,000, these resume blasting firms will send your resume to 1,000 to 10,000 headhunters and employers who seek such resumes. While we do not endorse these firms – and we are often skeptical about what appear to be inflated claims of effectiveness – nonetheless, you may want to explore a few of these firms. Good luck!

Prospect and Network

A second method of penetrating the hidden job market is through prospecting, networking, and informational interviews. This should prove to be your most effective job search strategy. Prospecting is a technique for developing personal contacts which will expand into interpersonal networks for the purpose of yielding important job search information. Your resume and letters play an important role throughout these processes.

Identify and Use Your Network

The interpersonal nature of the job search is well documented. Since the 1930s studies of blue collar, white collar, managerial, technical, and professional workers have found that no more than 20 percent of placements occur through formal mechanisms. From 60 to 90 percent of jobs are found informally – mainly through friends, relatives, and direct application. The U.S. Department of Labor reports that 63.4 percent of all workers use informal methods. Even with the highly structured government recruiting procedures, informal mechanisms play an important role in acquiring government employment.

Studies consistently show that formal and impersonal communications are the least effective means of getting a job: advertisements, public and private employment agencies, and job listings provided by organizations. The most widely used and effective methods are informal and personal: personal contacts and direct application. The **personal contact** is the major job-finding method, used by over 60 percent of all job seekers.

Studies also note that both employers and employees **prefer** the informal and personal methods. Both groups believe personal contacts result in more in-depth, accurate, and up-to-date **information** which both groups need. Employers feel these methods **reduce** their recruiting costs and hiring **risks**. Individuals who use personal contacts are more **satisfied** with their jobs; those who find jobs using formal methods tend to have a greater degree of job dissatisfaction. Those using informal methods tend to have **higher incomes**, and their jobs are in the highest income brackets.

> *From 60 to 90 percent of jobs are found informally – mainly through friends, relatives, and direct application.*

Insurance, real estate, and other direct-sales businesses use several face-to-face sales techniques which can be effectively adapted to your job search. The major techniques are **networking, pyramiding, and client referral systems**. Your job search goals and situations will be analogous to those of business:

1. Your goal is to sell an important high quality product – yourself – by shopping around for a good buyer.

2. The buyer wants to be assured, based upon previous performance and current demonstration, that he or she is investing in a high quality and reliable product.

3. Face-to-face communication, rather than impersonal advertising, remains the best way to make buying/selling decisions.

4. When buyer and seller exchange information on each other, the quality of information improves and the new relationship will probably be mutually supportive, beneficial, and satisfying.

The techniques involved in building networks, pyramids, and referral systems are relatively easy to learn and apply to your job search. However, you must first understand the nature of networks, pyramids, and referral systems before you can effectively apply them to your job search.

A **network** consists of you and people you know, who are important to you, and whom you interact with most frequently. Many of these people influence your behavior. Others may also influence your behavior but you interact with them less frequently. As illustrated on page 147, your network may consist of family friends, professional colleagues, fellow workers, your supervisor, and other who can assist you. Your network of relationships involves **people** – not data, things, or knowledge of a particular subject area.

Your Network of Relationships

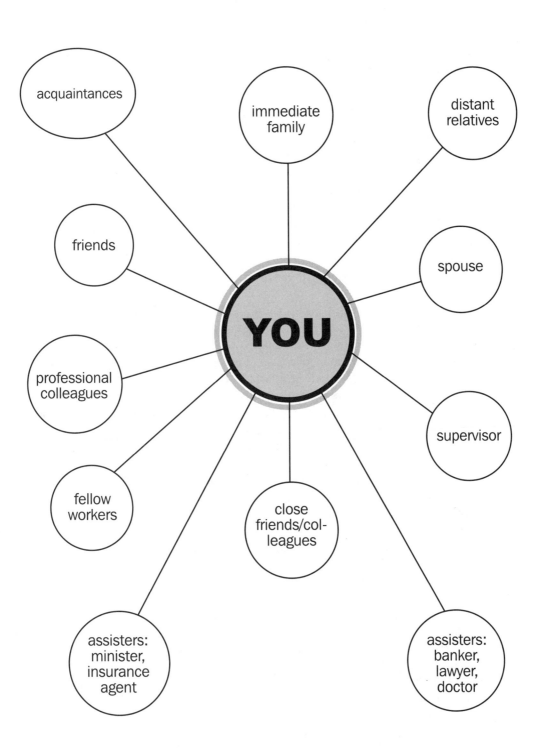

You begin using your network in the job search by asking several key questions:

- Who can help you?
- Who has information related to your job objective?
- Who knows others who might be helpful?

Address these questions to individuals in your network. Since others in your network have their own networks, their "contacts" may be useful to you. If you contact someone for information and advice, this person probably will refer you to individuals in his or her network.

Since most people like to give advice (perhaps everyone has a secret desire to be Ann Landers!) and they know other people who can do the same, you will be linking your network to their networks. If you address the same question to your relative (Uncle Joe in Dallas) and a former, and highly successful classmate, you will create new **opportunity structures** for uncovering information for your job search. An example of linking your network to those of your colleague, relative, and former classmate is illustrated on page 149. If you extend your network to include individuals you do not interact with regularly, you will create an incredible number of network linkages.

Develop a Contact List

The best way to get started in prospecting and building networks is to develop a list of potential job search contacts. Begin by listing the names of all the people you know. Include relatives, former employers, acquaintances, alumni, friends, bankers, doctors, lawyers, ministers, and professional colleagues. Perhaps only 15 of these people will be individuals you see and work with regularly. The others may be former friends, acquaintances, or your Aunt Betsy you haven't seen in ten years. If you have difficulty developing such a list, refer to the following checklist of categories to refresh your memory:

- ☐ Friends (take a look at your Christmas card and e-mail lists)
- ☐ Neighbors (current and past)
- ☐ Social acquaintances: golf, swim, tennis, PTA, social club members
- ☐ Classmates – from any level of school
- ☐ College alumni (get a list of those living locally)
- ☐ Teachers – your college professors, your children's teachers
- ☐ Anybody you wrote a check to in the past year
  - ____ tradespeople, drugstore owner
  - ____ doctor, dentist, optician
  - ____ lawyer, accountant, real estate agent
  - ____ insurance agent, stock broker, travel agent
- ☐ Manager of local branch of your bank
- ☐ Co-workers and former co-workers
- ☐ Relatives
- ☐ Politicians (local leaders often are businessmen/women or professionals in town who know everybody.)
- ☐ Chamber of Commerce executives in town
- ☐ Pastors, ministers (excellent resources)
- ☐ Members of your church

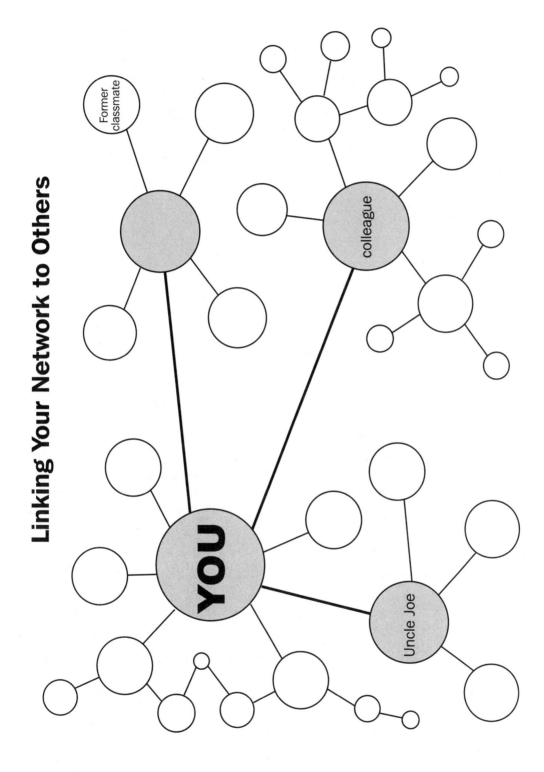

Linking Your Network to Others

❑   Trade association executives
❑   Professional organization executives
❑   Members of your professional societies
❑   Contacts you've made over the Internet
❑   People you meet at conventions
❑   Speakers at meetings you've attended
❑   Business club executives and members (Rotary, Kiwanis, Jaycees, etc.)
❑   Representatives of direct-sales business (real estate, insurance, Amway, Shaklee, Avon)
❑   Representatives of delivery services (Postal Service, UPS, Federal Express)
❑   Others

After developing your comprehensive list of contacts, classify the names into different categories of individuals:

■   Those in influential positions or who have hiring authority
■   Those with job leads
■   Those most likely to refer you to others
■   Those with long-distance contacts

Select at least 25 names from your list for initiating your first round of contacts. You are now ready to begin an active prospecting and networking campaign which should lead to informational interviews, formal job interviews, and job offers.

Organize and Link Your Networks to Others

Prospecting involves contacting people in your network and building new networks for information and job leads. Many people starting out in direct sales businesses quit at this point because they lack the prerequisites for success – patience, perseverance, and a positive attitude. After encountering two or three rejections, they develop a pessimistic attitude which prevents them from further venturing along the road to prospecting success. Successful prospecting techniques require you to:

■   Develop enthusiastic one-on-one appointments and informational interview presentations.

■   Be consistent and persistent in how you present your case.

■   Give prospecting a high priority in your overall daily routine.

■   Believe you will be successful given your persistence with these techniques; prospecting is a probability game involving both successes and failures.

Prospecting and networking, above all, require **persistence**. For example, it takes about 20 minutes to initiate a contact by telephone – longer by letter. If you contact at least one person in your immediate circle of contacts each day, your prospecting should yield 15 new contacts each week for a total investment of less than two hours. Each of these new contacts could possibly yield three additional contacts, or 45 new referrals. However, some contacts will yield more than three and others may yield none. If you develop contacts in this manner, you will create a series of small pyramids, as illustrated on page 152. If you expand your prospecting from one to three new contacts each day, you could generate 135 new contacts and referrals in a single week. If you continue this same level of activity over a two-month period, it is possible to create over 1,000 new contacts and referrals! At this pace, your odds of uncovering job opportunities, being invited to formal job interviews, and receiving job offers will increase dramatically.

The linkages and pyramids on page 152 constitute your **job search network**. Always remember to develop, nurture, and manage this network so it performs well in generating information and job leads. It will become your most important resource for acquiring job information, uncovering job leads, and contacting potential employers. When following through on new contacts, expect about half to result in referrals. However, a few of your contacts will continue to give you referrals beyond the initial ones. Consequently, you need to continually develop new contacts while maintaining communication with prior contacts. When conducting informational interviews, ask your contacts to keep you in mind if they hear of anyone who might be interested in your qualifications.

> *You need to continually develop new contacts while maintaining communication with prior contacts.*

While prospecting is an excellent way to create contacts, it also helps you develop a realistic objective, effective interview skills, and self-confidence. In using this system, you will seldom be turned down for an informational interview. You should uncover vacancies on the hidden job market as well as place yourself in a positive position to take advantage of such opportunities.

Never directly ask for a job while prospecting, networking, and conducting informational interviews. Asking for a job puts your contact under pressure; it is the quickest way to be politely shown the door. The basic principle behind networking is this: the best way to get a job is never ask for a job directly – always ask for information, advice, and referrals. By doing this, you will be interviewed, your resume will be read, and you eventually will be offered a job through one or more of your contacts.

Our prospecting system is similar to the networking techniques used in the direct-sales businesses. These proven, low-keyed sales techniques require persistence, a personable approach to people, and the ability to share a "product" and offer an opportunity to prospective buyers. This low-stress approach does not threaten individuals by asking them to buy something, or, in your case, give you a job. Some of the most successful businesses in the world have been built on this simple one-on-one networking and referral strategy. When adapted to the job search process, the same strategies have resulted in extremely successful job placements.

Conduct Informational Interviews

An informational interview is a low-stress, face-to-face meeting with a contact or potential employer for the purposes of getting:

1. **Information** on present or future job opportunities in your interest and skill areas.

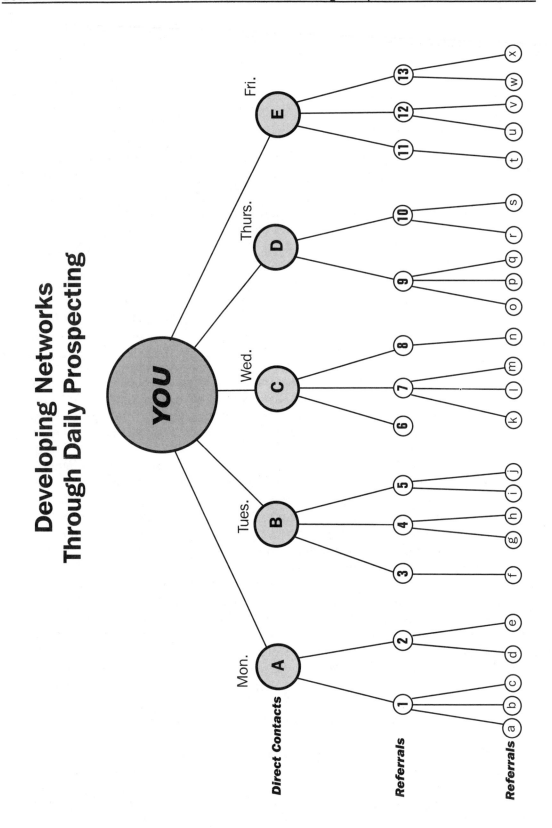

Developing Networks
Through Daily Prospecting

2. **Advice** on your job search campaign.

3. **Referrals** to other people who might be able to give you more information, advice, and referrals which, in turn, may lead to job interviews and offers.

If approached in the proper manner, at least 50 percent of your prospecting and networking activities should result in informational interviews over the telephone, Internet, or in face-to-face meetings. While a face-to-face meeting is preferable to a telephone or e-mail informational interview, be prepared to settle for a telephone or e-mail interview in cases where the individual is too busy to schedule a meeting. Face-to-face meetings with every prospect is an unnecessary waste of time for both you and your prospect. Such meetings take a great deal of time, much of which might be better spent on the telephone or over the Internet. Save face-to-face meeting times for people who really count in your network – the ones who are likely to generate job interviews.

> *The best way to get a job is never ask for a job directly; always ask for information, advice, and referrals.*

When initiating your networking activities, keep in mind that informational interviews have six major purposes:

1. **Gather current information** on the job market relevant to your specific interests (labor market conditions, potentially interested employers, trends).

2. **Acquire data** on any known specific vacancies (nature of work, job titles, working environment, interpersonal and political climates).

3. **Inform** your contact of your interests and qualifications as well as get his or her reaction to your resume.

4. **Get advice** on how to proceed with your job search.

5. **Obtain one or more referrals** to others who can give you additional information and advice on potential vacancies and job market conditions.

6. **Be remembered** for future reference.

You should conduct informational interviews with two audiences: (1) individuals with useful occupational information, and (2) potential employers. Do not confine your contacts to a single level in an organization or assume that people at the top are the most knowledgeable. Individuals at other levels can be helpful, too. Indeed, many middle-level managers know more about their organization and are more willing to talk with you than the influentials at the top. Furthermore, many organizations decentralize hiring power to operating units. Therefore, you must identify where to best target your efforts. There is no substitute for **knowing your organization.**

There's a myth that influential people don't want be the subject of informational interviews. In reality they don't want to be pestered by job seekers who abuse and misuse the informational interview to get a job through them. Whatever you do, don't abuse networking and informational interviews by using them as a guise to getting a job with the interviewee. If you do this, you will quickly be shown the door!

Why should influential people want to talk with you? They have any number of reasons to speak with you or see you within the context of an informational interview:

- Window-shopping for new talent
- Professional courtesy
- Acquire information from you
- Relaxation
- Curiosity
- Recruiting for a friend
- Sounding board – test out his or her ideas on you
- Ego – needs to live up to your expectations
- Desire to "play God" and help those who help themselves
- Internal politics – spread word on the grapevine that he or she is looking for new talent
- Need to save time and money
- Your persistence overcomes his or her resistance
- Unconscious fear – "there but for the grace of God go I"
- Pay back the world – he or she was once helped by others
- Reciprocity – he or she may need you someday
- Genuine desire to help others
- Discover genius or hidden talent
- Enjoys opportunity to criticize
- Coincidence of timing – he or she is actively looking

At the same time, be prepared to encounter individuals who may have another 20 reasons for not speaking with you or seeing you. In that case, you must reassess your approach, try again with these individuals, settle for a telephone or e-mail interview, or move on to others.

The procedure for conducting an informational interview can vary depending on your audience. Some people are successful in conducting "cold-turkey" interviews with important **strangers** in key positions. Others follow a four-step process with great success:

1. **Send an approach letter:** Follow the advice outlined in Chapter 9 on writing this letter. Do not enclose your resume.

2. **Make a telephone appointment:** This follows a few days after sending your letter. Try to set a specific time and date for a meeting. Avoid conducting a telephone interview.

3. **Conduct the interview:** Seek information, advice, and referrals. Leave a copy of your resume and ask to be remembered for future openings.

4. **Send a thank-you letter:** Be sure it is warm and sincere and follows the advice in Chapter 9.

The structure of a one-on-one informational interview should remain fairly consistent. Develop a script that is low-keyed, yet assertive enough to clearly communicate your objective and enthusiasm. Prior to the actual interview, role-play with a friend.

Remember that most people do not want to be put on the spot to be responsible for your employment fate. Therefore, try to promote a low-stress situation and develop a futuristic orientation. Most people like to give advice and be helpful. They are flattered when you ask for advice because you are saying that you value their opinions and knowledge. Such compliments will most likely result in willing cooperation and useful information. Many contacts will want to see you achieve your goals.

> *Ask your contact to critique your resume and suggest how to proceed with your job search.*

While your primary purpose is to gather information about future job possibilities, you should not hide the fact that you are looking for a job – if indeed you are. For example, you might say to your interviewee: *"While I don't expect you to have a job vacancy now, I would like to talk to you about future opportunities."* Bluntly asking for a job may make the person feel uncomfortable and prematurely end your relationship.

Your informational interviews should focus on **seeking information on opportunities and advice on your job objective.** You need such information and advice in order to make sound decisions about your future. Also, ask your contact to critique your resume and suggest how to proceed with your job search. Such a line of discussion should capture the empathy of your interviewer. After all, everyone has been involved in career planning and job hunting, and they will continue to be in the future. You will find that most contacts will refer you to other individuals for further information and advice.

Questions and Dialogue

Informational interviews are conversations which yield specific types of information. While this type of interview appears somewhat unstructured, you should maintain a basic structure to keep a conversation flowing. Let's look at some examples to illustrate how to conduct this interview. Your discussion might approximate the following:

Introduce Yourself

"Mr. Roberts, hello. It's a pleasure to meet you, and I really appreciate your taking some time to see me."

"As I said in my letter to you, I am exploring different job and career opportunities. Your type of work interests me very much. I want to learn more about (technical writing, accounting, sales, personnel administration, etc.). Let me repeat, I don't expect you to have or even know of a job vacancy."

Identify Job Requirements, Relationships, Environments

"If it's okay with you, I have some questions about this type of work:

- *What's involved in (occupation) in terms of regular tasks and activities?*

- *What skills and abilities are required to do a good job?*

- *What kinds of relationships with others are expected or necessary in performing the job?*

- *What is the work environment like in terms of pressure, deadlines, routines, new activities?"*

NOTE: discussion of work requirements should take 15-20 minutes.

Make a Transition

"This has been very helpful to me. You've given me information that I've not read nor even considered before."

Survey Occupational Outlook and Get Application Advice

"I'd like to shift the focus a bit and ask your opinion about the employment outlook in (occupation):

- *Are job prospects good, stable, or very competitive?*

- *What local organizations employ people in (occupation)?*

- *What's the best way to apply for jobs in (occupation)?"*

NOTE: discussion of employment outlook, job hunting, and application procedures should take approximately 10 minutes

Evaluate Your Resume

"If you don't mind, would you look over my resume? Perhaps you could comment on its clarity or make suggestions for improving it?"

Identify Occupational Opportunities

"How would someone with my background get started in (_____)? What kinds of positions could I qualify for?"

"You've been most generous with your time, and the information you've given me is most useful. It clarifies and reinforces a number of points for me. I have two final requests:

- *The jobs you thought might be appropriate for someone with my skills sound interesting and I'd like to find out more about those possibilities. Do you know individuals in those kinds of jobs who would be willing – like yourself – to provide me with additional information?*

NOTE: about half will provide you with multiple referrals

- *Finally, I would appreciate it if you could keep my resume for reference in case you hear of a vacancy appropriate for someone with my background and interests."*

Express Your Gratitude

"Thanks again for taking the time to see me. You've been very helpful and I appreciate it."

Be Thoughtful and Repeat

Upon completion of the informational interview, be sure to express your gratitude for the person's time and assistance. Make sure the person has your resume. Keep this interview to 30-45 minutes. However, don't be surprised if it runs longer than anticipated; many interviewers enjoy discussing their work and giving advice.

Within a day, write a thank-you letter (see Appendix C) in which you again express your gratitude for his or her assistance and emphasize once again that you would appreciate being kept in mind if he or she hears of any opportunities for someone with your qualifications. Some career consultants advise you to handwrite this note; others tell you to type it since typing looks much more professional than handwriting. We prefer the typed letter because it looks most professional. Handwritten notes or letters are too personal for this type of professional relationship. You may want to both e-mail and mail this letter.

Continue repeating the prospecting, networking, and informational interviewing. While your immediate goal is to get a job, your long-term goal is to build a career. Do not forget your contacts once you achieve your immediate objective. You owe them a debt of gratitude for helping you. After you get a job, inform them of your success and thank them once again for their assistance. In many cases, you may develop new and lasting relationships as a result of your job search.

Expected Results

Our networking and informational interviewing approach is based upon years of successful experience with thousands of clients. Most major professional career counseling firms teach this method to their clients, and they report excellent results. You, too, will be successful in getting job interviews and offers if you continue prospecting, networking, and conducting informational interviews. The odds are in your favor as long as you constantly repeat these activities. In general, your odds are about 50 percent that employers will meet with you based upon your approach letter. At the end of informational interviews, expect another 50 percent to refer you to three or four others. Consequently, if you feel you need more contacts, informational interviews, and referrals, just accelerate your level of prospecting and networking activities.

It is difficult to give precise estimates as to when you can expect your first formal job interview and offer based upon this approach (see our "Organization of Job Search Activities" chart in Chapter 5). Some people get lucky and follow through on their first referral with an informational interview that yields a job offer. Others repeat these activities for four to six months before receiving a job offer. A realistic prospecting plan is to initiate one new contact each day. Within the first month, you will have developed your initial contacts and completed your first round of informational interviews. During the second month, the number of informational interviews should increase considerably. Within two and a half to three months, firm job offers should be forthcoming. Again, job offers can occur at any time, from your first informational interview to your 100th interview six months later. But if you are consistent in making five new contacts each week and following through on your referrals, you should begin receiving job offers within two and a half to three months.

> *You, too, will be successful in getting job interviews and offers if you continue prospecting, networking, and conducting informational interviews.*

Keep Good Records

As you begin applying for many positions and networking for informational interviews, you will need to rely on something more than your memory. A good record-keeping system can help you manage your job search effectively. You can do this the old fashioned way by purchasing file folders for your correspondence and notes. Be sure to make copies of all letters you write, since you may need to refer to them over the telephone or before interviews. Record your activities with each employer – letters, resumes, telephone calls, interviews – on a 4" x 6" card and file it according to the name of the organization or individual. These files will help you quickly access information and evaluate your job search progress.

If you're computer savvy, you may want to electronically organize your recordkeeping activities using a database program. Check your current software programs for a contact manager, calendar, or tracking/follow-up program. Several software programs are now available for networking and tracking activities. Some, such as *WinWay Resume*, *ResumeMaker*, and *Sharkware*, are designed specifically for tracking job leads and following up specific job search activities. Many of the large employment websites, such as Monster.com, allow you to manage your resume and track applications online.

One of the simplest and most effective paper and pencil systems consists of recording data on 4" x 6" cards. If you respond to classified ads, clip the ad and paste it to the card. Label the card in the upper left-hand corner with a useful reference category and subcategory. For example, in applying for a management trainee position with a food company, your category might appear as follows: MANAGEMENT TRAINEE – food. In the upper right-hand corner, place the name of the company. At the bottom of the card identify the name, title, address, and phone number, and e-mail of your contact. This side of the card should approximate the following example:

MANAGEMENT TRAINEE – GENERAL FOODS
food

(ad)

Mr. James Lathrop
General Manager
4291 Grand Master Blvd.
Chicago, IL 60606
(312) 223-8012
E-mail: lathropj@netlink.com

On the reverse side of the same card, record all information pertinent to making contacts for this position. Organize this information by dates and the nature of the contact. Add any information which documents your continuing contacts. For example, this side of your card might look like the following:

7/9/05   –   sent resume (#14) with cover letter to Mr. Lathrop.

7/13/05   –   telephoned Mr. Lathrop to set up interview for 7/22. Spoke with secretary, Jean Staples.

7/18/05   –   received letter from Mr. Lathrop confirming appointment time and requesting information.

7/22/05   –   interviewed with Mr. Lathrop. See GENERAL FOODS file. Sent thank-you letter to Mr. Lathrop.

7/25/05   –   offered position at $68,000.

7/27/05   –   telephoned Mr. Lathrop to decline offer.

7/28/05   –   sent letter thanking Mr. Lathrop for opportunity; reaffirmed my continuing interest in the firm in another capacity.

Maintain similar records as you network and conduct informational interviews. However, these cards will be classified differently and therefore should be kept together in a separate category called "Networking." Organize these cards around the names of individuals. For example, at the top of a 4" x 6" card, place the name, address, and telephone number of your contact. Include any information which will clarify who this individual is in relationship to others and your job search. This information might appear as in the following example:

TEMPLE, Joan (Mrs.): 1156 Terrace Drive, Richmond, VA 24810
Tel. 703-212-8604, Fax 703-212-8605, E-mail: templej@aol.com

manager of Titan Corporation, security systems company. (see TITAN file info)

sister-in-law of John Graves. Received referral from John.

acquainted with Mary Cross, Dave Bairs, and Steve Rathing.

member of Grace Methodist church, Richmond Women's Network.

graduate of the University of Virginia – MBA, 2000. Classmate of Francis Catlin.

sailing enthusiast.

On the other side of this card, record all contact information. For example, you might include:

9/4/05   –   sent letter requesting informational interview via John Graves' recommendation.

9/8/05   –   Made phone call; set luncheon appointment for 2/14.

9/14/05   –   meeting; left resume; received 3 referrals – Smith, David, Alton (see notes in STAPLES file).

9/15/05   –   sent thank-you letter.

9/16/05   –   received phone call and 2 new referrals.

9/18/05   –   received phone call and invitation to interview.

You should also maintain active and inactive categories with both sets of cards. Keep the active file active by referring to each card once every two weeks. Make sure some activity has taken place between you and the contact within a four-week period. This may mean sending another letter or telephoning the contact. If no new entries have been made on the card within eight weeks, move it to the inactive category. However, it is best to keep your contacts alive by continually monitoring contact dates and following through with additional communication.

In addition to keeping an accurate set of 4" x 6" reference cards, be sure to keep all correspondence and notes in reference to your contact cards. This information can be best organized by using 9" x 12" file folders. Keep two sets of files. The first set should be organized by the names of contacts in your networking and informational interviewing campaigns. Copies of all correspondence coming to or from you should be included in these files. Also, include in each file all notes you take in reference to written communication, telephone conversations, and interviews. Include a copy of the specific resume you sent or left with the individual. If you are using a general resume, note in your file folders which resume – identified by coded number – applies to the folder.

You may wish to take this record-keeping system one step further by developing a master record sheet. While this record sheet duplicates the information on your 4" x 6" cards and in your file folders, it provides you with a chronological listing of contact information. In abbreviated form, this information is much easier to carry with you than the cards and folders. It also enables you to quickly overview your campaign as well as evaluate your progress. Use our Master Record Sheet on page 162 for developing your own form.

This record-keeping system will enhance the effectiveness of your campaign. If you receive telephone calls in reference to your application or networking activities, you can immediately refer to the 4" x 6" cards and file folders during the course of your conversation. If not, you may find yourself in the embarrassing position of trying to remember whom you are talking to in reference to what. When writing additional correspondence, you will be able to quickly and accurately refer to previous communication.

Your record-keeping system will also allow you to **monitor and evaluate your progress**. These are important capabilities to develop throughout your job search. If, for example, after applying for 50 positions you have not been invited to a single interview, re-evaluate your job search in reference to the published job market. Perhaps you are too aggressive, or maybe you need to be more dramatic, such as sending copies of your resume on colored paper. Or perhaps you need to make greater use of the telephone to initiate interviews. Randomly select five companies from your inactive file of 50 and contact the employers; ask them for advice on how you might improve your campaign. This type of evaluation can result in some useful advice from those who manage the advertised job market. In addition, it may result in converting an inactive contact into an active networking contact.

You should periodically conduct a similar evaluation on your prospecting, networking, and informational interviewing campaign. Try to increase your efficiency and effectiveness by first analyzing your program and then taking corrective action. If your prospecting is not yielding contacts, re-structure your prospecting campaign. Your approach to people may need to be revised. Consider doing less letter writing and more telephone calling or alter your script for developing contacts. Your major problem may be in the number of contacts you initiate. Your probabilities of getting interviews and job offers will be in direct proportion to the number of prospects you develop and networks you maintain and

Master Record Sheet

Name/ Organization address	Telephone No.	Contact Source	Contact Dates				Active	Evaluation/ Notes
			resume	letter	phone	interview		

expand. Your record-keeping system will give you an accurate picture of how diligent you have been in this regard. As your record-keeping system will confirm, you get results in direct proportion to the amount of time and effort you put into your job search.

The Art of Advertising

Your job search campaign has similar characteristics to the art of advertising. Good advertisers know you must alter your advertising campaign if the number of responses do not justify your expenditure of time, effort, and money. While the product is sometimes defective or no demand can be created for it, more often than not the problem lies in how you position and market the product. Demand for a product can usually be created if the product is clearly related to the needs and interests of the targeted audience and if the audience is continuously reminded that it is in their interests to acquire the product. The product must stress potential benefits and value to the consumer.

Results seldom occur overnight. Knowing how to effectively relate the product to the audience is often a trial and error process. Central to this process is a good record-keeping system which enables the advertiser to evaluate and adjust his or her campaign according to an improved understanding of the particular audience.

11

Implement and Follow Through With Persistence

IMPLEMENTATION IS ALL ABOUT translating your best laid plans into action and then following through with persistence. To write, produce, and distribute resumes and letters without implementing and following through is a sure way to kill your job search and push you into the legions of frustrated job seekers. Nonetheless, many job seekers fail to implement and follow through properly.

Making Things Happen Through Action

We've always been fascinated why people read "how-to" job search books but never seem to get their job search on track. Many people find such books "interesting" and "helpful." They may even attend a job search seminar or take a college course on the subject. Some even become book and seminar "junkies"; they repeat the process of reading more job search books and attending more seminars. Some get stuck trying to do a self-assessment, continuously asking themselves, *"Who am I?"* and *"Where am I going in life?"* They seem preoccupied with contemplating their future rather than interested in contacting, meeting, and getting feedback from potential employers. Others crank out resumes and cover letters which they send to only five employers. They wait and they wait and they wait. Then they wonder why there seem to be so few jobs available and why no one wants to hire them. They often repeat the lament of the frustrated job seeker, *"No one will hire me!"* Indeed, Ron addresses this and other key issues in *No One Will Hire Me!* (Impact Publications, 2004).

So they read another book and discover they did everything they were told to do, but, still, nothing seems to happen. Maybe the book was bad, or maybe they aren't good. All this "how-to" advice doesn't seem to work for them. In the meantime, they engage in a great deal of wishful thinking – believing the ideal job will come their way if only they read more books and attend more seminars that will reveal more secrets to job search success!

164

Let's be honest with ourselves about all the "how-to" advice you encounter in today's job market. Good jobs do not come by way of understanding a process, nor through osmosis or "big thinking." They only come your way if you take the necessary **actions** to bring them within the scope of your job search. You must take certain incremental actions and repeat them over and over again in the process of communicating your talents to employers. Those actions must go beyond reading more books and attending more job search seminars. It's time to free yourself of the books and get on with the business of making things happen on a daily basis.

> *Good jobs do not come by way of understanding a process, nor through osmosis....You must take certain actions and repeat them over and over again.*

Implement for Positive Results

The basic failure with most job searches is the inability to implement and follow through. Individuals may learn all the tricks to writing effective letters and resumes as well as how to network, conduct outstanding interviews, and negotiate terrific salaries. But if they don't translate their **understanding** into concrete and purposeful **repetitive actions**, they will go nowhere with their job search.

The process of translating understanding into action is what we call **implementation** – the ability to make things happen by putting into effect a plan of action. At the very heart of implementation is the repetitive process of **follow-up**. Without an effective follow-up campaign focused on all of your job search communications and actions, your job search is likely to flounder. You'll most likely receive no responses or *"Thank you but not now"* responses to your resumes and letters. You want to both take and receive action that moves you closer to your goals – job interviews and offers.

Commit Yourself in Writing

At the very least, implementation requires you to put together an action plan and commit yourself to seeing it become a reality. You may find it useful to commit yourself in writing to implementing your job search. This is a very useful way to get both motivated and directed for action. Start by completing the job search contract on page 166 and keep it near you – in your briefcase, on your desk, or in your computer.

In addition, you should complete weekly performance reports. These reports identify what you actually accomplished rather than what your good intentions tell you to do. Make copies of the performance and planning report form on page 168, and use one each week to track your actual progress and to plan your activities for the next week.

If you fail to meet these written commitments, issue yourself a revised and updated contract. But if you do this three or more times, we strongly suggest you stop kidding yourself about your motivation and commitment to finding a job. Start over again, but this time consult a professional career counselor who can provide you with the necessary structure to make progress in finding a job.

Job Search Contract

1. I will begin my job search on _____.
   (specific date)

2. I will involve _____ with my job
   search.   (individuals/groups)

3. I will complete my skills identification step by _____.
   (specific date)

4. I will complete my objective statement by _____.

5. I will complete my resume by _____.

6. I will complete my first round of job search letters (approach and cover)
   by _____.

7. I will begin my networking activities on _____.

8. Each week I will:

   - make _____ new job contacts.
   - write _____ job search letters.
   - conduct _____ informational interviews.
   - follow up on _____ referrals.

9. I expect my first job interview will take place during the week of
   _____.

10. I expect to begin my new job by _____.

11. I promise to manage my time well, according to my improved time
    management behaviors on pages 49-50, so that I can successfully complete
    my job search and find a high quality job.

   Signature: _____

   Date: _____

A professional may not be cheap, but if paying for help gets you on the right track and results in the job you want, it's money well spent. Don't be *"penny wise but pound foolish"* with your future.

Be Sure to Follow Up

Follow-up is a much neglected art, but it is the key to unlocking employers' doors and for achieving job search success. But many people fear following up. Like giving a speech, it requires initiating face-to-face communications with strangers! They would rather mail resumes and wait for a response by mail or telephone.

Follow-up occurs at the implementation stage of your job search. It is the single most important element for converting communications into action. Without an effective follow-up campaign, your letters and resumes will lose their impact. They will probably sit on someone's desk amidst numerous other letters and resumes. If you want high impact resumes and letters – ones that move readers to actions that eventually lead to job interviews and offers – you must engage in a series of follow-up activities that will give your resumes and letters their intended impact.

> *Without an effective follow-up campaign, your letters and resumes will lose their impact.*

Effective Follow-Up Methods

Follow-up means taking actions that get others to respond to you. Whether or not they respond in positive ways depends on the content of your follow-up activities. If you want to have maximum impact on employers, you must follow up both your resumes and letters with certain actions. The most effective follow-up actions are a telephone call and a thank-you letter.

Follow-up makes good sense given the nature of the employment process. Since employers are often inundated with resumes and letters, your follow-up actions will get their attention which, in turn, will likely get your resume and letter **read** and **reacted** to. Better still, your follow-up action will most likely result in getting **remembered** as a thoughtful person. Indeed, getting your resume and letters read and reacted to and your candidacy remembered are the three most important outcomes you should seek at the pre-interview stage of your job search. You get read, reacted to, and remembered when you follow up with a telephone call and thank-you letter.

Four high impact follow-up principles apply to both resumes and job search letters:

1. **Develop a 31-day follow-up filing system:** Your follow-up activities will quickly become chaotic if you do not develop an efficient and effective management system for handling your communications. We recommend creating a 31-day filing system. Ideally, this should consist of 31 hanging folders (8½" x 11") labeled numerically by each day of the month (1 through 31); use manila folders or an expandable file folder if you lack an appropriate filing cabinet or box. Once you communicate with an individual, take a copy of your correspondence – complete with a telephone number and appropriate notes – and place it in the folder with the date (ideally seven days from today)

Weekly Job Search Performance and Planning Report

1. The week of: _____.

2. This week I:

   - wrote ___ job search letters.
   - sent ___ resumes and ___ letters to potential employers.
   - completed ___ applications.
   - made ___ job search telephone calls.
   - completed ___ hours of job research.
   - set up ___ appointments for informational interviews.
   - conducted ___ informational interviews.
   - received ___ invitations to a job interview.
   - followed up on ___ contacts and ___ referrals.

3. Next week I will:

   - write ___ job search letters.
   - send ___ resumes and ___ letters to potential employers.
   - complete ___ applications.
   - make ___ job search telephone calls.
   - complete ___ hours of job research.
   - set up ___ appointments for informational interviews.
   - conduct ___ informational interviews.
   - follow up on ___ contacts and ___ referrals.

4. Summary of progress this week in reference to my Job Search Contract commitments:

   _____

   _____

   _____

   _____

   _____

   _____

in which you plan to make your next follow-up contact. Repeat this filing activity for all communication requiring a follow-up action. Each day pull the file for that date and conduct your follow-up actions. If you make a phone call and are unable to contact the person, move a copy of your correspondence to tomorrow's file and conduct another follow-up. Within a month you will have a very efficient and effective filing system which will enable you to systematically conduct follow-ups in a timely and organized manner. Better still, you will be pleasantly surprised to discover this basic filing system produces remarkable results! If you prefer using a computer program for tracking your contacts, try a contact management program, such as ACT! or Goldmine, or use the automated tracking and record-keeping programs identified on page 158.

2. **Follow up your resume and letters within seven days of mailing them:** Do not let too much time lapse between when you mailed your resume and when you contact the recipient. Seven days should give the recipient sufficient time to examine your communication and decide on your future status. If not, your follow-up actions will assist them in making a decision.

3. **The best follow-up for a mailed resume and letter is a telephone call:** Don't expect your resume recipient to take the initiative in calling you for an interview. State in your cover letter that you will call the recipient at a particular time to discuss your resume:

   "I will call your office on the morning of November 5 to see if a meeting can be scheduled at a convenient time."

   And be sure you indeed follow up with a phone call at the designated time. If you have difficulty contacting the individual, try no more than eight times to get through. After the eighth try, leave a message as well as write a letter as an alternative to the telephone follow-up. In this letter, inquire about the status of your resume and thank the individual for his or her consideration.

4. **Follow up your follow-up with a nice thank-you letter:** Regardless of the outcome of your phone call, send a nice thank-you letter based upon your conversation. You thank the letter recipient for taking the time to speak with you and reiterate your interest in the position. You can either e-mail or mail this letter.

Follow-Up Statements and Cheerful Persistence

Follow-up should play a central role in all of your job search communication. Especially when initially contacting potential employers through the mail, follow-up should be built into your letters in the form of a follow-up statement. Always close your letters with a follow-up statement rather than the standard but rather limp _"I look forward to hearing from you"_ close. Try to end with a closing that uses some variation of these follow-up statements:

"I will call your office on Tuesday, February 5, to see if your schedule would permit us to meet briefly."

"I know you're very busy. But I also know I could benefit greatly from your advice. I would like to call you on Thursday morning to briefly discuss my interests. I'll only take a few minutes of your time."

"I will call your office at 2pm on Thursday, April 23, to ask you a few questions about my interests and to see if we might be able to get together for a brief meeting in the near future."

"Would next week be a good time to discuss my interests? I'll call your office at 3pm on Tuesday, September 9, to check your schedule. I appreciate your time."

Each of these statements specifies **what** you will do and **when** you plan to do it – an anticipated follow-up action on your part. The reader knows what to expect next from you. At this stage he or she needs to do nothing other than **remember** you and your letter – the most important outcome you want to achieve when initially developing a communication link with your reader.

Conducting an effective follow-up by telephone is easier said than done, especially given today's frustrating voice mail systems. A typical follow-up may require three to seven phone calls because the person is unavailable or avoiding your call. With each phone call you may need to leave a message. However, similar to response rates to letters, don't expect busy people to return phone calls from strangers. Many people only do so after the third or fourth redundant phone message – guilt moves them to action!

Whatever you do, please do not show your irritation, anger, or disappointment in not having your phone calls returned. Some people feel insulted and express their irritation in their tone of voice or choice of words when they make their third, fourth, or fifth ineffective follow-up call:

"Well, I left two messages – one on Tuesday and another on Wednesday."

"Does he usually return his phone calls?"

"What should I do? I keep calling but he won't return my calls!"

"Did he leave a message for me?"

"How many more days should I wait before I call again?"

These responses communicate the wrong **attitude** toward someone who may be able to assist you. While they may accurately reflect what's happening, they lack tact and good job search manners. Keep your cool, and cheerfully continue leaving messages as if you understand this is what normally happens in the course of conducting follow-up calls. Remember, you are sowing the seeds of what will probably be a guilt-ridden and sympathetic individual who eventually, and apologetically, returns your calls.

A standard follow-up scenario goes something like this. You stated in your letter you would call at 2:30pm on Tuesday. When you call, you will probably have to go through one or two gatekeepers before you can make direct contact with the person you want to reach. The final gatekeeper will probably be a personal secretary or receptionist who is well versed in the art of screening important from not-so-important calls. When the final gatekeeper takes your call, the following exchange is likely to occur:

Secretary:	*"Mr. Carroll's office. How can I help you?"*
You:	*"Hi, this is Mary Harris calling for Mr. Carroll."*
Secretary:	*"I'm sorry, Mr. Carroll is not available."*
You:	*"When would you expect him to be free?"*
Secretary:	*"I really don't know. He's been in meetings all day. Could I take a message and have him return your call?"*
You:	*"Yes, would you please? My name is Mary Harris and my telephone number is _____. I'm calling in reference to a letter I sent Mr. Carroll on July 5. I mentioned I would be calling him today."*
Secretary:	*"I'll give him the message."*
You:	*"Thanks so much for your help."*

Don't hold your breath in expectation of getting a return call soon. The secretary will give him the message, but he probably will sit on it and do nothing until he's motivated to do so. Consequently, you will probably need to initiate another call. If you don't hear from the person within 24 hours, make another follow-up call. This time your conversation may go something like this:

Secretary:	*"Mr. Carroll's office. How can I help you?"*
You:	*"Hi, this is Mary Harris calling for Mr. Carroll."*
Secretary:	*"I'm sorry, Mr. Carroll is not available. Can I take a message?"*
You:	*"Yes. Can you tell him Mary Harris called. My telephone number is _____. I'm calling in reference to my letter of July 5. I also called yesterday and left a message."*
Secretary:	*"Oh, yes. I remember your call. I did give him the message. However, he's been extremely busy. I'll make sure he gets the message again."*

You may get a return call, but don't hold your breath. You will probably need to initiate yet another call or two before you make direct contact. Again, wait 24 hours to call again. With a third call you will most likely have the attention of both the secretary and the letter recipient. Both may start to feel somewhat guilty for not taking your call. The secretary especially feels responsible because she obviously has been ineffective vis-a-vis both you and her boss. The letter recipient is beginning to collect a pile of message notes indicating the same person is waiting for a return call. At this point the secretary is likely to make certain decisions: the next time you call she will make a special effort to remind her boss that you have called several times, and it would be nice to return the call or give a more hopeful response than *"I'll give him the message"*; or she will ask her boss if she should relay any special message to Mary Harris should she call again. Your fourth follow-up call may result in a change in dialogue with the secretary:

Secretary:	*"Mr. Carroll's office. How can I help you?"*
You:	*"Hi, this is Mary Harris calling for Mr. Carroll."*
Secretary:	*"Yes, I remember you called earlier. I'm sorry Mr. Carroll hasn't been able to get back with you. He's been so busy these past few days. When I spoke with him yesterday, he said he would call you today around 4pm."*

Making several follow-up phone calls demonstrates your persistence. While it's unfortunate you may have to make so many calls, especially if they are expensive long-distance calls, that's the reality of communicating in today's busy business world. Such persistence eventually pays off because you become **remembered** and because individuals **feel guilty** about not returning your calls after receiving the same message over and over again from the same person.

> *Persistence pays off because you become remembered and because many people feel guilty not returning your calls.*

You might also try to follow up by e-mail. However, many people treat e-mail from strangers as junk mail – an unwelcome intrusion into their lives worthy of a quick delete. Don't expect to increase your response rate, nor the quality of your response, by resorting to impersonal e-mail. In fact, many people resent having what they consider to be a private channel of communication – their e-mail – invaded by strangers.

Follow Up Your Follow-Up

Once you make telephone contact, be sure to follow up this follow-up call with a nice thank-you letter. Again, your goal is not just to get useful job information. Your goal should also include being **remembered** for future reference. You want busy people to remember you, because they are likely to refer you to other busy people who may be looking for individuals with your qualifications. In other words, the thank-you follow-up letter becomes an important building block in the expansion of your network for information, advice, and referrals. Job seekers who follow up their follow-up calls with a thank-you letter are more likely to be remembered that those who merely hang up the phone and move on to other follow-up calls.

Follow-Up Means to Follow Up

It's funny what you learn about people through their letters. Today more and more job seekers close their letters with an effective follow-up statement, but they never follow up. They simply don't do what they say they will! Indeed, the last three letters we received from job seekers included the date and time they would call us to follow up. They wrote nice letters – modeled after the advice of "how-to" job search letter books – but we have yet to hear from them. Somewhere along the way to the mailbox no one told them they actually had to follow up their letter! Yes, we remember these people, but unfortunately we remember them for what they did to us – wasted our time with a canned follow-up statement they had no intention of doing anything about.

You simply can't do more damage to your job search than failing to follow up according to expectations. Many people say they will call on Thursday afternoon, but they never call. It's as if the action follow-up statement has become a routine and meaningless closing for job search letters. Many job seekers merely go through the motions of including a "canned" closing statement. Indeed, one wonders how much else in the letter is "canned" or "creatively plagiarized" from examples of "outstanding" cover letters.

Whatever you do, make sure your letters represent **you**. Moreover, make sure you **do** exactly what you say you will do. If you tell your reader you will call them at 2:30 on Thursday afternoon, make sure you call exactly at that time. The person may have penciled in this time on their calendar to speak with you. If you fail to do so, the individual is likely to remember you in negative terms – this job seeker doesn't follow through or make appointments! You simply can't recover from such an initial negative impression. You will be wasting both your time and the time of the reader.

Evaluate Your Follow-Up Competencies

Let's evaluate the potential effectiveness of your implementation and follow-up activities. Respond to each of the following statements by indicating how you dealt with each follow-up action:

Follow-Up Actions	Yes	No
1. Completed the "Job Search Contract."	1	3
2. Completed my first "Weekly Job Search Performance and Planning Report."	1	3
3. Ended my letter with an action statement indicating I would contact the individual by phone within the next week.	1	3
4. Made the first follow-up call at the time and date indicated in my letter.	1	3
5. Followed up with additional phone calls until I was able to speak directly with the person or received the requested information.	1	3

6. Maintained a positive and professional attitude
during each follow-up activity. Was pleasantly
persistent and tactful during all follow-up calls.
Never indicated I was irritated, insulted, or
disappointed in not having my phone calls returned.   1   3

7. Followed up the follow-up by sending a thank-you
letter genuinely expressing my appreciation for
the person's time and information.   1   3

TOTAL

Add the numbers you circled to the right of each statement to get a cumulative score. If your score is higher than "7," you need to work on improving your implementation and follow-up competencies. Go back and institute the necessary changes in your implementation and follow-up behavior so your next resumes and letters will be a perfect "7"!

12

Electronic Resumes and Internet Job Searching

MOST OF THE PRINCIPLES outlined in this book apply to 95 percent of all resumes written and distributed today. Many of the remaining resumes, which are growing in number, follow other important writing and distribution principles. This chapter examines the special case of electronic resumes, which come in several different forms: text, formatted, PDF, web page, web portfolio, video, and multimedia. If you plan to write a resume that will be transmitted via e-mail and the Internet, or produce a video or multimedia resume, you should find this chapter useful.

Resumes in an Electronic Era

Automated applicant tracking systems, employment databases, the Internet, videos, and multimedia have transformed the resume writing, production, distribution, and screening processes. These technologies are changing the methods by which employers arrive at screening and hiring decisions. While only a few years ago employers primarily asked mailed, faxed, and scannable resumes, today more and more employers require applicants to submit their resumes by e-mail or to go to company websites where they are requested to complete online forms that produce profiles of candidates in lieu of a resume. Consequently, job seekers need to become Internet-savvy in terms of how they both write and distribute their resume, especially their format options.

The Internet and computerized applicant tracking systems are increasingly responsible for linking candidates to employers, especially for entry-level positions in large companies. These and related technologies are significantly altering the way individuals write and distribute resumes as well as how employers initially screen candidates. In today's job market, you need to become acquainted with these technologies since your next resume may be initially "read" by computers before it gets passed on to the people who have the power to hire. Before mailing, faxing, e-mailing, or uploading your resume to an

---

Your resume must first satisfy technological requirements before it has the opportunity to grab the attention of employers.

---

employer's website, you need to know the specific submission requirements of an employer. For example, does Employer X want you to e-mail a plain-text or formatted resume, complete an online resume form, or submit a PDF resume, web resume, or web portfolio? If you don't know the answer to these questions, or if you can't provide your resume in employer-requested or acceptable electronic formats, you may not be considered for a position. For, in the end, your resume must first satisfy software requirements before it has the opportunity to grab the attention of employers.

The Changing Electronic Resume

During the past few years, electronic resumes were primarily defined as scannable and e-mailable resumes. When advised to write an electronic resume, job seekers were given lists of do's and don'ts on how to write a scanner-friendly resume (eliminate special emphasizing elements) as well as one that could be e-mailed as an ASCII or plain-text document (eliminate standard formatting). As a result, job seekers often wrote two types of resumes: (1) a pretty paper resume that could be mailed, faxed, or transmitted by e-mail as a Word or WordPerfect attachment or in PDF format, or (2) an "ugly duckling" resume to be transmitted virus-free in the body of an e-mail message as an ASCII or plain-text document. They also were alerted to posted resumes – complete resume forms for entering their resume into online searchable resume databases operated by such online employment sites as <u>Monster.com</u>, <u>CareerBuilder.com</u>, and <u>Hotjobs.Yahoo.com</u>. The result was often a mini-resume or resume profile that could be periodically updated online. All you needed to do was to follow the online instructions for completing each section of an online resume template or form.

How times have changed within just a few years. Today, given the widespread use of the Internet and recent changes in e-mail programs and software, the era of the scanned and "ugly duckling" resume is about over. Scanning technology is now old and inconvenient technology for employers who increasingly rely on the Internet for applications and communications. Very few employers scan resumes and fewer and fewer employers request that resumes be transmitted as ASCII or plain-text documents. The issue for employers, especially those with large companies, is one of volume: they are inundated with resumes. Many resumes come from Internet-savvy students and recent graduates who blast their resumes to numerous employers via the Internet. Unable to handle the sheer volume of resumes they receive by mail, fax, and e-mail, employers have decided to more efficiently manage this process by primarily relying on the Internet for acquiring resumes and screening candidates. As a result, many employers now refuse to accept mailed or faxed resumes. Instead, they require candidates to submit their resumes to a specific e-mail address in a variety of alternative forms: plain-text, formatted, PDF, and HTML.

The current, and perhaps long-term, trend is to require applicants to post their resumes to a company website which automatically places resumes into a searchable database. Similar to rigid application forms, where one must complete each pre-defined section, many of these websites have their own resume format requirements. They require some effort on the part of the applicant to meet the specific resume standards of the employer. By requiring candidates to complete an online resume form, employers are able to eliminate many not-so-serious "clip and paste" and "resume blasting" candidates, acquire all requested qualifying data, and efficiently search and retrieve resumes in the company's own online database. In many cases, the online resume form actually produces a candidate profile rather than a standard resume. This website-generated profile becomes the key to getting screened in or screened out of consideration for a position.

Types of Electronic Resumes

In today's job market you will encounter several different types of electronic resumes that are more or less accepted by employers, depending on their particular requirements:

1. **ASCII or plain-text resumes:** These are the original "ugly duckling" e-mailable resumes shorn of standard formatting and highlighting elements. They also are known as text-only, simple-text, or unformatted resumes. Candidates send a text-only version of their resume in the body of an e-mail message. Such unadorned resumes are virus-free and can be easily forwarded to others as well as entered into resume databases. Since these resumes are not easy to read given their lack of standard formatting and highlighting elements, readers tend to focus on the language and content of such resumes. Writers of such resumes should pay particular attention to the use of keywords.

2. **Formatted resumes:** These resumes are produced in a standard word processing program, such as Word or WordPerfect, and transmitted as an e-mail attachment. Similar to resumes outlined in this book, they look like standard formatted resumes and include all the "dress for success" elements associated with traditional resumes. Some employers prefer not receiving such resumes since they may harbor viruses when transmitted as an attachment. Writers of such resumes should focus on all resume elements, from format and emphasizing techniques to keywords and language, outlined in this book.

3. **PDF resume:** This type of resume is similar to the formatted resume, but it is saved in PDF (Portable Document Format) form. Such resumes can be e-mailed, posted on websites, viewed online, or submitted to resume databases. The recipient must be able to open and view such resumes using Adobe Acrobat Reader or PDF viewer.

4. **HTML or web page resume:** This type of resume actually becomes a web page with its own unique URL. It can be produced with a variety of graphic and color elements as well as incorporate photos, video clips, audio files, and hyperlinks. It can be easily designed using such popular, inexpensive, or free web page development programs as FrontPage, Dreamweaver, or Netscape Composer.

5. **Online portfolio:** This is the ultimate online resume website and marketing tool. Similar to a paper portfolio but functioning as a website, the online portfolio includes a web resume with hyperlinks to a variety of sections that emphasize qualifications and provide proof of performance: objectives and/or philosophy, photos, video clips, audio files, letters of recommendations, work samples, and

testimonials. Going far beyond a standard resume format, the online portfolio attempts to provide a complete career profile of a candidate's background and qualifications.

6. **Posted resumes:** Required by online employment sites and employer websites, these are basically fill-in-the-template resumes. Just follow the instructions and complete each section accordingly. You may be able to clip and paste much of the required information from your standard resume. However, some of these forms may require a great deal of original writing. The end result is often a mini-resume or candidate profile rather than a full-blown standard resume. Such forms enable employers to quickly enter information into a searchable company resume database. The key to writing these resumes is to follow the instruments and include lots of keywords in the resume since resumes will be searched by keywords.

Whatever you do, make sure you understand the resume requirements of each employer. All employers are not the same when it comes to electronic resumes. Some will only accept resumes posted into the resume database of their company website, whereas others will accept formatted resumes and web resumes. The new rule for writing and submitting electronic resumes is simple: Make no technology assumptions about employers; know the electronic resume requirements of each. When in doubt, ask about the organization's preferred format.

"Software Sensitive" Resumes

If you know an employer uses an automated applicant tracking system for screening, viewing, storing, and retrieving resumes, you need to write a resume that responds to such a system. Some of the most widely used automated applicant tracking systems include the following:

■ Applicant Tracking Software	www.trak-it.com/AT-Overview.html
■ AtWork Technologies	www.atwork.com
■ HireWorks, Inc.	www.hire-works.com
■ HR Power Guide	www.notjustsurveys.com/HR
■ PeopleSoft	www.peoplesoft.com
■ People-Trak	www.people-trak.com
■ Preferred Hire Plus	www.preferredhire.com
■ Recruiting Solutions International	www.recruitingsoftware.com
■ ResumeWare	www.resumeware.com
■ StaffingSoft	www.staffingsoft.com
■ Talent Secure	www.talentsecure.com
■ UnicornHRO	www.softwareplus.com
■ WebHire	www.webhire.com

Most of these programs are popular with large organizations (having more than 1,000 employees) that receive a huge volume of unsolicited resumes which are difficult, if not impossible, to adequately read, screen, store, retrieve, and reply to by traditional human means, i.e., the human resources department or the hiring authority is overwhelmed by the sheer volume of resumes received. Many of these companies also have a large number of entry-level positions. The software enables companies to literally screen, store, retrieve, and reply to hundreds of resumes in their database within a few hours.

How do you know if you should be sending a resume that will be entered into a searchable database? This is not rocket science. If you are sending your resume to numerous well-known companies which have 5,000 or more employees, assume that they will be using an automated applicant tracking system. If you are uncertain whether or not a company is using such a system, pick up the telephone and call the company. Simply ask them, *"What are your resume submission requirements?"* If you are unclear about their answer, try this question: *"Do you use an automated applicant tracking system?"* If they do, ask if they have any specific guidelines you should follow for preparing your resume. In many cases the company may include such guidelines on their home page.

Electronic resumes require close attention to the choice of resume language. The search-and-retrieval software of automated applicant tracking systems literally takes **keywords** selected by employers and matches them with similar keywords found on resumes. If, for example, an employer is looking for a human resources specialist with 10 years of progressive experience in developing training programs for mining engineers and who also is proficient in using PowerPoint and developing multimedia presentations, a search for candidates meeting these qualifications may result in making matches with 15 resumes in the database. The employer receives hard copies or summaries of the resumes and further sorts the batch of candidates through more traditional means, such as telephone screening interviews.

When writing an electronic resume, you must focus on using **proper resume language** that would be most responsive to the search-and-retrieval software. This means knowing what keywords are best to include in such a resume. The best keywords used in such resumes should be **nouns** rather than verbs. Nouns such as "operations research," "teams," "C++," and "Lotus 1,2,3" identify specific assets or capabilities employers look for when filling positions. Keywords often encompass the jargon of particular fields. Traditional "dress for success" elements, such as layout, typefaces, emphasizing, paper texture, and color, are important at the second stage when being evaluated by the hiring official **after** the resume has been retrieved electronically. The degree to which your resume is "software sensitive" will largely determine how many employers will contact you. If your resume lacks an appropriate mix of keywords, it will be passed over as unacceptable for further consideration. For a good overview of hundreds of keywords by profession, see Wendy S. Enelow's *Best KeyWords for Resumes, Cover Letters, and Interviews* (Impact Publications).

The structure of resume elements also changes with electronic resumes. While conventional resumes may include objectives and personal statements, most of the information included in such categories will not be read on electronic resumes. Instead of starting with a powerful objective and summary of qualifications, electronic resumes should begin with a powerful **Keyword Preface** which literally front-loads the resume with a list of 20 or 30 words the computer or employer must see in order to screen you in for consideration. A good example of such a keyword preface is found in Peter Weddle's *Electronic Resumes for the New Job Market* (Impact Publications):

> Human Resource Management and Development. Ten Years Experience in Health Care Industry. Compensation and Benefits. Employee Relations. Staffing. Union Relations. EEO/AA. Succession Planning. Vice President of Human Resources for 1,000 Employee Company. SPHR.

Other categories that should appear on such resumes include Abilities, Experience, Special Awards and Recognition, Special Licenses and Certifications, and Training. Again, each section should be rich in keywords (nouns) employers seek when screening resumes. If your resume lacks such keywords, your chances of being considered "qualified" by both the computer and recruiter will be greatly diminished!

In contrast to conventional resumes, your electronic resume should:

- Incorporate as many keywords (nouns) as possible throughout each section of your resume.

- Begin with a "Keyword Preface" or "Keyword Summary" in lieu of an Objective and/or Summary of Qualifications.

- Include the acronyms and jargon of your profession since they may be included in a keyword search.

- If presented as an unformatted resume, eliminate special emphasizing elements, such as underlining, italics, boxes, shading, and graphics.

- Run more than two pages if necessary. Use three or four pages to detail your work experience and skills, which should include additional keywords.

When in doubt on how to best write this type of resume, always contact the employer for guidelines on their particular resume requirements. For more information on writing and distributing such resumes, we highly recommend the following books which focus on the latest developments relevant to electronic resumes:

Resumes for Dummies, Joyce Lain Kennedy (John Wiley & Sons)
e-Resumes, Susan Britton Whitcomb and Pat Kendall (McGraw-Hill)
e-Resumes, Pat Criscito (Barrons)

You also may want to examine these electronic resume books:

Cyberspace Resume Kit, Fred E. Jandt and Mary B. Nemnich (JIST)
Electronic Resumes and Online Networking, Rebecca Smith (Career Press)
Internet Resumes, Peter D. Weddle (Impact Publications)

Author Rebecca Smith (*Electronic Resumes and Online Networking*) also operates a website that provides online assistance for writing an electronic resume:

Rebecca Smith's eResumes & Resources   www.eresumes.com

Resumes for E-Mail and Internet Transmission

Since electronic resumes are designed to be e-mailed or transmitted over the Internet, the Internet becomes the medium for writing, transmitting, viewing, and screening resumes. Within the past 10 years the Internet has taken off as an important job market medium. It is transforming the way employers recruit candidates and the way job searchers gather information, network, identify job vacancies, and communicate with employers. Supplementing the paper job market of classified ads and mailed or faxed resumes, the Internet is an electronic advertised job market that now hosts nearly 100,000 sites that deal with jobs and employment. Many of the largest sites function as resume clearinghouses and networks for linking candidates with vacancies via an electronic resume. Financed by employers who advertise jobs on these sites (usually $300 for four weeks) or pay fees for accessing resumes available through the site's database, most of these sites are free to job seekers, who can post their resumes online. At the same time, many employers have their own home pages that include an employment section with instructions on how to submit an electronic resume. Applicants are instructed to either e-mail their resume or post it to the site's resume database. An e-mail submission follows standard procedures most Internet users can follow.

If you've saved your resume in a standard word processing program, you can easily copy it and then paste it into your e-mail program for transmission. However, the end result will not be the same as the original word-processed document because of formatting problems. The person receiving your resume via e-mail will most likely view a garbled document. If an employer asks you to e-mail your resume as an ASCII or plain-text file, you'll need to convert your word-processed resume by doing the following:

- Go to your resume that's saved on your word processing software. Open the file and then save it as an ASCII text, plain-text, or text-only file. Convert your word-processed resume into an ASCII text file using a different name and the file extension *.txt* (for example, *resume.txt*).

- Take out the formatting which would include any special characters or emphasizing techniques not supported by the ASCII character set. This would include boldface, italics, underlining, boxes, bullets, different font sizes, shading, or graphics. You can use characters such as "*" and ">" to substitute for bullets or boxes. Any key you can press on your keyboard, other than function keys, is part of the ASCII character set.

- Capitalize headings for emphasis and left-align each.

- Use a 10-point Courier font; avoid proportional fonts.

- Limit the number of characters to 60 per line.

- Use your "Enter" or "Return" key to break each line rather than let it automatically wrap to the next line.

- Start all text to the left and line-space to different sections rather than use the "Tab" key.

When you're ready to submit your resume via e-mail, paste it into your e-mail program and hit the "Send" button. However, before you transmit it to an employer, it's a good idea to test your composition by e-mailing it to yourself or a friend to see how it looks at the receiving end.

Internet Distribution

Once you've mastered the basics of writing and transmitting your resume by e-mail, you should be ready to distribute your resume to hundreds of sites on the Internet. You'll find three different ways to go about doing this, each involving a different approach to the online job market:

1. Submitting your electronic (ASCII) resume to various job sites that welcome free submissions because they have active resume databases that are regularly accessed by paying employers.

2. Composing mini-resumes or profiles which are basically questionnaires you complete online and which conform to the site's resume format. Your answers to each question eventually result in a mini-resume that gets entered into the site's resume database.

3. Transmitting your electronic resume directly to employers based upon instructions found in a classified ad, vacancy announcement, or the employment section of a company's home page.

The first two approaches are the online equivalent to the "broadcast" or "shotgun" approach to distributing paper resumes; it produces few results for job seekers. The third approach is more targeted and thus may produce results for a few job seekers.

If you plan to distribute your resume online, you should familiarize yourself with the major websites that offer opportunities to post your resume online. As we noted earlier, you will find more than 100,000 sites that deal with jobs and employment, and many of them welcome electronic resumes. Finding these sites takes lots of time, patience, and a conviction that you might be doing something productive. If you're just getting started in using the Internet for conducting a job search, we recommend visiting a few major gateway sites. Five of the most comprehensive such sites include:

- AIRS   www.airsdirectory.com/jobboards
- MyJobSearch   www.myjobsearch.com
- The Riley Guide   www.rileyguide.com
- Quintessential Careers   www.quintcareers.com
- JobHuntersBible   www.jobhuntersbible.com

The AIRS website is the key gateway site for locating over 5,000 job boards with resume databases. Many of these sites welcome resume submissions by candidates.

Some of the most popular online employment sites that include a mixture of job listings, job search tips, employer profiles, resume databases, discussion groups, articles, and resource centers include the following:

- Monster.com   monster.com
- JobCentral.com   jobcentral.com
- America's Job Bank   www.ajb.dni.us
- CareerBuilder   careerbuilder.com
- NationJob   nationjob.com

- Yahoo Hot Jobs — http://hotjobs.yahoo.com
- Jobs.com — jobs.com
- CareerJournal — careerjournal.com
- CareerFlex — careerflex.com
- Employment911.com — employment911.com
- EmploymentSpot — employmentspot.com
- JobFactory — jobfactory.com
- Job Sniper — jobsniper.com
- Vault.com — vault.com
- WetFeet.com — wetfeet.com
- MyJobSearch — myjobsearch.com
- PlanetRecruit — planetrecruit.com
- 4Work — http://4-work.com.8media.org
- BestJobsUSA — bestjobsusa.com
- Career Shop — careershop.com
- Job Sleuth — jobsleuth.com
- MonsterTrak — monstertrak.monster.com
- Brass Ring — brassring.com
- Career.com — career.com
- JobBank USA — jobbankusa.com
- Net-Temps — net-temps.com
- CareerTV — careertv.net
- Preferred Jobs — preferredjobs.com
- ProHire — prohire.com
- CareerExchange — careerexchange.com
- Career Magazine — careermag.com
- Employers Online — employersonline.com
- EmployMax — employmax.com
- WantedJobs — wantedjobs.com
- JobFactory — jobfactory.com
- MindFind — mindfind.com
- NowHiring.com — nowhiring.com
- RecruitUSA — recruitusa.com
- Recruiters Online Network — recruitersonline.com
- kForce.com — kforce.com
- Dice.com — dice.com
- Washington Post — washingtonjobs.com

Most employment websites have a very similar structure and purpose. Over 80 percent of all employment websites function as job boards with separate sections for job seekers and employers. As such, they usually include two key components:

- Job postings
- Resume database and/or job alerts

Some sites include a job alert section in lieu of a resume database. This allows job seekers to automatically receive by e-mail any new job postings that meet their specific interest criteria. Most sites are free to job seekers. Employers pay various user fees to post jobs and search resume databases.

Many employment websites include some combination of the following services designed to attract repeat traffic to their sites:

- Job Search Tips
- Featured Articles
- Career Experts or Advisors
- Career Tool Kit
- Career Assessment Tests
- Community Forums
- Discussion or Chat Groups
- Message Boards
- Job Alert ("Push") E-mails
- Company Research Centers
- Networking Forums
- Salary Calculators or Wizards
- Resume Management Center
- Resume and Cover Letter Advice
- Multimedia Resume Software
- Job Interview Practice
- Relocation Information
- Reference Checkers
- Employment or Career News
- Free E-mail For Privacy
- Success Stories
- Career Newsletter
- Career Events
- Online Job Fairs
- Affiliate Sites
- Career Resources
- Featured Employers
- Polls and Surveys
- Contests
- Online Education and Training
- International Employment
- Talent Auction Centers
- Company Ads (buttons and banners)
- Sponsored Links
- Special Channels for Students, Executives, Freelancers, Military, and other groups

> *How do you plan to get employers to find you on the Internet?*

Huge mega employment sites such as Monster.com include over 80 percent of these add-on services. Most sites, however, are very basic in their orientation – primarily include job postings and resume databases and maybe a newsletter designed to capture e-mails of job seekers who must register in order to receive the newsletter. Ron and Caryl Krannich review many of these websites in their two companion Internet employment books: *America's Top Internet Jobs Sites* and *The Directory of Websites for International Jobs*. Margaret Dikel and Frances Roehm also survey hundreds of Internet employment websites in *The Guide to Internet Job Searching*. Bernard Haldane Associates's *Haldane's Best Employment Websites for Professionals* summarizes the best employment websites in the United States, Canada, and the United Kingdom. See the order form at the end of this book for information on these and other Internet employment resources.

HTML Resumes and Home Pages

Given the new generation of software that enables individuals to easily create their own home pages, many job seekers are creating an HTML (Hypertext Markup Language) resume and putting it on their home page. If you are computer and Internet savvy, creating such a resume and a home page is not all that difficult these days. Numerous books, such as Kristina Ackley's and Hilary Benoit's *Online Web Design* (Impact Publications), outline how to do this. In fact, many web browsers, such as Netscape, have online sites that teach how to create your own home page.

But the important question is whether or not such a resume and home page will make any difference to your job search. Probably not, but you never know. While you can easily produce these online documents, how do you plan to get employers to take notice and invite you to a job interview? After all, you cannot e-mail an HTML resume – only the hyperlink. You must market your site to employers, who must take the time to access your site. Unless you are exceptionally well qualified or you are in a field where an HTML resume demonstrates your skills, such as computer graphics or graphic arts, we really don't expect many busy employers to go looking for your resume and home page on the Internet. You would need to develop a very active Internet marketing strategy to get employers to find your site. On the other hand, a home page may be useful for networking purposes – communicate to friends and colleagues in a graphic form that you are conducting a job search. Use your own judgment here. An HTML resume and home page probably won't hurt your job search, and it may actually help if you do some creative marketing.

e-Portfolios

More and more job seekers also are creating e-portfolios to showcase their professional capabilities. Also known as online portfolios, web portfolios, or digital portfolios, these are essentially stand-alone websites primarily devoted to showcasing an individual's accomplishments. Such portfolios can include a variety of elements for quickly communicating one's qualifications to recruiters and potential employers:

- Resume
- Career success stories
- Goals and philosophy
- Endorsements and testimonials
- Photographs, graphics, and illustrations
- Audio and video presentations
- PowerPoint presentation
- Sample interview
- Biography
- Professional blog
- Contact information

Information on how to create such online portfolios, along with examples, can be found in these three new books:

Executive Job Search for $100,000 to $1 Million+ Jobs, Wendy S. Enelow and Louise Kursmark (Impact Publications)

e-Resumes: A Guide to Successful Online Job Hunting, Pat Criscito (Barrons)

Create Your Digital Portfolio, Susan Amirian and Eleanor Flanigan, Ph.Ds (JIST)

Keep in mind that e-portfolios tend to include a variety of written, audio, photographic, and video elements that can work both for you and against you in getting a job interview. Don't assume they are superior presentations of your qualifications just because they are technically sophisticated and comprehensive. Such online productions may present too much information about you. Always ask yourself this question before investing time and money in creating a digital portfolio: Will it generate more job interviews than a well-crafted and targeted one- or two-page resume? When in doubt about how to best create a digital portfolio, contact a career expert who specializes in developing such presentation tools.

Your Internet Act

The Internet is literally a two-edge sword – it can work for or against you, depending on the nature of your presence on the Internet. More and more employers "Google" candidates' names before inviting them to job interviews in order to acquire additional information that may be beyond the control of the candidate. Such searches may uncover unexpected information about you that could either enhance or diminish your candidacy.

Some information you can control on the Internet while other information may be beyond your control. If you've already created a personal profile or blog online that is likely to be found when using a search engine, make sure it presents you in the best professional light possible. Indeed, you are well advised to enter your name in several search engines to learn what type of presence you already have on the Internet. First impressions count, whether in a face-to-face encounter or on the Internet or telephone. If you have committed some "Internet indiscretions," consider cleaning up your Internet act **before** contacting employers about job opportunities. If not, you may be passed over in silence or asked some embarrassing questions during a job Internet about what the interviewer discovered on the Internet.

Video and Multimedia Resumes

If you are in a creative field, such as film, multimedia, music, art, or theater, you may want to consider producing a video or multimedia resume that simultaneously demonstrates your skills in your particular field. But individuals in other fields should be cautious in using such unconventional resume formats. Keep in mind that most employers are busy people who really don't have the time or equipment to view video or CD-ROM productions – unless they indicate such a resume is acceptable (call and ask if in doubt). Also, video and multimedia resumes introduce elements of a job interview – verbal and nonverbal communication – that may be best left to the job interview.

If you do submit a video or multimedia resume, make sure it represents your best professional effort. If you are not talented in these mediums and try to do it yourself on the cheap (just let your video camera roll!), chances are your video or multimedia resume will quickly eliminate you from consideration. Indeed, like putting a picture on a resume, you may not look as good on video as you think you do. You can easily be screened out at this stage by how you look and sound – too young, too old, too heavy, too ugly, too flashy, too slick, too nervous, too funny sounding, too loud, too talkative, too strange, too unenthusiastic. Carefully think through this alternative before investing your time and money in such a production. Better still, "field test" your video production by asking people whose opinions you respect to critique the video from the perspective of an employer.

Question Electronic Effectiveness

We're fascinated with the application of new technology to the job search, but we've not been seduced by its many exaggerated claims that a new "revolution" is likely to displace more conventional job finding methods, including traditional paper resumes and letters, face-to-face networking, and just showing up. Like so many new technological developments, there's an initial tendency to exaggerate and over-rely on technology. The main revolution is for employers in large companies who are now better able to manage their recruitment process through the use of the Internet. The verdict is still out for job seekers and small companies. Indeed, while definitely benefiting large employers, the Internet may be less useful for most job seekers and the small businesses that employ over 80 percent of the workforce. In fact, we've yet to meet many job seekers who have actually found jobs on the Internet or small employers who use the Internet to recruit. In the meantime, most employment sites are basically hyped as mediums for selling advertising to large companies that find it cheaper to post vacancy announcements online ($300 for four weeks) than to purchase classified ads in newspapers and magazines ($500 to $10,000) or use headhunters (25-35% of the successful candidate's first-year salary).

Despite our performance concerns, we strongly recommend incorporating the Internet in your job search. It's a rich resource for researching jobs and employers, networking for information and advice, surveying job listings, and applying for jobs online. More and more employers, including small companies, will continue to use the Internet to recruit candidates. However, similar to playing the classified ad game with conventional resumes, for job seekers the Internet is a very crowded medium filled with lots of hype, hope, and dead ends. Like so much of the advertised job market, the Internet can be a great time waster if not used properly and focused around a well organized job search that includes a strong networking component. For all the Internet's bells and whistles, many job seekers find the Internet interesting and useful but disappointing in terms of ultimate job search outcomes – interviews that result in job offers.

13

Welcome Opportunities

I F YOU HAVE CAREFULLY FOLLOWED each of the preceding chapters, you should be well on your way to writing high impact resumes and letters for communicating your qualifications to employers. As we said from the very beginning, this type of written communication takes time and effort because it must be linked to other steps in the career planning and job search processes. The additional work involved should result in producing first-class resumes and letters. If properly marketed, they should have a high probability of motivating employers to invite you to a job interview as well as generate referrals to other employers.

Building on Basic Foundations

If you decide to take the easy way out by editing our resume and letter examples, by all means study our models of the career planning and job search processes on pages 42 and 43. They stress a simple principle: **you should know where you are going before you get started**. You wouldn't take a major trip without a map or a guidebook, would you?

Writing resumes and letters without a basic foundational understanding of where you are coming from (skills and competencies) and where you are going (objective) is a sure way to conduct an aimless and ineffective job search. While you eventually will find some kind of job, you probably won't find a job that is **right for you**.

Communicating your objective and competencies in resumes and letters is the first step in developing high impact written communication. Knowing your audience also is important. You should target employers by investigating them. You do this by conducting library and online research and talking to knowledgeable people.

Follow our principles, rules, and advice on developing form and content. But proper form and content are not enough. Your resume and letters must reach your intended audience. Connecting with the right people is possible if you prospect, network, and conduct informational interviews with your resume and letters. In so doing, you will open doors by communicating that you are purposeful and competent. You should demonstrate your value by emphasizing what you can do well.

Your Next Steps

While this book takes you through most career planning steps, it does not direct you through the final two steps – interviewing and negotiating the job offer. These are subjects of other books. Formal interviews and negotiations come **after** you achieve initial impact. Prepare for these critical steps like you organize your resume and letters – with purpose and thoroughness.

Connecting with the right people is possible if you prospect, network, and conduct informational interviews with your resume and letters.

Finding a job that is right for you will take time, patience, and hard work. Our 22 principles for achieving a successful job search (pages 55-58) are especially important for **implementation and follow-through**. If you have difficulty in this regard, develop a job search management scheme as outlined in Chapter 5; find someone to monitor your daily progress.

Optimism With Pragmatism

Regardless of what others tell you, it is not easy to find a job that is right for you. It requires work. For some people, this may be the hardest work they ever do! Surely it is one of the most important activities of your career.

The job search becomes difficult because of its very personal and ego-involved nature. You lay your ego on the line when you apply for a position, ask for employment assistance, or interview for a job. You condense years of experience and value into a one- or two-page resume. When you conduct the job search, you open important aspects of your life to total strangers.

But rejections are part of the job search game. You will likely receive several rejections before you get the acceptances that count – an interview and job offer. The best way to handle rejections is to:

- Recognize your value as going beyond immediate job search situations.

- Practice marketing techniques that minimize the number of rejections you might receive, such as networking.

- Don't become too ego-involved by taking yourself and each up and down in the job search too seriously.

- Remember the probabilistic nature of any job search.

- Keep busy by moving on to new job leads, networking, and following up, In other words, it may not be good to dwell too long on any one job search situation.

We recommend an optimistic/pragmatic job search perspective. In part, you are playing a **probability game** where the outcomes are similar to the combinations of apples and oranges that come up in a slot machine. The longer you keep at it, the more rejections – and acceptances – you are likely to encounter. However, unlike the casino, luck is only a part of the equation. The greater the quality and effort you put into your job search, the more you are likely to get out of it.

> *Rejections are part of the job search game. Learn to handle them as you continue along the road to getting acceptances.*

Employers look for a special "fit," but you may not fit at a particular time and in a particular place. Like the slot machine, the right combination of apples and oranges will come up as long as you keep at it. While persistence and patience will pay off, a well planned job search with high impact resumes and letters should increase your probability of success.

Luck Will Come Your Way

We hope you will avoid the many pitfalls and emotional thumps other job seekers experience. Writing high impact resumes and letters will get you off to a good start and prepare you for the other job search steps.

Luck will come your way if you prepare to seize opportunities. Good luck and enjoy your job search. Whatever you do, make sure you give it direction with high impact resumes and letters.

14

The Savvy Job Hunter –
110 Questions and Answers

THE PREVIOUS CHAPTERS OUTLINED numerous principles for writing, producing, distributing, and following up resumes and letters. As we noted earlier, there are no definitive rules for writing resumes and letters; most principles and rules are more or less useful, depending on your purpose and your targeted audience. In this chapter we address numerous questions most frequently raised by job seekers concerning the writing, production, distribution, and follow-up of resumes and letters. Taken together, these questions and answers provide a quick overview of the major issues affecting resumes and job search letters.

Resume Writing

1. Is it best to write my own resume or hire a professional resume writer to do it for me?

It depends on how good you are at writing your own resume and how much you are willing to spend on hiring a professional. Some people can do it on their own by following the advice and examples in this book. Others, however, have difficulty being objective about themselves, putting all the elements altogether, and writing in the language of employers. After all, many of them were taught from childhood not to talk about themselves! While we prefer that you write your own resume because it will more accurately reflect your interests, skills, abilities, and goals, we recognize that professional help is sometimes needed at critical stages of the job search. If this is something you have difficulty doing, by all means seek professional help. Paying a professional to put together a winning resume will more than pay for itself. Make sure your professionally produced resume follows many of the principles outlined in this book. If you are interested in using a professional resume writer, you are well advised to contact the professional resume writers who contributed to this book (see Appendix D) as well as explore the resources on these professional resume writing websites:

- Professional Association of Resume
  Writers and Career Coaches   www,parw.com

- Professional Resume Writing and
  Research Association   www.prwra.com

- National Resume Writers' Association   www.nrwaweb.com

- Career Masters Institute   www.cminstitute.com

At the same time, check out some of these websites which are sponsored by professional resume writers. Most of them will give you a free resume critique prior to using their fee-based services:

- A&A Resume	aandaresume.com
- A Advanced Resume Service	topsecretresumes.com
- Advanced Career Systems	resumesystems.com
- The Advantage	advantageresume.com
- Cambridge Resume Service	cambridgeresume.com
- Career-Resumes	career-resumes.com
- CertifiedResumeWriters	certifiedresumewriters.com
- College-Resumes.com	college-resumes.com
- eResumes & Resume Writing Services (Rebecca Smith's)	eresumes.com
- e-resume.net	e-resume.net
- ExecutiveAgent.com	executiveagent.com
- Free-Resume-Tips	free-resume-tips.com
- Leading Edge Resumes	leadingedgeresumes.com
- Resume Agent	resumeagent.com
- Resume.com	resume.com
- ResumeMaker	resumemaker.com
- Resume Writer	resumewriter.com
- WSACORP.com	www.wsacorp.com

2. **How much would it cost to have a professional write my resume?**

The cost depends on the level of service you desire. If you only want someone to word-process a draft of what you've done, the cost may only be $50. On the other hand, if you're using someone who will actually write your resume from scratch, it could cost anywhere from $200 to $700. Executive-level resume writing services will cost the most.

3. How can I contact a professional resume writer and what types of questions should I ask?

When shopping for a professional resume writer, be sure to ask questions concerning prices and what you'll get for your money, such as the number of copies to be provided to you. Ask to see samples of their work and request references. Also, ask about their experience in using the Internet and writing electronic resumes. While many professional resume writers are listed in the Yellow Pages or found by conducting an online keyword search via one of the major search engines, especially www.google.com, you might want to explore the many professional resume writing websites mentioned above under the first question on page 192.

4. How long should it take to write a resume?

It's not difficult to write a resume in a couple of hours if you just creatively plagiarize examples from other resumes. However, this "quick and easy" writing approach most likely will not result in a resume that really reflects your best self. As we've noted in previous chapters, your resume should represent the "unique you." If you do first things first – assess your interests, skills, and abilities and then formulate a clear objective **before** writing each resume section – you may take one to two weeks to complete your resume. Indeed, you should spend a great deal of time doing first things first and then refining your resume so it fits on one or two pages. If done properly, this exercise requires hours of hard work. But the final product will be first-

> *If done properly, writing your resume requires hours of hard work.*

class and clearly communicate your qualifications to employers. If you decide to use an inexpensive professional resume writer, chances are you will end up with a quick one- to two-hour resume written by someone who doesn't know much about you, other than what you tell them in a brief interview. Again, we prefer that you write your own resume based on a thorough understanding of yourself. Better still, do the necessary front-end work – assess your skills, state your objective, and draft your resume – and then use the professional to fine-tune the final product.

5. At what stage in my job search should I write my resume?

We recommend writing the resume at the very beginning of your job search – make this a thorough two- to three-week job search orientation project. By so doing, you'll force yourself to engage in a series of assessment, research, and networking activities that should result in focusing your job search on your interests, skills, abilities, values, and goals. If you do this, your resume will become the driving force around which you organize all other job search activities. We also recommend conducting an annual career check-up – regardless of whether or not you are looking for a job. Look over your last resume, reassess your goals, consider incorporating new accomplishments, and make whatever changes you feel are necessary in order to keep your resume up-to-date and in line with your career goals. You never know when you may need this updated resume. Best of all, this annual career check-up exercise forces you to rethink where you are going and what you want to do in the future. If and when you need to re-enter the job market, you will be well prepared with your annually revised resume. And who knows? A new opportunity may come knocking on your door with a request to see your resume!

6. How important is a resume to finding a job?

Resumes are extremely important for getting job interviews – not jobs. In fact, many people still believe a resume should result in a job. Resumes have no such magical quality. Indeed, we have yet to meet an employer who hired people based on their resume. They screen candidates for job interviews and hire only after interviewing candidates – no interview, no job. The resume is one of the most important **steps** in the process of getting a job. Since most employers you encounter in your job search are strangers who know little or nothing about you, it's extremely important that you put together a first-class resume to clearly communicate your qualifications to employers.

7. Is it always necessary to write a resume?

Not always, but a resume is essential when applying for most professional positions. Alternatives to resumes include the curriculum vitae (CV), portfolios, applications, and letters. CVs, which are basically lengthy resumes that showcase professional activities, publications, and memberships, are mainly used by educators and international job seekers. **Portfolios**, which include work examples, are used extensively by artists, advertising copywriters, other creatives, and consultants. **Applications** tend to be completed in lieu of a resume and are most frequently used by blue collar and hourly workers. **Letters** may substitute for resumes on occasion. In some cases, such as when individuals are hired through employment firms, the employer may never see a resume or even an application. In these cases, the individual is screened by the employment firm and sent to the employer for an interview. The employer hires based upon the interview.

> *We have yet to meet an employer who hired people based on their resume.*

8. My resume is 10 years old. Is it best to just update it or should I start from scratch and develop an all-new resume?

It's best to start over. Not only have you and perhaps your goals changed during the past 10 years, the principles of resume writing also have changed. Ten years ago you probably only wrote one type of resume. Today, you may want to write two different types of resumes – conventional and electronic. Make sure your resume clearly reflects both your and employers' expectations.

9. Should I write one resume or do I need several different resumes?

It depends on how you plan to market yourself through different mediums and with different employers. The "one-resume-fits-all-situations" is not the best resume for today's job market. If you plan to conduct a conventional job search, you need to write a **conventional resume** as outlined in this book. If you plan to conduct a job search on the Internet or send your resume via e-mail, you'll need to write different types of **electronic resumes** as outlined in Chapter 12. At the same time, you may want to customize your resume for particular positions and employers. If you word-processed your resume, you have the flexibility to change the content of your resume in response to the particular requirements of specific employers. The more you can customize your resume around the needs of specific employers, the better will be your chances of getting invited to an interview. Even executives making more than $100,000 a year need to have an electronic version of their resume.

10. How long should my resume be?

The general rule is one to two pages, depending on your experience. For someone first entering the job market, or with less than five years of work experience, the one-page resume should be fine. If you have a considerable amount of experience, go to a two-page resume. Avoid going over two pages since employers generally lose attention after reading one or two pages. At the same time, you may break this one- to two-page rule in certain cases, especially if you are applying for a position within your company (see the example on pages 256-259), in education, or for an international job. Educators, for example, prefer CVs (curriculum vitae), which can run five

> _Employers generally lose attention after reading one or two pages._

to 20 pages and include all types of detailed information on educational activities, from presenting conference papers and publishing articles to chairing committees and receiving research grants. International job seekers often encounter employers who want to see lengthy resumes that include all types of details on international activities; in fact, many of them will reject candidates who present only a one- to two-page resume. They view it as too brief and superficial for their needs. Even some executives may want to go to five-page resumes that detail their specific accomplishments. However, since many executives are recruited through executive recruiters, they will be advised by their recruiter as to the appropriate length of their resume. Electronic resumes can run more than two pages and include a complete work history with a rich selection of keywords.

11. What's the best way to start writing the resume?

Here's one of the best tips for getting started in writing each section of a resume. Would you normally start at the top, bottom, or middle? Most people start at the top and that's where they get stuck and frustrated. You'll find this whole process will go much faster and will be less frustrating if you start from the bottom and then work up. This strategy focuses on doing the easiest things first – write the factual sections on educational background, professional affiliations, and work history. These sections should go quickly and set the stage for completing the more difficult sections. After doing these sections you can concentrate on the more analytical parts of other sections, such as work experience, statement of qualifications, and your objective. Many resume writers, including the professionals, find the various parts of the resume come together much better if they approach this writing exercise from the bottom up.

12. Is it ever appropriate to handwrite a resume?

Not in the U.S. However, if you are applying for a job in Europe, you may be requested to handwrite your resume. Many European employers still use handwriting analysts to screen candidates for personality characteristics. These analysts supposedly can tell through your handwriting whether or not you are "fit" for the job.

13. Is it okay to handwrite notes on the resume?

Do this if you're sending your resume to your mother or lover! This is not the time and place to practice time management skills by scribbling brief notes on correspondence. Your resume should represent your *best* professional effort at presenting your qualifications to employers. Handwritten notes are too personal. Worst of all, they distract from your professionalism. They give your resume a killer "personal touch" for getting you screened out from consideration. If you have something to say that can't be said on the resume, put it in your cover letter.

> *Your resume should represent your best professional effort.*

14. What should come first on a resume?

Always follow the principle of putting the most important information first. On a resume this means starting with your name and contact information – mailing address and telephone number and perhaps your fax number, pager number, and/or e-mail address. Immediately follow this section with important summary information – "Objective" and "Summary of Qualifications." These three elements make a strong five-second impression – who you are, what you want to do, what you have done, and what major strengths (competencies) you will most likely bring to a new employer.

15. Should I include an e-mail address?

By all means, especially if you are over 40. An e-mail address communicates that you are up-to-date for today's job market – someone who knows how to communicate. You can probably speak the language of younger people in the organization. In addition, the employer can always contact you by e-mail.

16. Is it okay to use a P.O. Box number rather than a street address on my resume?

Avoid using post office box numbers unless you are truly in transition from one street address to another. Post office box numbers do not enhance your image. Indeed, they may communicate the wrong messages – you appear transient or secretive. Always try to use a street address, unless for some reason it communicates the wrong message (you are unfortunate enough to have an embarrassing street name, such as Big Trouble Lane).

17. Should I include both a home and work telephone number?

Yes, if you want to be contacted as soon as possible. However, be careful with in-cluding your work number, especially if you don't want your current employer to know you are job hunting. Alternatively, you may want to only use your home phone number but enlist an answering service to handle your messages. If you're very mobile and carry a cell phone or beeper, include those numbers.

18. Since no one is at home during the day, should I use an answering machine to take calls?

Yes, if you're afraid you might miss any important calls and especially if you prefer not taking employment calls at your place of work. However, keep your message short, simple, friendly, and professional. Avoid voice mail programs that include bells and whistles or comical characters. Try to check your messages at least once a day and return calls promptly. If you've included your cell phone number and receive a voice message on your cell phone, return the call as soon as possible and from a non-public area.

19. In addition to my telephone number, should I include a fax number, pager number, or e-mail address on my resume?

Yes. The principle for including such information is this: How can I best be contacted at all times? If an employer cannot contact you in a timely manner, chances are you may be eliminated from consideration as *"more trouble than you're worth."*

20. I have a home page. Should I also include the URL on my resume?

Be careful here. It depends on what's on your home page. If your home page is a blog that's basically your personal diary, don't include it since it probably contains observations that could turn off potential employers. Ask yourself these questions: Will the information enhance my resume, further communicate my qualifications to employers, and persuade the reader to invite me to a job interview? Or have I included a lot of personal information that might distract from my professionalism? If your website includes your photo, information about your family and pets, and insights into an unconventional lifestyle, it should not see the light of day as part of your job search! Use this principle for including or excluding this information: If your home page is not designed to directly relate to and thus enhance your resume, candidacy, and professional image, do not volunteer this information on your resume. On the other hand, you may want to create a separate home page which only contains your web resume or develop a web portfolio (see Chapter 12).

21. I belong to a couple of online social networks that include my photo and personal information. Do you think employers will check me out online?

Assume employers will attempt to gather as much information as possible on you before both inviting you to an interview and offering you a job. Many employers routinely "Google" candidates for information. Using various search engines, they can quickly find out if you have an presence on the Internet. This could be a website, blog, online portfolio, or a news item about you. Be sure to "Google" yourself before conducting a job search. Make sure there is nothing on the Internet that could raise red flags about your candidacy. If these is, try to eliminate those items that are within your control to change.

22. I look great! Should I include my photo on the resume?

Not unless you are seeking a position in modeling, theater, movies, or other occupations where how you look is key to the selection process. For most positions, a photo becomes a two-edged sword – 50 percent of your audience may like your photo but the other 50 percent may hate it. The problem is that you don't know which 50 percent will like it! Regardless of how much you love your photo and yourself, it's inappropriate to include a photo on most resumes. Exceptions to this rule arise when employers request a photo – often international employers – or it is expected in your professional field, such as modeling.

23. What other things should I avoid putting on my resume?

Avoid any extraneous information that does not support your objective or communicate your qualifications to employers. The first thing to leave off your resume is the word "Resume"; it's obvious what it is. Avoid including your height, weight, age, sex, religion, health, politics, names and ages of children, spouse's occupation, parent's occupation, and other personal information that is not a bona fide job qualification. Also, do not include references or salary history/requirements. Apply this simple guiding inclusion/exclusion principle for packing a suitcase: *"When in doubt, throw it out!"* Your focus should be on communicating just enough information about your qualifications so the employer will be interested enough to invite you to a job interview.

> *Your focus should be on communicating just enough information so the employer will be interested in inviting you to an interview.*

24. Is it really necessary to write an electronic resume in today's job market?

Yes. How frequently you use it will depend on what position you're applying for, whom you're applying to, and whether or not you're using e-mail and online resume databases to market your qualifications. In today's fast-paced job market, invariably employers will request that you send your resume via e-mail.

25. Do many people get jobs by posting their resumes on the Internet?

We hope so, but probably not as many as one might expect, given all the talk about conducting an Internet job search. In fact, many job seekers may be wasting a lot of time and effort using the Internet to find a job. Recent studies show that fewer than 20 percent of job seekers eventually get a job via their Internet job search efforts. In spite of all the Internet hype, we really don't know how effective the Internet is for job seekers in terms of actually getting interviews that result in jobs. It probably depends on your background. If you are in computer and high-tech fields or have exotic skills that are difficult to find through other recruitment channels, you may get lucky with the Internet. Ironically, it's especially effective for employers who can quickly screen hundreds, if not thousands, of candidates through Internet employment (they call them "Internet recruitment") sites. Indeed, thousands of employers now include the Internet in their recruitment strategies. After all, it's much cheaper to advertise ($300 for four weeks) on the Internet than to purchase classified ads ($1,000 - $5,000) or use headhunters (they receive 25-35% of the individual's first-year salary). In many respects, the Internet is a high-tech resume "broadcast" medium where you can expect to get few "hits" unless you are exceptionally well qualified. Be sure to use the Internet in your job search, but don't spend a disproportionate amount of time looking for a job on the Internet. Like classified ads, job sites on the Internet are only one of many resources to include in your job search.

26. How can I get my resume on the Internet?

It's a daunting task! The Internet includes over 25,000 employment sites. Most sites allow you to post your resume free of charge in various resume databases which are accessed by employers. The best way to find these sites is to use one of the search engines, such as <u>Google.com</u>, and search under keywords such as "Jobs," "Careers," "Employment," and "Resumes." Also, examine the URLs, electronic resume, and Internet job search books identified in Chapter 12 (pages 180-185). These resources include the URLs of hundreds of key Internet sites that allow you to post your resume online. Many of these sites provide detailed instructions on how to submit an electronic resume. In many cases this will be a mini-resume created by responding to a series of fill-in-the-blank (windows) questions.

27. What's the best layout for the resume?

We prefer the two-column resume: section headers run down the left side and detailed information for each section is included on the right. Avoid three-column resumes. The layout should be pleasing to the eye, which means it incorporates lots of white space and avoids overcrowding. However, other attractive layouts include centered or left-flush headings followed by subheadings and text. Always keep in mind that your reader has very limited time to read your resume. Try to make his or her reading task easy by offering a very eye-pleasing layout that helps the reader quickly read and retain the contents of your resume.

28. How wide a margin should I have top to bottom and on either side?

The smallest margin should be one inch all around. Otherwise the resume begins looking very cramped because it lacks sufficient white space.

29. What typeface seems to work best?

Stay with a standard typeface that is easy to read. The most readable are **Times Roman**, Bookman, and **Arrus BT**, which is used in this book. Other popular typefaces are **Helvetica**, **Arial**, and **Verdana**. While less readable, these latter three have a modern look. Any of these typefaces should be used for scannable resumes. If you decide to vary typefaces, don't use more than two different ones. If you use more than two, the resume may be irritating to read. Keep the type size between 10 to 14 point for the text and between 13 and 16 point for headings. Otherwise the type size will be too small or too large to read. Use the same typeface and size throughout a scannable resume.

30. What type of emphasizing techniques seem to work best?

Be careful not to create too much variation. Use two but no more than three emphasizing techniques. The most common ones are **bold**, CAPITALIZATION, *italics*, underlining, bullets (•), boxes (■), and asterisks (*). We prefer using bold and boxes. Do not use italics, underlining, shading, and graphics when writing a scannable resume.

31. How should the categories be ordered?

It depends on your level of experience and the type of resume you select. If you have little or no direct work experience and your educational background appears to be your best qualification, put your education at the very top, just after your contact information and objective. If you have a great deal of experience, put your experience near the top. For most people using a chronological resume, the sequence of categories will be as follows:

1. Contact Information
2. Objective
3. Summary of Qualifications
4. Professional Experience
5. Education
6. Professional Affiliations

Combination and functional resumes will include other categories such as Work History. If you write a scannable resume, a Keyword Summary should replace the Objective and Summary of Qualifications.

32. Do I really need to include an objective on my resume?

We strongly recommend including an employer-centered objective. This objective becomes the central focus around which all other elements on the resume relate. It's especially important to include an objective on your resume if you have little or no experience. Individuals with a great deal of experience can substitute a "Qualifications Summary," "Career Profile," "Core Competencies," or "Summary/Achievements" for an "Objective." This section highlights, in bulleted form, four or five key skills and accomplishments that characterize the individual's career. Ideally this sections should quickly summarize one's predictable performance patterns. As such, it can nicely substitute for an objective. It tells an employer what you are likely to do for them. In this case, you can still include an objective on the resume, just before the "Qualifications Summary," or include it in your cover letter.

33. What's the best way to state an objective?

Your objective should be employer-centered rather than self-centered. It should communicate what it is you want to do for the employer rather than what you want from the employer. It should focus on performance and expected outcomes.

34. Should I include a "Summary of Qualifications" section in addition to an objective?

Yes, it's a good idea to capture the essence of your qualifications in three to five bulleted items immediately following the objective. This section essentially functions as a "Keyword Summary" for conventional resumes. It helps focus the reader's attention on your key qualifications. It's especially important to include this section since most resume readers spend no more than 30 seconds reading the complete resume. A "Summary of Qualifications" follows one of the most important writing principles – that you should always "put the most important information first" so it will get read and remembered first.

35. I only completed two-and-a-half years of college before flunking out. Should I be honest and admit that I wasn't able to get my degree?

You should include the highest level of education attained, which in this case is two-and-a-half years of higher education. Any higher education is better than none at all. Therefore, state your education in a positive way – for example, *"Completed 2½ years of college majoring in sales and marketing."* The circumstances under which you left college without a degree should not be included on the resume. After all, you could have run out of money, received a job offer you couldn't refuse, decided you had enough education and training for the type of career you wanted to pursue, or you're still in the process of completing your degree. If the employer asks you during the interview why you did not complete college, be prepared to give a positive and honest answer. Until it's addressed in the job interview, your education should be presented in the best possible light. This is not the time nor place to confess your weaknesses or be *"honest but stupid."*

36. Should I include my high school diploma under "Education"?

Only if it's one of your most important qualifications. If you've just graduated from high school, include it on your resume. Most employers assume you have at least a high school diploma by the mere fact that you are literate enough to write a resume and letter. If you've earned a B.A., M.A., or Ph.D., leave your high school diploma off the resume. To include it when you have higher education degrees looks like you're having great difficulty finding items to include on your resume!

37. How many jobs should I include on my resume?

It's not necessary to include all of your jobs, especially if they are very dated and show little relationship to your current profession. The rule of thumb is to go back 10 to 15 years. Keep in mind that employers want to **predict** your future performance based upon knowledge of your past performance. Include those jobs that best communicate your predictable future performance – skills and achievements during the past 10 years. Include jobs you held 15 or 20 years ago only if they enhance your objective and show progressive career development. Avoid including jobs that appear irrelevant to your objective or may distract the reader from your qualifications. Try to always keep your reader "on message" by focusing on what you want them to most know about your qualifications. This means giving less attention to your history and more attention to your achievements. Remember, you want just the right mix of useful information to motivate the reader to invite you to a job interview.

38. I was convicted of a felony and spent two years in Allen State Correctional Facility in Pennsylvania. How should I handle my incarceration on a resume?

There's no need to include such a red flag on a resume. Indeed, the resume is not the place to confess your weaknesses and thus prematurely eliminate yourself from consideration. You can handle your time gap several different ways; for example, stating that you were employed by the State of Pennsylvania (if you were doing prison work there) during those two years, if you're using a chronological resume, or switching to a functional resume that does not include employment dates. At some time, usually during the job interview, you will need to disclose your criminal record to an employer. For assistance with questions relating to incarceration or red flags in one's background, see the Krannichs' and Enelow's three books on this subject: *Best Resumes and Letters for Ex-Offenders, The Ex-Offenders' Job Hunting Guide,* and *Job Interview Tips for People With Not-So-Hot Backgrounds* (Impact Publications).

> *Try to always keep your reader "on message" by focusing on what you want them to most know about your qualifications – your achievements.*

39. I've had so many different jobs that I may look like a job-hopper who doesn't know what she wants to do. How should I handle all these different jobs on my resume?

You sound like a good candidate for a combination or functional resume. A chronological resume will accentuate your frequent job changes. If you use the combination or functional resume format, you can summarize common skills and accomplishments that crosscut your different jobs. If you list work history, try to group two or three jobs together into a summary statement about your work experience. If, for example, you held four different jobs during a four-year period, and each involved some aspect of customer relations, group them together in this type of summary statement: *"Customer Service: Maintained excellent customer relations in a variety of challenging work settings, from retail trade to telemarketing, 2001-2005."*

40. Should I put my most recent job first or last?

First. Follow the principle of "reverse chronology," which conforms to our principle of putting the most important information first. Put your most recent job first and continue in reverse chronological order over a 10-year period.

41. Should I include volunteer experience?

Include it if it supports your objective and enhances your qualifications in the eyes of the employer. Individuals with little or no work experience – especially those re-entering the job market after an lengthy absence – should definitely include their volunteer experience. Remember, volunteer experience is work, even though it may not be financially compensated work. Make sure you analyze your volunteer experience like you do any other jobs – identify your skills and accomplishments and include them on your resume.

42. What do employers really look for on resumes?

Employers look for **predictors of future performance**. They want to know what it is you will do for them rather than your unique history. The best predictors of your future performance are clear statements of your skills and accomplishments – what it is you have done, can do, and will do in the future.

43. Should I staple my two-page resume?

Yes and no. This is not a big deal. If the recipient wants to make copies or scan your resume, a staple will be a minor inconvenience or irritant. Use a nice paper clip as an alternative to stapling the pages together. If you're afraid the second page will get misplaced without a staple, include a footer at the bottom of the first page stating that this is "Page 1 of 2" and then on the top of the second page include your name and page number, as in the following two examples:

JOHN STEVENS   Page 2
_____

JOHN STEVENS
Page 2 of 2
_____

44. How should I best discuss my experience?

Focus on your **accomplishments** rather than discuss your assigned duties and responsibilities. Your language should incorporate a rich assortment of keywords consisting of action verbs and nouns that clearly communicate your accomplishments to prospective employers. Whenever possible, include statistics and examples that serve as **supports** to indicate how well you performed in previous jobs.

45. Should I include special awards, training, or hobbies on my resume?

It depends. Will they enhance your qualifications in the eyes of the employer or will they distract and raise unnecessary questions about you? If they do not enhance your objective, leave these items off. Remember, your resume should not be a compendium of your history – only those things that count the most for communicating your qualifications.

46. Should I include salary requirements on the resume?

Never. Salary is something you **negotiate** after you have had a chance to (1) determine the value of the position and (2) demonstrate your value to the employer during the job interview.

47. Should I include references on my resume?

No. Provide a list of references only if requested to do so. Also, take a list of references with you to the job interview where you may be asked for them. And don't forget to inform your references that you are looking for a job and that they might expect to hear from employers soon. Be sure to send them a copy of your resume so they can better stress your positives.

48. How can I give my resume an extra personal touch?

You really don't want to do this. Insecure individuals and manipulators seem to feel they need to do this. Most employers do not appreciate a personal touch which sometimes verges on psychological manipulation or bribery. You want to give them your best **professional touch.** You do this by concentrating on the content and language of your resume. Remember, the employer needs to fill a specific position. You need to demonstrate that you are the best "fit" for that position – your skills and accomplishments for the employer's position and money. Paper size and color, typeface style, staples, envelope size, and type size are peripheral to what you really should be focusing on – communicating your qualifications loud and clear to the employer. Focus on what and how you're going to best write each resume section.

49. What's the best type of resume to use in today's job market?

It depends on your experience and goals. What's best for you may not be best for the employer. Most employers expect to receive a chronological resume that outlines progressive work experience – complete with names of employers and inclusive dates of employment. Remember, they are looking for work patterns which are best viewed chronologically. For example, does the candidate have a pattern of career advancement, a stable job history, and a record of progressive accomplishments? Or does the candidate appear unfocused in his career, hopping from one job to another? How long does she normally stay with a single employer? The frequency of job moves can raise red flags about an individual's overall career development and focus.

> *Employers look for work patterns, which are best viewed chronologically.*

50. I have little work experience. What type of resume should I write?

While the chronological resume remains the best resume for most employment situations, a combination or functional resume may work best for you if you have little work experience, an unstable work history, or are in the process of making a career change. A chronological resume will tend to accentuate your lack of work experience. In this case, the combination resume may be the perfect solution.

51. When should I use a functional resume?

Seldom. You should avoid this type of resume since it often raises more questions about your qualifications than it answers because it tends to be vague and unfocused for readers who expect to see progressive employment dates and positions. It also may raise suspicions that the writer is trying to hide something by using broad functional categories and language. Only individuals with little or no work experience, especially those first entering the job market or re-entering after a lengthy absence, or those making a major career change should use a functional resume. This resume stresses your objectives and skills in the absence of direct work experience.

52. How should I handle time gaps on my resume?

If you have significant time gaps, avoid using a chronological resume, which by its very nature accentuates inclusive employment dates. Instead, use a combination or functional resume. Whenever you do state employment dates, state them as inclusive years, such as 1995-1998 or 2003-2006, rather than include the day and month you started or stopped working for an employer, such as May 1, 2002 to March 7, 2004. Even if you use a chronological resume where employment time gaps may appear obvious, don't worry about it too much. Just be prepared to explain the time gaps during the job interview.

53. How do I handle dates when specifying work history?

We prefer putting inclusive employment dates at the end of the experience statements rather than at the beginning. The reasoning behind doing this is simple – the most important points you wish to stress are your skills and accomplishments, not your employment dates. Put the dates at the end of each employment description to satisfy the curiosity of employers.

54. If a job title did not accurately reflect my duties and responsibilities, is it okay to create one that more accurately reflected my work?

It's okay to change your job title as long as you do so honestly. Your goal should be to give the employer accurate information on what you have done, can do, and will do in the future. If, for example, your official job title was "Receptionist" but 80 percent of your work was actually in public relations, use a job title that best reflects your work but which is also honest. In this case, you might write:

"Public Relations: Developed press releases, contacted media, and arranged interviews with both print and electronic media. Increased the number of media contacts by over 300 percent in the first six months and maintained contact with more than 50 key media contacts each week. Began as a receptionist but job expanded into a public relations position supporting sales and marketing operations."

Even though your employer did not change your official job title (or your salary!), this description is both accurate and honest as well as demonstrates initiative and progressive career development.

55. How honest should I be on my resume?

Always be honest, but avoid being stupid! Honesty can be communicated many different ways. Honesty in the job search does not mean you are required to confess your weaknesses and tell employers what is wrong with you. Indeed, many job seekers say the stupidest things in the name of honesty. Tell the truth but don't volunteer the whole bloody truth. For example, it is not necessary to volunteer why you left a position, especially if you were fired. Nor should you confess a criminal record or a negative financial history. Neither should you inflate your skills, accomplishments, and education. Many job seekers do this and get caught and rejected because of such deception. Everything you do during your job search should be positive, upbeat, and **honest.**

56. Is it okay to exclude certain skills or work history that may make me appear over-qualified for a job?

Yes. This is another one of those *"be honest but not stupid"* situations. This problem arises for some people in today's job market who appear over-qualified for what they really would like to do. There is no rule that says you must fully disclose all of your work history and education – only what's relevant to the position in question. For example, if you have a law degree but you really want to work as a paralegal, then don't include your law degree on your resume. If you do, you will probably disqualify yourself since you will appear over-qualified for the position and thus "unfit." Your goal should be to get the interview. During the interview you can talk about your legal background and explain why you really want to be a paralegal rather than a lawyer.

57. What language style should I use in describing my experience?

Be succinct and use lots of keywords which consist of action verbs (primarily for conventional resumes) and nouns (primarily for scannable and electronic resumes). Keep your sentences short and to the point.

58. How do I refer to myself on the resume?

It's not necessary to directly refer to yourself. If you use action verbs in completing each resume section (directed, supervised, marketed, completed, etc.), the reader assumes you are the subject. Never refer to yourself as "I." Doing so gives your resume a very self-centered tone.

59. Should I include personal information on my resume?

The general rule for including personal information is "No." By all means avoid including such extraneous information as age, sex, height, weight, marital status, spouse, children, race, and religion. This information does nothing to enhance your candidacy. In fact, it may raise negative questions about you and your judgment. As for hobbies and other interests, only include those that might enhance your candidacy.

60. I'm 21 years old and I'll be graduating from college in 10 months. But I have hardly any work experience. I'm not sure what I want to do or what to put on my resume. What should I do to attract employers?

There's lots you can do between now and graduation to better position yourself with employers. Your strongest assets appear to be (1) your education, (2) your youth, and (3) your willingness, enthusiasm, and drive to work. Make sure you do a skills assessment and develop a strong employer-oriented objective that communicates both your enthusiasm and willingness to work and learn. Examine your education carefully in terms of skills you've thus far learned and applied. Do a careful analysis of any work experience, be it an internship or volunteer work, to identify your strongest skills and accomplishments. Write a functional or combination resume and include powerful cover letters with each resume you send to employers or others. Be sure to network for information, advice, and referrals, and be persistent in your job search. And between now and graduation, become more entrepreneurial – do some volunteer work or create an internship that best relates to your career goals. Also, don't overlook sales positions since many are entry-level and require little previous work experience. Your long-term career growth may be dependent on having at one time had sales experience which teaches you to become very entrepreneurial within a company and learn the bottom line – key experience and skills required for today's companies. As many employers will tell you, we are all in sales, whether we like it or not! The sooner you learn this, the better for your long-term career growth.

61. Is it necessary to do a video or multimedia resume?

It depends. Only if requested to do so or if it is appropriate for a particular occupational field, such as modeling, sales, film, theater, art, music, or multimedia. Be very careful in using these types of visual and high-tech resumes. They are not for everyone, and despite marketing hype about these "new resumes," only a few people probably use them successfully. They may have unintended consequences for you. Ask yourself these questions: *"What is it you're trying to communicate in these mediums that you can't communicate in a paper or electronic resume? Is this an appropriate medium at this stage in your job search?"* If you volunteer a video resume, you may in fact put yourself at a disadvantage. A video includes key verbal and nonverbal elements that should be communicated at the job interview – not at the resume stage. Like putting a picture on your resume, your video may be disliked by 50 percent of those who see it! Be careful in confusing what elements should go into a resume versus those elements which you are in a better position to control in a face-to-face job interview.

62. How many drafts of the resume should I complete before going into final production?

As many as you need to get it perfect. Keep drafting and re-drafting your resume until it becomes a quick and well focused read. Ask yourself this question: *"In 30 seconds will the employer know exactly what I have done, can do, and will do for him or her?"* If it's not perfectly clear and impressive enough to motivate the employer to invite you to an interview, keep drafting your resume until you get it right. It must have immediate and lasting impact – a memorable document. Evaluate your resume properly before sending it to your targeted audience.

63. What's the best way to evaluate my drafts?

You need to conduct two different types of evaluations – internal and external. The internal one involves you assessing various aspects of your resume according to the checklist of evaluation criteria outlined in Chapter 8. The external evaluation involves giving your resume to individuals who are competent to assess your resume according to the external evaluation criteria in Chapter 8. Your best evaluation will come from individuals who are in hiring positions.

64. I don't have time to do an external evaluation and multiple drafts. The resume has to be sent tomorrow. What do I do?

Complete the database forms in Chapter 7, write each section beginning at the bottom and working up, do an internal evaluation (Chapter 8), and ask one or two people you trust to look it over. You may be able to complete this whole process in five hours. After you send this resume, take the time to go back and redraft your resume according to our previous advice on how to write a high impact resume.

Resume Production

65. What size paper works best?

Use standard size 8½" x 11" paper. Smaller or larger size papers may set your resume apart from others, but such odd sizes will not enhance your candidacy. In fact, it may not make a lot of difference what size paper you use. In the end, most employers will make judgments based upon the quality of your resume content rather than on paper size or other "dress for success" elements that sometimes candidates confuse with the importance of producing compelling content.

66. What color paper works best?

Stay with conservative white, off-white, or light gray papers. Two-tone paper – a light gray with a one-inch white margin top/bottom and left/right – seems to work very well for many executives. However, if you are applying for a position in art or graphic design, you might want to use less conventional colors.

67. How important is the paper quality?

Again, you're trying to present your best professional effort. In so doing, print your resume on good quality bond paper – 20 lb. or heavier. The paper should have a very professional look and it should feel substantial – just like your candidacy! You'll find lots of good quality paper available at any major office supply store.

68. What color ink should I use?

Black is fine in most cases. If you are using a color printer or have a choice of inks with a print shop, you might consider using dark blue ink on light gray paper or dark brown ink on off-white paper. Avoid any unconventional colors unless you are applying for an unconventional position.

69. Should I type, word-process, or typeset my resume?

You're best off word-processing your resume and producing it on a laser printer. Using a computer gives you the flexibility to run as many copies as you wish, as well as customize each resume for individual employers. Computer-generated resumes also are relatively inexpensive. Typewriters are old technology that give you weak production capabilities for producing a first-class resume. Typesetting also is old technology. You need someone who can produce camera-ready copy – a desktop publisher or graphic artist who works in such programs as Word, WordPerfect, PageMaker, Quark, or Ventura. If you don't have a computer, you are well advised to get one and acquire word processing skills. Today's job market requires individuals who are computer literate. If you have someone else generate your resume on a computer, make sure their price includes giving you a copy of the disk. Since you may want to revise your resume later, having it on disk will make the revision process much easier. You may want to use an off-the-shelf software resume production program, such as *WinWay Resume*, *ResumeMaker*, or *Custom Resume Creator*.

70. How many copies should I make?

As many as you need. If you word-process your own resume, you have the flexibility of producing one copy at a time, depending on whom or how many people you plan to send it to. If you have someone else word-process your resume, you probably only need a few copies and an original from which you can make additional copies on a good quality copy machine. If you have your resume typeset, you'll probably want to run at least 100 copies, depending on the cost and your distribution plans.

71. How much should it cost to produce my resume?

It depends on what you want. If you have your resume professionally printed, it can cost you $100 or more. If you pay to have it word-processed, it may cost $25 to $75. If you're making copies from originals, each copy will cost from $0.10 to $0.25. If you're having your resume copied from an original, we recommend purchasing your own high quality paper and supplying it to the printer when making copies. If not, you have to select a house paper that may not project the image you want to convey with your resume.

Resume Distribution

72. Who should get my resume?

As many people as possible – not just employers who are trying to fill vacancies. Make sure you spread the word that you are looking for a job. Contact your relatives, friends, colleagues, former teachers, and other people in your network and let them know about your job search. Send them a copy of your resume for their reference. They just might know someone who would be interested in your qualifications. And, of course, you want to send your resume to employers who appear to have job vacancies. Depending on your skills and experience, you might also want to send your resume to several headhunters who specialize in your occupational field.

73. Is it best to broadcast my resume to hundreds of employers or target it toward only a few employers?

It's always best to target your resume to specific employers whom you know are hiring for specific positions related to your qualifications. The broadcast method gives you a false sense of making progress in the job market because you are sending out lots of resumes and letters to lots of employers. You'll be lucky to get a one-percent response rate from such junk mailings. However, if you are in a high-demand field, such as information technology, have unique skills, demonstrate lots of experience, and make more than $100,000 a year, the broadcast letter may work better for you. You might want to broadcast your resume to two audiences – headhunters and employers. Several firms, which we identified in Chapter 10 (page 145), specialize in broadcasting resumes primarily to headhunters via e-mail. If you want to try your luck, for anywhere from $24 to over $4,000, these resume blasting firms will send your resume to 1,000 to 10,000 headhunters and employers who seek such resumes. While we do not endorse these firms – and we are often skeptical about what appear to be inflated claims of effectiveness – nonetheless, you may want to explore a few of these firms.

74. I've heard that employment firms will send my resume to hundreds and thousands of firms. Is it a good idea to use these firms?

It's hard to say. Many of these firms work on the "dark side" of the job market – sell worthless services to vulnerable job seekers who don't know any better. The firms will tell you they get great results for their clients and they may share a few anecdotes to convince you that their approach works. We're very suspect of such claims, especially anecdotal evidence rather than statistics of the number of individuals who actually got interviews and job offers. This is a broadcast method that we know gets very low results. You'll probably waste your time and money working with such firms. Try this approach: Ask them to structure their fees according to their performance – you only pay them when you get so many interviews and offers. See how they respond to such performance criteria. Chances are they will pitch you the old advertising line – their mailing will "expose" you to several hundred eyeballs. You can easily do this yourself, or hire a $49.95 resume e-mail blaster (see page 145), and get the same meager results!

75. When I do an informational interview, should I start by giving the person I'm interviewing a copy of my resume?

No! Doing so sends the wrong message – that you're looking for a job through this person – and negates the purpose of this interview, which is to get information, advice, and referrals. Take a copy of your resume to the interview but only mention your resume at the very **end** of the interview. At that time ask the individual if he or she would be so kind as to review your resume in light of your conversation and make suggestions as to how to best improve it for the types of jobs you were discussing. Afterward, be sure to send a revised copy of your resume to this person with a nice thank-you note that expresses your sincere gratitude for their time and helpful advice.

76. Should I send my resume to headhunters?

Not everyone should and can use headhunters or executive search firms, especially individuals seeking entry-level positions or those with little work experience. Remember, headhunters work for employers who have very special needs which are reflected by the fact that employers are willing to pay headhunters 25 or 30 percent of your first-year salary rather than recruit through less expensive classified ads, employment firms, or online advertising sources. Headhunters tend to specialize in particular occupational fields or work on a contingency basis for particular employers. Furthermore, they generally fill positions paying annual salaries of $60,000 or more, preferably in the $100,000+ range. If you make more than $60,000 a year and have specialized skills of interest to headhunters, by all means send them a resume and cover letter indicating your interest in working with them. Headhunters are always looking for well qualified individuals to include in their databases. The best sources for contacting headhunters are *The Directory of Executive Recruiters* (Kennedy Information, annual), **Oya's Directory of Recruiters** (www.i-recruit.com), and **Recruiters Cafe** (www.recruiterscafe.com). The first resource (*The Directory of Executive Recruiters*) is a book which includes a CD-ROM, provides information on occupational specialties, indicates contingency-based firms, and gives complete contact information. It's also linked to an executive-level resume blasting service: www.executiveagent.com. The second resource (www.i-recruit.com) is a gateway website for locating recruiters in 14 major occupational categories. The third resource (www.recruiterscafe.com) helps users find local search firms by agency name, geographic focus, and industry specialization.

> *Before you contact recruiters, make sure you have the right mix of skills and experience relevant to particular recruiters.*

It's okay to broadcast your resume and letters to these firms. But before you contact these firms, make sure you have the right mix of skills and experience relevant to particular recruiters. Otherwise, you will waste your time and money trying to get into the headhunter business. Executive-level talent is well advised to get their resumes posted on this combination of free and fee-based websites. The first two sites below are free; the last three sites are fee-based:

▪ Recruiters Online Network	www.recruitersonline.com
▪ 6FigureJobs	www.sixfigurejobs.com
▪ ExecuNet	www.execunet.com
▪ ExecutivesOnly	www.executivesonly.com
▪ Netshare	www.netshare.com

77. What size envelope should I use to mail my resume?

We prefer sending resumes and cover letters in 9" x 12" envelopes. These envelopes get more attention than the regular #10 business envelope and they keep your resume and letter flat. However, it's perfectly acceptable to send your resume in a #10 business envelope – but nothing smaller. If you really want to get an employer's attention, send your resume in a Federal Express box.

78. Should I ever use attention-getting delivery methods and mediums, such as putting my resume in a shoe box or sending it via a singing messenger?

It depends on your occupational field, the employer, and the position. The old resume in the shoe box trick (*"Now that I've got my shoe in the door, how about an interview?"*) still works for people applying for aggressive sales positions. A singing messenger might be appropriate for other sales positions or for positions in creative fields. A multimedia resume might be terrific for someone applying for a position in multimedia or graphic arts. A resume embedded in the front page of a newspaper, with an attention-getting headline, might be very effective for someone applying for a position in journalism. No doubt about it – these methods and mediums do get attention. The really important question is this: Do they produce results, i.e., invitations to job interviews? Use your own judgment on this issue based upon sound knowledge of your audience. Research the position, employer, and organization before using such unconventional approaches.

79. Is it best to send my resume and letter by a next-day delivery service that will give my letter special attention and a sense of urgency?

This is one of those *"six one way, half a dozen another"* situations. Yes, sending your letter and resume in a colorful next-day delivery envelope (Federal Express, UPS, Express Mail, etc.) will get your letter to its destination faster and with more attention, but it may not make much difference in terms of the final outcome – an invitation to a job interview. Concentrate on the contents of your message, which should grab the attention of the recipient and motivate them to call you for an interview.

80. Should I type or handwrite the address on the envelope and use a mailing label?

Always type the address – with or without a mailing label. Remember the principle of *"demonstrating your best professional effort"* throughout your job search. Handwritten addresses personalize your message too much and may appear unprofessional and manipulative.

81. Is it best to use a postage stamp or use a meter strip for postage?

Use a nice postage stamp – avoid flowers, animals, and ugly and controversial people. It may not make much difference if you use a meter strip, although some people may think you're stealing postage from your current employer in affixing such postage.

82. When should I fax or e-mail my resume?

Only fax or e-mail when requested to do so. More and more employment ads do request that you e-mail a resume. Many companies also include their website address in their ads. Make sure you visit their sites before sending your resume. You may learn certain things about the company that would help you customize your resume and letter to the particular position and company. Also put a copy of your resume in the mail with a note stating you faxed or e-mailed it.

83. Is it a good idea to fax or e-mail the employer informing him or her that my resume will be arriving shortly by mail?

This can be a very effective approach to getting the attention of employers. It is used by public relations firms in sending press materials to the media. It's basically a "heads-up" approach – informs the recipient that he or she can expect to receive something from you very soon. This also becomes one important step in a three-step approach to delivery and follow-up:

1. Fax or e-mail a short message saying your resume and letter will be arriving within the next few days.
2. Resume and letter arrives by mail or special delivery service.
3. Telephone call placed within five days to follow up on receipt of your resume and letter.

Resume Follow-Up

84. How long should I wait before following up on the resume and letter?

Follow up within three to five working days after the expected receipt of your resume and letter. If you wait longer, chances are important initial screening decisions may have already been made. You want to follow up before or during this decision-making process.

85. Is it best to follow up with a copy of the original resume and letter, a new letter, or a telephone call, fax, or e-mail?

We prefer a telephone call. It's quick and gives you immediate feedback. Best of all, you may get to talk to a real person and conduct an initial screening interview! Additional letters, faxes, and e-mail are likely to go unanswered.

86. If I fax or e-mail my resume and letter, how should I follow up?

Immediately follow up with a hard copy of your correspondence. Wait three to five working days and then follow up with a telephone call. If you can't get through to a person, leave voice mail and then follow up with a fax or e-mail.

87. If I make a follow-up phone call but can't get through to the right person, what should I do next?

Leave a message with a person or on voice mail. Keep the message short and sound upbeat, enthusiastic, and professional. Include your name and telephone number for a return call.

88. When is the best time to make a follow-up phone call?

Try a Tuesday, Wednesday, or Thursday early in the morning (7:30am to 8:45am) or late in the afternoon (4:30pm to 6:30pm). Mondays and Fridays tend to be very busy days for many employers. And the hours between 9am and 4:30pm are often very busy with meetings and other business. Since many employers arrive early and leave late, you might get lucky and contact them directly during these early and late hours.

89. What should I say if I get a receptionist or other gatekeeper when I make a follow-up phone call?

Start by introducing yourself and asking to speak to the party you are calling: *"Hi, this is Mary Jackson calling for Mr. Sebring."* This introductory statement will either get you directly through to your party or you will be asked a few screening questions, such as, *"What should I say you're calling in regards to?"* or *"Mr. Sebring is not available. Would you like to leave a message or would you like his voice mail?"* Be sure to leave a message either with the person or on the voice mail. Make this message short and to the point: *"This is Mary Jackson calling in reference to my letter of May 7th. My phone number is 711-321-1234."* This is not the time and place to leave a lengthy message about what you want. You'll either get a call back or you won't.

90. If I get voice mail when I make a follow-up phone call, should I leave a message or try again later?

Leave a nice follow-up message, which should include your name, phone number, and purpose of your call. If you hang up without leaving a message, chances are you'll encounter the same voice mail message the next time you call. Many busy people routinely use their voice mail to screen most of their calls. Therefore, it's important that you leave a short message and that you sound friendly, enthusiastic, and non-threatening. Don't leave a message that will motivate the person to avoid you. Rather than aggressively and presumptuously say *"I sent you my resume last week. When can I expect to hear from you about an interview? Please call me back at 711-321-1234. I'll be here all day,"* say *"Hi, this is Mary Jackson. Just following up on my letter of last week. My number is 711-321-1234. Talk to you later."*

In the second response you are not asking the person to return your call but it's implied by the fact that you left your telephone number. The person can expect to *"talk to you later"* whether or not he initiates the call. Your plan is to talk to him, which may mean making several additional follow-up calls.

91. How many times should I make follow-up phone calls before I give up or use some other follow-up methods?

Be pleasantly persistent. Remember, most employers are very busy people who screen their calls through voice mail. You may have to make five to eight calls before getting a reply. After the eighth call, give up and write a nice follow-up letter instead. Throughout this sometimes frustrating follow-up process, you must remain upbeat, friendly, and nonaggressive. After the fifth or sixth unanswered follow-up call, chances are the individual will begin feeling guilty for not returning a call from such a pleasant and persistent person. There's a high probability you will receive a return phone call by the eighth attempt. It may not come directly from the person you're trying to contact (an assistant may return your call), but the message given to you will be from that person. Chances are that person reread your resume before returning your phone call. And that's exactly one of the outcomes you want from this follow-up exercise – be read and remembered in a positive manner.

92. I really can't afford to make long distance phone calls to research the employer or follow up my resume and letter. Will I be at a disadvantage for not doing so?

If you are serious about getting a job, you simply can't afford not to make the necessary long distance phone calls! **Call** to get the name of a person to whom you should address your correspondence. **Call** to follow up on all of your communication. If you are concerned about costs, perhaps early in your job search you should check with your long distance carrier to determine if you are paying too much for long distance phone calls. Many carriers charge $0.10 or less per minute even during the day, and many long distance Internet calls are free. Since long distance calls are very inexpensive, you would be *"penny wise and pound foolish"* not to make long distance phone calls relating to your future employment. Whatever you do, don't be cheap at this critical stage in your job search. You owe it to yourself to spend a few dollars here and there to get the job you want. And, yes, you will be at a disadvantage if you're too cheap to make those long distance phone calls.

Job Search Letters

93. Is it really necessary to include a cover letter with my resume?

Yes. If you send a resume without a cover letter, you send an incomplete message to an employer. In fact, your cover letter may be more important to getting the interview than the resume. Many employers report having selected candidates based on their cover letter rather than their resume. In a cover letter you have more room to express your enthusiasm and personality than on a resume. It's these personal qualities expressed in the cover letter that may set you apart from other candidates who may appear equally qualified from a reading of their resumes.

94. What letter style works best?

You basically have four different styles to choose from – semi-blocked, modified-blocked, fully-blocked, or square-blocked. We prefer the fully-blocked style where all paragraphs begin left-flush. However, the other styles also work well. We also prefer left-justifying our letters. Fully justified letters look too formal and mass produced. However, whether you left-justify or fully justify your letters may not make a difference in terms of outcomes – getting invited to interviews. Select a style, be consistent, and concentrate on producing high impact letter **content**.

95. What are the best types of letter to write during a job search?

There is no one best type of letter to write. It depends on your situation. However, two types of powerful letters are often overlooked during a job search. Many employers report the importance of receiving **thank-you letters** – letters that express important social graces, project personality characteristics, and indicate a desire for the position. Such letters can make a big difference in being accepted or rejected for a position. **T-letters**, which are often used in lieu of a resume and cover letter, quickly get attention and increase the probability of being invited to a job interview. You should seriously consider incorporating such letters into your job search. Whatever you do, don't limit your letter writing to standard cover letters. You need to write a variety of different letters throughout your job search.

96. How long should my cover letter be?

Usually one page. However, if it runs two pages, be sure it doesn't overwhelm your resume. The principle of "less is more" is applicable to both your resume and letter.

97. What should I include in my cover letter?

Express your interest in the position, state your most important skills and achievements in direct reference to the employer's skill requirements, and state when you will call the employer. Don't repeat what's in your resume. Make sure the tone of your letter is very employer-centered, enthusiastic, and energetic.

98. What's the best way to begin a cover letter?

Open with an attention-grabbing question or statement. For example, *"Are you looking for someone who can increase sales by 30 percent a year? I have done so for the past five years as . . ."* Whatever you do, avoid such standard openers as *"Please find enclosed a copy of my resume in response to . . ."* This is a dull and formal opener that may stop the reader at the end of the first sentence. It does not separate you from the competition. It does little to express your enthusiasm, energy, and personality. It's simply deadly and may kill your resume!

99. What's the best way to end a cover letter?

Always close with an **action statement** in which you indicate that you will be following up your resume and letter with a telephone call. For example,

> *"I'll give you a call the afternoon of October 7th to answer any questions you might have concerning my candidacy."*

Without such an action statement, you may not hear from the employer. By closing with an action statement, you indicate that you are a "heads-up" candidate who needs to be **read and remembered** because you will be calling in a few days.

100. Is it necessary to address my letter to a specific person or name, or is "Dear Sir/Madam" sufficient?

Always try (make a phone call) to get a name of a specific person to whom you should address your letter, resume, and follow-up phone call. Without a name, you will have difficulty conducting a follow-up. However, if you are unable to get a name, or if your inquiries result in instructions *to "just send it to Personnel or Human Resources,"* send your correspondence to the required department. Avoid standard anonymous salutations such as "Dear Sir/Madam" or "To Whom It May Concern." We prefer leaving the salutation off altogether and go directly from your return address to the body of your letter.

101. How does a cover letter differ from a broadcast letter?

A broadcast letter can be in the form of either a generic cover letter or a letter unaccompanied by a resume. Since a broadcast letter may be sent en masse to hundreds of employers, it must be high energy and toot the writer's horn. It should be very accomplishment-oriented. On the other hand, cover letters focus on the relationship between the a specific position and the applicant's qualifications. They are custom-designed around the needs of the employer.

102. What other types of job search letters should I write?

A cover letter is only one of several types of job search letters you should be writing throughout your job search – from start to finish. You should consider writing six other types of letters: start-up, network, resume, follow-up, thank-you, and special. One of the most important and effective letters is the thank-you letter. In fact, it may be more important than a cover letter in landing interviews and getting job offers. Be sure to write such letters.

103. Should a thank-you letter be handwritten or word-processed?

Word-processed. Again, this is business correspondence in which you are demonstrating your best professional effort. Handwritten thank-you letters are okay for social occasions (you loved the party) and in the real estate and insurance businesses where salespeople try to "personalize" financial relationships with potential clients. They are inappropriate for most job search situations. However, whether you handwrite or type your thank-you letters may not make a great deal of difference in terms of outcomes – getting invited to job interviews.

104. When approaching a potential employer without prior contacts, should I send my resume and letter to the personnel or human resources department?

Neither. Most personnel and human resources departments do not make hiring decisions. They may announce vacancies, process paperwork, handle benefits, and hire for positions within their departments, but most do not hire for positions in other departments. You need to research the organization and find out who makes the hiring decisions in your occupational area and then address your letter to that individual. The person who usually has the power to hire is found in an operational unit that has the actual hiring need. This also is the person, or persons, who will interview candidates. You will waste your time and effort by sending an unsolicited resume and letter to personnel or human resources.

105. Should my letter be printed on the same paper as my resume?

In most cases the answer is "yes." Everything should match, including the envelope. Remember, you're demonstrating your best professional effort in your paper presentation. Matching papers present a good professional image. However, should you choose a special resume paper, such as a light gray paper with a white border, print your accompanying cover letter on matching white paper.

106. If an employment ad asks to state one's "salary history" or "salary requirements," should I do so in my letter?

Yes in the case of "salary history," but calculate your total compensation package which could be 45% above your yearly salary figure. In the case of "salary requirements," state "open" or "negotiable." You want to negotiate your salary requirements based upon (1) demonstrating your value to the employer during the interview and (2) learning the value of the position in question. And when you do get to the negotiation stage, make sure your "salary requirements" are stated as a range rather than a specific dollar figure. By stating a range, you leave room to negotiate a higher salary than an employer may initially offer.

107. What else should I include with my cover letter other than my resume?

Nothing unless requested by the employer. Sending unsolicited photos, transcripts, and samples of work distracts from your message and makes you look desperate. Such items would be most appropriate to include in a "portfolio." Include them only if requested to do so.

108. Is it okay to use a different size paper for the cover letter than for the resume?

Keep them the same size. A smaller size paper tends to communicate a more personal message. Remember, this is business correspondence that should demonstrate your best professional effort.

109. I'm thinking of sending a telegram in lieu of a letter. Is that a good idea?

In some quarters, such as sales, an unusual letter in the form of a telegram may get you special attention and thus would be perfectly acceptable. However, in other occupational areas, especially more conservative circles, writing a conventional letter and sending it by conventional means is more appropriate. If you want to get special attention, mail your letter using a Federal Express, UPS, Express Mail, or other special delivery envelope.

110. Am I finished writing letters once I accept a job offer?

You should still write one more letter to your new employer – a post-hire thank-you letter. This letter helps set the stage for developing your new relationship as well as confirms to the employer that you were probably the correct hiring decision.

Appendix A

Resume Transformations

THE FOLLOWING EXAMPLES REPRESENT an actual case study. While it is not a typical case, it does emphasize some important employment problems which can be handled with different types of resumes.

Except for the names and dates, everything appearing in these resumes is true, including misspelled words. They illustrate our principle of being truthful but not stupid. One of the major differences among these resumes is that the truth is more advantageously communicated – for both the applicant and employer – in some resumes than in others.

The individual in this case held several full-time positions as typist, secretary, receptionist, and sales clerk while working her way through college. After graduation, she continued in her former occupation. Wanting to break out of the *"once a secretary, always a secretary"* pattern, she had several resume options for changing careers. Which ones do you think best present her qualifications to employers?

The first resume on pages 221-222 represents the **traditional chronological or "obituary" resume**. It omits an objective, emphasizes dates and job titles, includes extraneous information, and lacks visual appeal. This resume communicates all the wrong things – the individual lacks a focus, is a job hopper, and can answer the telephone and type. It also includes several errors related to spelling, use of personal pronouns, personal statements, and references. While this resume accurately compiles the individual's work history, it presents the individual's qualifications at the lowest and least flattering levels.

The **improved chronological resume** on page 223 presents this person's qualifications in a much more professional manner. It stresses skills and accomplishments in relationship to an objective. The individual presents those jobs which should strengthen her objective. However, the "Education" and "Experience" sections do not clearly support the objective; the chronological organization of "Experience" leads the reader to conclude that Gail S. Topper has little relevant experience related to the type of sales position she desires. While much better than her previous resume, this type of resume appears inappropriate for someone who is trying to make a major career change.

The **functional resume** on page 224 presents another picture of this individual's qualifications. Here, employment dates and job titles are eliminated in favor of presenting transferable skills and accomplishments. While this resume is ideal for someone entering the job market with little job related experience, this resume does not take advantage of this individual's work experience with specific employers.

The **combination resume** on page 225 is ideal for this particular person. It minimizes employment dates and job titles, stresses transferable skills and accomplishments, and includes work history. The individual appears purposeful, skilled, and experienced.

The **resume letter** on page 226 also is a good alternative for this person. It is designed to open doors without the traditional resume. The individual can present one of the resumes – preferably the combination resume – to the employer at some later date.

The secretarial experience does not appear on the chronological, functional, or combination resumes. If it did, it would tend to stereotype this individual prior to being invited to an interview. It is important, however, that this individual be able to explain the secretarial experience during the interview, especially how it will make her a particularly good salesperson – knows the particular equipment and problems from the perspective of those who will encounter them on a day-to-day basis.

Traditional Chronological Resume

RESUME

Gail S. Topper	Weight:	122 lbs.
136 W. Davis St.	Height:	5'4"
Washington, DC 20030	Born:	8/4/60
202-465-9821	Health:	Good
	Marital Status:	Married

Education

1985-1988 George Mason University, Fairfax, Virginia. I received my B.A. in Comunications.

1982-1984 Northern Virginia Community College, Annandale, Virginia. I completed my A.A. degree.

1977-1981 Harrisonburg High School, Harrisonburg, Virginia.

Work Experience

2/14/92 to present: Secretary, MCT Coporation, 2381 Rhode Island Ave., Philadelphia, Pennsylvania 19322.

2/30/89 to 2/9/91: Secretary, Martin Computer Services, 391 Old Main Rd., Charleston, South Carolina 37891.

4/21/88 to 2/20/89: Secretary, STR Systems, Inc., 442 Virginia Ave., Rm. 21, Washington, D.C. 20011.

9/28/87 to 1/4/88: Typist, NTC Corporation, 992 Fairy Avenue, Springfield, Virginia 22451.

1/9/87 to 7/30/87: Secretary, Foreign Language Department, George Mason University, Fairfax, Virginia 22819

3/1/85 to 9/14/86: Salesclerk, Sears Reobuck & Co., 294 Wisconsin Avenue, Boston, Massachusetts 08233

5/3/82 to 2/1/84: Salesclerk, JT's, 332 Monroe St., New Orleans, Louisiana 70014.

1977-1981: Held several jobs as cook, counter help, salesclerk, typist, and secretarial assistant.

Community Involvement

1992 to prsent: Sunday school teacher. Grace Methodist Church. Falls Church, Virginia.

1988: Volunteer. Red Cross. Falls Church, Virginia.

1984: Stage crew member. Community Theatre Group. New Orleans, Louisiana

1983: Extra. Community Theatre Group. Annandale, Virginia.

Hobbies

I like to swim, cook, garden, bicycle, and listen to rock music.

Personal Statement

I have good mannual dexterity developed by working back stage in theatrical productions and working with various office machines. I can operate IBM Mag Card A and II typeriters, dictaphones, IBM 6640 (ink jet printer), various duplicating machines, and several copying machines. Familiar with addressograph. I am willing to relocate nad travel.

References

John R. Teems, Manager, Martin Computer Services, 391 Old Dominion Rd., Annandale, Virginia 20789

James Stevens, Secretary, STR Systems, Inc., 442 Virginia Ave., Rm. 21, Washington, D.C. 20011.

Alice Bears, Assistant Personnel Director, MCT Corporation, 2381 Rhode Island Ave., Philadelphia, Pennsylvania 19322

Also contact the Office of Career Planning and Placement at George Mason University.

Improved Chronological Resume

GAIL S. TOPPER
136 West Davis Street
Washington, DC 20030   202-465-9821

OBJECTIVE: A professional sales position . . . leading to management . . . in information processing where administrative and technical experience, initiative, and interpersonal skills will be used for maximizing sales and promoting good customer relations.

EDUCATION: **B.A. in Communication, 1988**
George Mason University, Fairfax, Virginia.
- Courses in interpersonal communication, psychology, and public speaking.
- Worked full-time in earning 100% of educational and personal expenses.

TECHNICAL EXPERIENCE: **MCT Corporation, 2381 Rhode Island Avenue, Philadelphia, PA 20033:** Office management and materials production responsibilities. Planned and re-organized word processing center. Initiated time and cost studies, which saved company $30,000 in additional labor costs. Improved efficiency of personnel. 1992 to present.

Martin Computer Services, 391 Main Rd., Charleston, SC 37891: Communication and materials production responsibilities. Handled customer complaints. Created new tracking and filing system for Mag cards. Improved turnaround time for documents production. Operated Savin word processor. 1989 to 1991.

STR Systems, 442 Virginia Avenue, Rm. 21, Washington, DC 20011: Equipment operation and production responsibilities. Operated Mag card and high speed printers: IBM 6240, Mag A,I,II,IBM 6640. Developed and organized technical reference room for more effective use of equipment. 1988-1989.

SALES EXPERIENCE: **Sears Roebuck & Co., 294 Wisconsin Avenue, Boston, MA 08233:** Promoted improved community relations with company. Solved customer complaints. Reorganized product displays. Handled orders. 1985 to 1987.

JT's, 332 Monroe St., New Orleans, LA 70014: Recruited new clients. Maintained inventory. Developed direct sales approach. 1982 to 1984.

Functional Resume

GAIL S. TOPPER

---

136 West Davis Street   Washington, DC 20030   202-465-9821

OBJECTIVE: A professional sales position . . . leading to management . . . in information processing where administrative and technical experience, initiative, and interpersonal skills will be used for maximizing sales and promoting good customer relations.

EDUCATION: **B.A. in Communication, 1988**
George Mason University, Fairfax, Virginia.
- Courses in interpersonal communication, psychology, and public speaking.
- Worked full-time in earning 100% of educational and personal expenses.

AREAS OF EFFECTIVENESS

SALES/ CUSTOMER RELATIONS: Promoted improved community relations with business. Solved customer complaints. Recruited new clients. Re-organized product displays. Maintained inventory. Received and filled orders.

PLANNING/ ORGANIZING: Planned and re-organized word processing center. Initiated and cost studies, which saved company additional labor costs and improved efficiency of personnel. Developed and organized technical reference room for more effective utilization of equipment. Created new tracking and filing system for Mag cards which resulted in eliminating redundancy and improving turnaround time.

TECHNICAL: Eight years of experience in operating Mag card and high speed printers: IBM 6240, Mag A, I,II,IBM 6640, and Savin word processor.

PERSONAL: Excellent health . . . enjoy challenges . . . interested in productivity . . . willing to relocate and travel.

REFERENCES: Available upon request.

Combination Resume

GAIL S. TOPPER

136 West Davis Street	Washington, DC 20030	202-465-9821

OBJECTIVE: A professional sales position . . . leading to management . . . in information processing where administrative and technical experience, initiative, and interpersonal skills will be used for maximizing sales and promoting good customer relations.

AREAS OF EFFECTIVENESS

SALES/
CUSTOMER
RELATIONS: Promoted improved community relations with business. Solved customer complaints. Recruited new clients. Re-organized product displays. Maintained inventory. Received and filled orders.

PLANNING/
ORGANIZING Planned and re-organized word processing center. Initiated time and cost studies, which saved company additional labor costs and improved efficiency of personnel. Developed and organized technical reference room for more effective utilization of equipment. Created new tracking and filing system for Mag cards which resulted in eliminating redundancy and improving turnaround time.

TECHNICAL: Eight years of experience in operating Mag card and high speed printers: IBM 6240, Mag A,I,II,IBM 6640, and Savin word processor.

EMPLOYMENT
EXPERIENCE: MCT Corporation, Philadelphia, PA
Martin Computer Services, Charleston, SC
STR Systems, Inc., Washington, DC
NTC Corporation, Springfield, VA

EDUCATION: **B.A. in Communication, 1983**
George Mason University, Fairfax, Virginia.
- Courses in interpersonal communication, psychology, and public speaking.
- Worked full-time in earning 100% of educational and personal expenses.

PERSONAL: Excellent health . . . enjoy challenges . . . interested in productivity . . . willing to relocate and travel.

Resume Letter

136 W. Davis St.
Washington, DC 20030
January 7, _____

James C. Thomas, President
Advanced Technology Corporation
721 West Stevens Road
Bethesda, MD 20110

Dear Mr. Thomas:

Advanced Technology's word processing equipment is the finest on the market today. I know because I have used different systems over the past eight years. Your company is the type of organization I would like to be associated with.

Over the next few months I will be seeking a sales position with an information processing company. My technical, sales, and administrative experience include:

- Technical: eight years operating Mag card and high speed printers: IBM 6240, MAG A,I,II,IBM 6640, and Savin word processor.

- Sales: recruited clients; maintained inventory; received and filled orders; improved business-community relations.

- Administrative: planned and re-organized word processing center; created new tracking and filing systems; initiated time and cost studies which reduced labor costs by $40,000 and improved efficiency of operations.

In addition, I have a bachelor's degree in communication with emphasis on public speaking, interpersonal communication, and psychology.

Your company interests me very much. I would appreciate an opportunity to meet with you to discuss how my qualifications can best meet your needs. I will call your office next Monday, January 18, to arrange a meeting with you at a convenient time.

Thank you for your consideration.

Sincerely yours,

Gail S. Topper

Gail S. Topper

Appendix B

Resume Styles

THE FOLLOWING RESUME EXAMPLES reflect different educational and experience levels. The resume on page 228 is for a high school graduate with vocational skills and experience. The resume on page 229 is for a junior college graduate with a non-traditional background. The resume on page 230 is appropriate for a recent B.A. graduate.

The example on pages 231 and 232 differs from all others. Especially appropriate for individuals with an M.A. or Ph.D. degree, or for individuals with specialized research, publication, and other production experience, this example includes an add-on supplemental sheet which lists relevant qualifications. The main resume is still one page. The add-on sheet is designed to reinforce the major thrust of the resume without distracting from it.

The example on pages 233 and 234 is for a professional with a great deal of experience. It incorporates the use of a qualifications summary which includes many keywords. This is a powerful employer-centered resume that stresses major accomplishments.

The final example on page 265 is the classic "T" letter. It can substitute for a resume because it targets one's qualifications on the specific needs of the employer. Many job seekers report remarkable success with this type of resume substitute.

JOHN ALBERT
1099 Seventh Avenue
Akron, OH 44522
322-645-8271

OBJECTIVE: **A position as architectural drafter** with a firm specializing in commercial construction where technical knowledge and practical experience will enhance construction design and building operations.

EXPERIENCE: <u>Draftsman</u>: Akron Construction Company, Akron, OH. Helped develop construction plans for $14 million of residential and commercial construction. (1990 to present)

<u>Cabinet Maker</u>: Jason's Linoleum and Carpet Company, Akron, OH. Designed and constructed kitchen counter tops and cabinets; installed the material in homes; cut and laid linoleum flooring in apartment complexes. (1987 to 1990)

<u>Carpenter's Assistant</u>: Kennison Associates, Akron, OH. Assisted carpenter in the reconstruction of a restaurant and in building of forms for pouring concrete. (Summer 1986)

<u>Materials Control Auditor</u>: Taylor Machine and Foundry, Akron, OH. Collected data on the amount of material being utilized daily in the operation of the foundry. Evaluated the information to determine the amount of materials being wasted. Submitted reports to production supervisor on the analysis of weekly and monthly production. (Summer 1985)

TRAINING: <u>Drafting School, Akron Vocational and Technical Center</u>, 1989. Completed 15 months of training in drafting night school.

EDUCATION: <u>Akron Community High School</u>, Akron, OH. Graduated in 1988.

PERSONAL: Single...willing to relocate...prefer working both indoors and outdoors...strive for perfection...hard worker...enjoy photography, landscaping, furniture design and construction.

REFERENCES: Available upon request.

GARY S. PLATT
2238 South Olby Road, Sacramento, CA 97342
712-564-3981

OBJECTIVE

A position in the areas of systems analysis and implementation of Management Information Systems which will utilize a demonstrated ability to improve systems performance. Willing to relocate.

RELATED EXPERIENCE

Engineering Technician, U.S. Navy.
Reviewed technical publications to improve operational and technical descriptions and maintenance procedures. Developed system operation training course for high-level, nontechnical managers. Developed PERT charts for scheduling 18-month overhauls. Installed and checked out digital computer equipment with engineers. Devised and implemented a planned maintenance program and schedule for computer complex to reduce equipment down-time and increase utilization by user departments. (1991 to present)

Assistant Manager/System Technician, U.S. Navy, 37-person division.
Established and coordinated preventive/corrective maintenance system for four missile guidance systems (9 work centers) resulting in increased reliability. Advised management on system operation and utilization for maximum effectiveness. Performed system test analysis and directed corrective maintenance actions. Interfaced with other managers to coordinate interaction of equipment and personnel. Conducted maintenance and safety inspections of various types of work centers. (1987 to 1990)

Assistant Manager/System Technician, U.S. Navy, 25 person division.
Supervised system tests, analyzed results, and directed maintenance actions on two missile guidance systems. Overhauled and adjusted within factory specifications two special purpose computers, reducing down-time over 50%. Established and coordinated system and computer training program. During this period, both systems received the "Battle Efficiency E For Excellence" award in competition with other units. (1984 to 1986)

EDUCATION

U.S. Navy Schools, 1989-1993:
Digital System Fundamentals, Analog/Digital Digital/Analog Conversion Techniques, UNIVAC 1219B Computer Programming, and Technical Writing.

A.S. in Education, June 1987:
San Diego Community College, San Diego, CA
Highlight:
    Graduated Magna Cum Laude
    Member, Phi Beta Kappa Honor Society

CHERYL AYERS

2589 Jason Drive
Ithaca, NY 14850

202-467-8735
E-mail: cayers@aol.com

OBJECTIVE: A research, data analysis, and planning position in law enforcement administration which will use leadership, responsibility, and organizational skills for improving the efficiency of operations.

EDUCATION: **B.S. in Criminal Justice**, 1996
Ithaca College, Ithaca, NY
- Major: Law Enforcement Administration
- Minor: Management Information Systems
  G.P.A. in concentration 3.6/4.0

AREAS OF EFFECTIVENESS:

Leadership
Head secretary while working at State Police.
Served as Rush Chair and Social Chair for Chi Phi Sorority. Elected Captain and Co-Captain three times during ten years of cheerleading.

Responsibility
Handled highly confidential information, material, and files for State Police. Aided in the implementation of on-line banking system. In charge of receiving and dispersing cash funds for drive-in restaurant.

Organization
Revised ticket system for investigators' reports at State Police. Planned schedules and budget, developed party themes and skits, obtained prop material, and delegated and coordinated work of others during sorority rush.

Data Analysis
Program in Fortran, Cobal, and RPG II.
Analyzed State Police data on apprehensions; wrote report.

PERSONAL: Excellent health . . . single . . . enjoy all sports and challenges . . . willing to relocate.

REFERENCES: Available upon request from the Office of Career Planning and Placement, Ithaca College, Ithaca, NY.

MICHELE R. FOLGER
733 Main Street
Williamsburg, VA 23572
804-376-9932

OBJECTIVE: A manager/practitioner position in public relations which will use research, writing, and program experience. Willing to relocate.

EXPERIENCE: **Program Development**
Conducted research on the representation of minority students in medical colleges. Developed proposal for a major study in the field. Secured funding for $845,000 project. Coordinated and administered the program which had major effect on medical education.

Initiated and developed a national minority student recruitment program for 20 medical colleges.

Writing
Compiled and published reports in a variety of educational areas. Produced several booklets on urban problems for general distribution. Published articles in professional journals. Wrote and presented conference papers.

Research
Gathered and analyzed information concerning higher education in a variety of specialized fields. Familiar with data collection and statistics. Good knowledge of computers.

Administration and Management
Hired and trained research assistants. Managed medium-sized office and supervised 30 employees.

Public Relations
Prepared press releases and conducted press conferences. Organized and hosted receptions and social events. Spoke to various civic, business, and professional organizations.

WORK HISTORY: ATS Research Associates, Washington, DC
Virginia Education Foundation, Richmond, VA
Eaton's Advertising Agency, Cincinnati, OH

EDUCATION: M.A., Journalism, College of William and Mary, 1997.
B.A., English Literature, University of Cincinnati, 1991.

REFERENCES: Available upon request.

SUPPLEMENTAL INFORMATION   MICHELE R. FOLGER

Public Speaking

- "The New Public Relations," New York Public Relations Society, New York City, April 8, 2005.
- "How to Prepare an Effective Press Conference," Virginia Department of Public Relations, Richmond, Virginia, November 21, 2004.
- "New Approaches to Public Relations," United States Chamber of Commerce, Washington, D.C., February 26, 2003.

Professional Activities

- Delegate, State Writers' Conference, Roanoke, VA, 2005.
- Chair, Journalism Club, College of William and Mary, 2004.
- Secretary, Creative Writing Society, University of Cincinnati, 2003.
- Co-Chair, Public Relations in the United States Conference, College of William and Mary, 2000.
- Chair, Women's Conference, Junior League of Cincinnati, 1999.

Publications

- "The Creative Writer Today," Times Literary, Vol. 6, No. 3 (September 2004), pp. 34-51.
- "Representation of Minority Medical Students," Medical Education, Vol. 32, No. 1 (January 2003), pp. 206-218.
- "Recruiting Minority Students to Medical Colleges in the Northeast," Medical College Bulletin, Vol. 23, No. 4 (March 2001), pp. 21-29.

Reports

- "Increasing Representation of Minority Students in 50 Medical Colleges," submitted to the Foundation for Medical Education, Washington, DC, May 2004, 288 pages.
- "Urban Education as a Problem of Urban Decay," submitted to the Urban Education Foundation, New York City, September 2002, 421 pages.

Continuing Education

- "Grantsmanship Workshop," Williamsburg, Virginia, 2004.
- "Developing Public Relations Writing Skills," workshop, Washington, DC, 2002.
- "New Program Development Approaches for the 1990's," Virginia Beach, Virginia, 2000.
- "Research Design and Data Analysis in the Humanities," University of Michigan, 1998.

Educational Highlights

- Assistant Editor of the Literary Times, University of Cincinnati, 1995.
- Earned 3.8/4.0 grade point average as undergraduate and 4.0/4.0 as graduate student while working full time.
- M.A. Thesis: "Creating Writing Approaches to Public Relations."

David Watson

2211 Bailey Drive
Houston, Texas 77777
Tel. 123-456-9876
E-mail: davidw@wireme.com

Objective

A challenging position using skills in **Financial Analysis, Security Analysis, Budget Analysis,** and **Investment Strategies** that will be used to:

- strengthen a company's financial position
- identify new investment opportunities
- develop effective financial strategies
- forecast and manage future performance

Qualifications Summary

Detail- and results-oriented individual with strong analytical and entrepreneurial skills in accounting and financial systems. Adept at using statistical and other forecasting models for creating budgets, improving business operations, and developing investment strategies. Proven ability to create and implement effective cost management systems. Over 8 years of progressive responsibility and expertise in financial environments dealing with:

Financial Analysis/Planning	Investment Analysis	Accounting
Strategic Planning	Cash Management	Contracting
Credit Analysis	Budget Analysis	Valuation
Mergers and Acquisitions	Financial Management	Research
E-commerce	Risk Management	Project Management

Experience and Accomplishments

Finance

- Managed financial operation of government contractor with $15 million in assets and $25 million in annual revenue. **Results:** Saved over $50,000 in annual accounting costs by strengthening leadership over all accounting, payroll, banking, and risk management functions.

- Analyzed financial statements and other related reports, using ratio analysis to identify possible weaknesses in the company's financial operations and recommended remedial actions. **Results:** Improved procedures enabled company to develop aggressive marketing strategy for generating an additional $5 million in revenue.

- Developed and administered new defined contribution, profit sharing, and cafeteria plans. **Results:** Employee turnover reduced by 20 percent over a 12-month period.

- Prepared reports that summarized and forecasted company business activity based on past, present, and expected operations. Used various forecasting techniques, such as regression, moving averages, and other econometric models, to establish the forecasted figures. **Results:** Earnings forecasts, which were 95 percent accurate in the first six months, established new investment strategy for a 20 percent annual growth rate.

- Created the operational, cash, and capital budgets of several small companies. Introduced simplified small business accounting software programs to manage day-to-day accounting functions. **Results:** Saved each business over $30,000 annually by eliminating the need to hire a full-time accountant.

Accounting

- Defended employer before Contract Board of Appeals. **Results:** Saved employer over $200,000 in disallowed contract costs emanating from a FTAC audit.

- Performed all facets of accounting, including accounts payable, receivable, payroll functions, and general ledger account reconciliation and bank reconciliation statements. **Results:** Eliminated the need for two part-time bookkeeping positions and thus saved employer over $40,000 a year in personnel costs.

- Prepared corporate financial statements, including income statements, balance sheets, and cash flow statements for both internal and external reporting. **Results:** Improved on-time reporting by 300% within first six months and developed attractive financial portfolio for generating $8 million in outside investment.

- Introduced a budgetary system that inculcated a culture of cost control awareness. **Results:** Streamlined the service delivery system of a training company and saved over $100,000 annually in wasteful processes.

- Developed sensitivity models for determining break-even sales volume for each corporate division. **Results:** Improved profitability of five divisions by 15 percent within six months and eliminated one unprofitable division which saved the company more than $200,000.

Professional Experience

DELTA COMPUTER SERVICES, Orlando, FL   1999 – Present
Controller

THE TRAINING GROUP, Atlanta, GA   1994 – 1998
Senior Accountant

SEVEN SMALL BUSINESSES   1992 – Present
Part-time consultant in various aspects of accounting

Education

University of Illinois   MBA, Finance   1999

- Developed award-winning e-commerce business model for reaching undergraduate students
- Interned with KPMG as Investment Analyst

Vanderbilt University   BA, Accounting   1994

- Graduated with Honors, 3.8/4.0
- Worked full-time in earning 100% of educational and personal expenses

Computer Skills

- Microsoft Word   - Excel   - Access   - PowerPoint
- PageMaker   - PhotoShop   - Lotus Notes

Memberships and Affiliations

- Society of Investment Analysts   - American Society of Accountants
- American Association of Individual Investors   - Toastmasters International

October 10, _____

Emily Thomas
James David Corporation
123 Fort Wayne Boulevard
Tampa, Florida 12345

Dear Ms. Thomas:

I'm responding to your job announcement that appeared on the CareerWeb site yesterday for a Public Relations Specialist. My resume is available online (#281481) with CareerWeb and I e-mailed a copy to you yesterday per your instructions.

I believe I may be the perfect candidate for this position given my more than eight years of progressive, results-oriented experience in Public Relations:

Your Requirements	**My Qualifications**
5+ years of experience in PR	8+ years of experience in PR as well as sales and marketing. I understand the important relationship between PR and sales and marketing.
Strong interpersonal skills	Consistently praised on annual performance appraisal as *"adept in working well with both co-workers and clients."* Twice received "Employee of the Year" Award.
Ability to bring in new accounts	Maintained and significantly expanded (20% annually) client base of key accounts that generate 30% of employer's total revenue base – up from 5% when hired three years ago.
Energetic and willing to travel	Work well with deadlines and stressful situations. Energy and enthusiasm cited by clients as a main reason for working with Joan Riley. Love to travel and do so frequently in working with clients and participating in professional activities.

In addition, I know the importance of building strong customer relations and developing innovative approaches to today's new PR mediums. I love taking on new challenges, working in multiple team and project settings, and seeing clients achieve results from my company's efforts.

I believe there is a strong match between your needs and my professional interests and qualifications. Could we meet soon to discuss how we might best work together? I'll call your office Thursday at 2pm to see if your schedule might permit such a meeting.

I appreciate your consideration and looking forward to speaking with you on Thursday.

Sincerely,

Joan Riley

Joan Riley

Appendix C

Effective Job Search Letters

T HE FOLLOWING TYPES OF LETTERS are written in reference to our discussion of letter writing in Chapter 9. In addition, they relate to several resumes appearing in Appendix B.

The resume letters on pages 237 and 238 are designed for the high school graduate (John Albert) and the M.A. degree recipient (Michele R. Folger) in Appendix B. The cover letters on pages 239 and 240 relate to the A.S. and B.A. graduates (Gary S. Platt and Cheryl Ayers) in Appendix B. The approach letters on pages 241 and 242 are designed for the high school graduate (John Albert) in Appendix B and the B.A. graduate (Gail S. Topper) in Appendix A.

Six types of thank-you letters are presented on pages 243-248: the standard post interview, post informational interview, response to a rejection, withdrawal from consideration, acceptance of a job offer, and terminating employment. These are some of the most powerful job search letters anyone can and should write. They may have a greater impact on employers than your resume or interview.

All of these letters follow the principles outlined in Chapter 9 on how to write effective job search letters. Pay particular attention to closing paragraphs that initiate follow-up actions.

Resume Letter

1099 Seventh Avenue
Akron, OH 34522

August 25, _____

Michael C. Marvis, President
MARVIS CONSTRUCTION COMPANY
1121 Jackson Blvd.
Akron, OH 24520

Dear Mr. Marvis:

Your recently completed shopping complex on Eighth Avenue is well designed and compatible with the existing neighborhood. I am particularly impressed with how you placed the parking area next to the main access points for the restaurant and theatre complex.

I am especially interested in your work because my background is in architectural drafting. I know good design, and I want to associate with a firm that will fully use my talents. My qualifications include:

- Three years of architectural drafting experience; helped develop plans for $14 million of residential and commercial construction.

- Three years handling all aspects of construction – building and installing cabinets, reconstructing commercial building, pouring concrete.

- Collected and evaluated data for controlling quality of construction.

- Trained as a draftsman.

At present I am seeking an opportunity to use my skills in developing projects similar to your Eighth Avenue shopping complex. I would appreciate an opportunity to meet with you to discuss our mutual interests. I will call your office next week to arrange a convenient time.

I look forward to meeting you.

Sincerely,

John Albert

John Albert

Resume Letter

773 Main Street
Williamsburg, VA 23572

November 12, _____

Barbara Thompson, President
SRM ASSOCIATES
421 91st Street
New York, NY 11910

Dear Ms. Thompson:

I just completed reading the article in <u>Business Today</u> on SRM Associates. Your innovative approach to recruiting minorities is of particular interest to me because of my background in public relations and minority recruitment.

I am interested in learning more about your work as well as the possibilities of joining your firm. My qualifications include:

- research and writing on minority recruitment and medical education

- secured funding for and administered a $845,000 minority representation program

- published several professional articles and reports on creative writing, education, and minorities

- organized and led public relations, press, and minority conferences

- M.A. in Journalism and B.A. in English

I will be in New York City during the week of December 10. Perhaps your schedule would permit us to meet briefly to discuss our mutual interests. I will call your office next week to see if such a meeting can be arranged.

I appreciate your consideration.

Sincerely yours,

Michele R. Folger

Michele R. Folger

Cover Letter
(Referral)

2237 South Olby Road
Sacramento, CA 97342

July 17, _____

David Myers
Vice President
FULTON ENGINEERING CORPORATION
1254 Madison Street
Sacramento, CA 97340

Dear Mr. Myers:

John Bird, the Director of Data Systems at Ottings Engineering Company, informed me that you are looking for someone to direct your new management information system.

I enclose my resume for your consideration. During the past 10 years I have developed and supervised a variety of systems. I have worked at both the operational and managerial levels and know how to develop systems appropriate for different types of organizations.

I would appreciate an opportunity to visit with you and examine your operations. Perhaps I could provide you with a needs assessment prior to an interview. I will call you next week to make arrangements for a visit.

Thank you for your consideration.

Sincerely,

Gary S. Platt

Gary S. Platt

Cover Letter
(Response to Advertised Position)

2589 Jason Drive
Ithaca, NY 14850
April 3, _____

Sharon A. Waters
Personnel Director
NEW YORK STATE POLICE DEPARTMENT
892 South Park
Albany, NY 11081

Dear Ms. Waters:

I enclose my resume in response to your November 1 listing in the Ithaca College Placement Office for a research and data analyst with your department.

The position interests me for several reasons. My education and work experience have prepared me for this position. On May 15 I will receive my B.S. degree in Criminal Justice, with specialties in research and data analysis. I am familiar with the New York State Police operations based upon my work in your Albany office this past summer and upon my research on apprehension rates.

The position you outline is one which I feel I can enhance with my technical background as well as my active leadership roles which involve extensive planning, organizing, and communicating. I am a responsible person who is concerned with performance and accountability.

I would appreciate an opportunity to discuss with you how I might best meet your needs. I will call your office next week to inquire about an interview.

Thank you for your consideration.

Sincerely,

Cheryl Ayers

Cheryl Ayers

Approach Letter
(Referral)

1099 Seventh Avenue
Akron, OH 44522

December 10, _____

Janet L. Cooper, Director
Architectural Design Office
RT ENGINEERING ASSOCIATES
621 West Grand Avenue
Akron, OH 44520

Dear Ms. Cooper:

John Sayres suggested that I write to you in regards to my interests in architectural drafting. He thought you would be a good person to give me some career advice.

I am interested in an architectural drafting position with a firm specializing in commercial construction. As a trained draftsman, I have six years of progressive experience in all facets of construction, from pouring concrete to developing plans for $14 million in commercial and residential construction. I am particularly interested in improving construction design and building operations of shopping complexes.

Mr. Sayres mentioned you as one of the leading experts in this growing field. Would it be possible for us to meet briefly? Over the next few months I will be conducting a job search. I am certain your counsel would assist me as I begin looking for new opportunities.

I will call your office next week to see if your schedule permits such a meeting.

Sincerely,

John Albert

John Albert

Approach Letter
(Cold Turkey)

136 West Davis St.
Washington, DC 20030
October 2, ____

Sharon T. Avery
Vice President for Sales
BENTLEY ENTERPRISES
529 W. Sheridan Road
Washington, DC 20011

Dear Ms. Avery:

I am writing to you because you know the importance of having a knowledgeable, highly motivated, and enthusiastic sales force market your fine information processing equipment. I know because I have been impressed with your sales representatives.

I am seeking your advice on how I might prepare for a career in your field. I have a sales and secretarial background – experience acquired while earning my way through college.

Within the coming months I hope to begin a new career. My familiarity with word processing equipment, my sales experience, and my Bachelor's degree in communication have prepared me for the information processing field. I want to begin in sales and eventually move into a management level position.

As I begin my job search, I am trying to gather as much information and advice as possible before applying for positions. Could I take a few minutes of your time next week to discuss my career plans? Perhaps you could suggest how I can improve my resume – which I am now drafting – and who might be interested in my qualifications. I will call your office on Monday to see if such a meeting can be arranged.

I appreciate your consideration and look forward to meeting you.

Sincerely,

Gail S. Topper

Gail S. Topper

Thank-You Letter
(Post Interview)

1947 Grace Avenue
Springfield, MA 01281
November 17, _____

James R. Quinn, Director
Personnel Department
DAVIS ENTERPRISES
2290 Cambridge Street
Boston, MA 01181

Dear Mr. Quinn:

Thank you for the opportunity to interview yesterday for the Sales Trainee position. I enjoyed meeting you and learning more about Davis Enterprises. You have a fine staff and a sophisticated approach to marketing.

Your organization appears to be growing in a direction which parallels my interests and career goals. The interview with you and your staff confirmed my initial positive impressions of Davis Enterprises, and I want to reiterate my strong interest in working for you. My prior experience in operating office equipment plus my training in communication would enable me to progress steadily through your training program and become a productive member of your sales team.

Again, thank you for your consideration. If you need any additional information from me, please feel free to call.

Yours truly,

Gail S. Topper

Gail S. Topper

Thank-You Letter
(After Informational Interview)

921 West Fifth Street
Denver, CO 72105

July 18, _____

James R. Taylor
Assistant Manager
ASSOCIATED FINANCIAL ADVISORS
241 Skyline Road
Denver, CO 71088

Dear Mr. Taylor:

Joan Karvin was right when she said you would be most helpful in advising me on a career in finance.

I appreciated you taking time from your busy schedule to meet with me. Your advice was most helpful and I have incorporated your suggestions into my resume. I will send you a copy next week.

Again, thanks so much for your assistance. As you suggested, I will contact Mr. David James next week in regards to a possible opening with his company.

Sincerely,

John Perkins

John Perkins

Thank-You Letter
(Responding to Rejection)

1947 Grace Avenue
Springfield, MA 01281

September 14, ____

Sharon T. Avery
Vice President for Sales
BENTLEY ENTERPRISES
529 W. Sheridan Road
Washington, DC 20011

Dear Ms. Avery:

Thank you for giving me the opportunity to interview for the Customer Services Representative position. I appreciate your consideration and interest in me. I learned a great deal from our meetings.

Although I am disappointed in not being selected for your current vacancy, I want you to know that I appreciated the courtesy and professionalism shown to me during the entire selection process. I enjoyed meeting you, John Roberts, and other members of your sales staff. My meetings confirmed that Bentley Enterprises would be an exciting place to work and build a career.

I want to reiterate my strong interest in working for you. Please keep me in mind should another position become available in the near future.

Again, thank you for the opportunity to interview. Best wishes to you and your staff.

Yours truly,

Gail S. Topper

Gail S. Topper

Thank-You Letter
(Withdrawing from Consideration)

733 Main Street
Williamsburg, VA 23512

December 1, _____

Dr. Thomas C. Bostelli, President
NORTHERN STATES UNIVERSITY
2500 University Drive
Greenfield, MA 03241

Dear Dr. Bostelli:

It was indeed a pleasure meeting with you and your staff last week to discuss your need for a Director of Public and Government Relations. Our time together was most enjoyable and informative.

As I discussed with you during our meetings, I believe one purpose of preliminary interviews is to explore areas of mutual interest and to assess the fit between the individual and the position. After careful consideration, I have decided to withdraw from consideration for the position.

My decision is based upon several factors. First, the emphasis on fund raising is certainly needed, but I would prefer more balance in my work activities. Second, the position would require more travel than I am willing to accept with my other responsibilities. Third, professional opportunities for my husband would be very limited in northwest Massachusetts.

I want to thank you for interviewing me and giving me the opportunity to learn about your needs. You have a fine staff and faculty, and I would have enjoyed working with them.

Best wishes in your search.

Sincerely,

Janet L. Lawson

Janet L. Lawson

Thank-You Letter
(Accepting Job Offer)

2589 Jason Drive
Ithaca, NY 14850

August 19, ____

Sharon A. Waters
Personnel Director
NEW YORK STATE POLICE
Administrative Division
892 South Park
Albany, NY 11081

Dear Ms. Waters:

I want to thank you and Mr. Gordon for giving me the opportunity to work with the New York State Police. I am very pleased to accept the position as a research and data analyst with your planning unit. The position requires exactly the kind of work I want to do, and I know that I will do a good job for you.

As we discussed, I shall begin work on July 1, _____. In the meantime, I shall compete all the necessary employment forms, obtain the required physical examination, and locate housing. I plan to be in Albany within the next two weeks and would like to deliver the paperwork to you personally. At that time we could handle any remaining items pertaining to my employment. I'll call next week to schedule an appointment with you.

I enjoyed my interviews with you and Mr. Gordon and look forward to beginning my job with the Planning Unit.

Sincerely,

Cheryl Ayers

Cheryl Ayers

cc: Mr. Edward Gordon, Administrator,
    Planning Unit

Thank-You Letter
(Terminating Employment)

1099 Seventh Avenue
Akron, OH 44522

August 2, _____

Mr. James T. Thomas
Chief Engineer
AKRON CONSTRUCTION COMPANY
1170 South Hills Highway
Akron, OH 44524

Dear Jim,

I am writing to inform you that I will be leaving Akron Construction Company on September 12 to accept another position.

As you know, I have developed an interest in architectural drafting which combines my drafting skills with my artistic interests. While I was vacationing in Houston recently, a relative approached me about an opening for someone with my background with a large architecture and engineering firm. I investigated the possibility and, consequently, received an offer. After careful consideration, I decided to accept the offer and relocate to Houston. I will be working with Brown and Little Company.

I have thoroughly enjoyed working with you over the past two years, and deeply appreciate your fine supervision and support. You have taught me a great deal about drafting, and I want to thank you for providing me with the opportunity to work here. It has been a very positive experience for me both personally and professionally.

I wanted to give you more than the customary two weeks notice so you would have time to find my replacement. I made the decision to relocate yesterday and decided to inform you immediately.

Best wishes.

Sincerely,

John Albert

John Albert

Appendix D

Resumes and Letters From Career Professionals

THE FOLLOWING COLLECTION OF resumes and letters comes from the files of four professional resume writers and career coaches who share their work in this edition of *High Impact Resumes and Letters*. As we discussed in the Preface and on pages 63 and 191-193, you may want to use the services of such professionals at various stages of your job search. These are talented individuals who specialize in writing resumes and job search letters. Many of them also offer related career coaching services. Once you have completed this book, you should be able to specify exactly what types of professional career services will best meet your needs.

Whatever you do, don't hesitate to contact a career professional for assistance when it comes time to write your resume and letters. What little money you spend on their services will more than pay for itself if your expertly crafted documents turn into invitations to job interviews that eventually result in job offers!

The following career professionals contributed the resume examples that appear in this Appendix:

Louise Garver, MA, CMP, CPRW, CEIP, MCDP, JCTC
Career Directions LLC
Website: www.CareerDirectionsLLC.com
E-mail: CareerPro@cox.net
Tel. 860-623-9476
Fax 860-623-9473

Susan Guarneri, MS, NCCC, DCC, MCC, CPRW, CERW, CCMC, CEIP
Websites: Resume-Magic.com
         CareerMagicCoach.com
E-mail: Resumagic@aol.com
Tel. 866-881-4055
Fax 715-546-8039

Don Orlando, MBA, CPRW, JCTC, CCM, CCMC
The McLean Group
E-mail: Yourcareercoach@aol.com
Tel. 334-264-2020
Fax 334-264-9227

Janice M. Shepherd, CPRW, CEIP, JCTC
Write On Career Keys
Bellingham Washington
Tel. 360-738-758
Fax 360-738-1189
Website: www.writeoncareerkeys.com
E-mail: janice@writeoncareerkeys.com

The following examples are organized by each career professional. In so doing, you will get an inside view of how such professionals approach their subjects. Better yet, you will be able to see the differences in approaches and styles to resume and letter writing. You'll also be able to benefit from the analyses offered by career professionals, such as Susan Guarneri (pages 251-286) who carefully walks us through her rationale for crafting a particular type of resume and letter and then shares with us the actual outcomes for her clients.

One theme that runs throughout these examples is that there are no hard-and-fast rules on resume and letter writing. While ideally you should try to keep your resume to one or two pages, in some of these examples, resumes run three or more pages. But look carefully at the extensive backgrounds and experiences of these clients. Such lengthy resumes work well in certain cases. You'll also see the use of "core competencies" for communicating skills and accomplishments. And you'll see a variety of attractive layouts. But most important of all, you'll see what talented professional resume writers produce for their clients – stand-out resumes that grab the attention of potential employers.

Susan Guarneri

MS, NCCC, DCC, MCC, CPRW, CERW, CCMC, CEIP
Susan Guarneri Associates/CareerMagicCoach
6670 Crystal Lake Road
Three Lakes, WI 54562
Websites: Resume-Magic.com
CareerMagicCoach.com
E-mail: Resumagic@aol.com
Tel. 866-881-4055
Fax 715-546-8039

With more than 20 years of experience in the career field, Susan's work represents the very best among career counselors and consultants. Known as the Career Assessment Goddess, she is the only National Certified Career Counselor with additional certifications in personal branding, career coaching, and professional resume writing.

Susan has provided extensive resume writing, career consulting, and outplacement services to thousands of individuals as well as Fortune 500 companies, colleges, and non-profit agencies. Her articles and sample resumes and cover letters have appeared in major professional publications, books, and websites. In addition, Susan has been interviewed on Richard Bolles's live radio show, *JobTalk*, on "How to Create a Better Resume."

In the following examples Susan brings together a unique, powerful, and informative set of resumes and letters that provide the reader with an inside view of a top professional's decision making processes and the hard work involved in packaging clients who pose special challenges for career professionals. Indeed, these are not slam-dunk resumes designed for perfect clients. Each client poses special issues and challenges, as you will see in the story threads that run throughout Susan's analyses. In her own words Susan candidly explains what she did and why, from focusing on special skills to selecting particular type styles. Especially important, she reveals results-oriented outcomes for her clients.

While Susan includes Objectives on three of her resume examples (Cossich, Massingill, and Mace), the remaining resumes present powerful summary statements of targeted accomplishments at the very beginning – an excellent choice that is reinforced throughout the rest of the clients' resumes.

We invite you to carefully examine each of Susan's examples, along with her compelling stories and analyses of each. In so doing, you'll learn a great deal about the resume and letter writing processes of a top professional. You also may discover why it's often good to have a talented professional to work with since, after all, you may be too close to your subject to discover what's best for you!

Kevin T. Blackmore, Jr.

17 Prospect Heights Avenue	Home: 908-527-7441
Union, NJ 07083	Mobile: 908-351-1113
	Kevblack@newmedia.net

MARKETING ASSOCIATE / ADVERTISING ASSOCIATE
Client Relationship Management / Business Customer Acquisition

- **College graduate** with unique blend of experience in customer acquisition, sales/marketing, operations management, client relationship management, and team building in commercial (B2B) marketplace.

- **Creative, energetic developer** of high-level (95%) repeat and referral business. Enhanced revenues, expanded customer account base, and boosted client retention by selling and cross-selling full-service, custom-designed flooring solutions for discriminating buyers within a highly competitive market.

- **Solid customer relationship management skills,** with ability to build on credibility and gain clients' respect and trust quickly. Motivated team player willing to "go the extra mile," partnering with customers and contractors to devise optimal design options for projects ranging from $10,000 to $40,000. Additional proven skills and experience in:

■ Client Relationship Management	■ Consultative Sales	■ Opportunity Identification
■ Operations / Project Management	■ Communications	■ Account Development
■ Customer Acquisition Strategies	■ Revenue Growth	■ Training & Team Management

EDUCATION & TRAINING

Bachelor of Arts, Visual Communications – Kean University, Union, NJ – May 2005
Courses: Interactive Media Design, Photography, PhotoShop, Graphic Design, Visual Communications

Technology Summary: Windows XP/ME, Microsoft Office 2000/2003/XP (Word, Excel), QuarkXpress 5, Adobe Illustrator 10, Adobe PhotoShop 7, Macromedia Flash 5, Internet, PC and Mac platforms.

PROFESSIONAL EXPERIENCE

CAPITOL TILE, MARBLE, & FLOORING – Union, NJ   1998 – present
Family-owned subcontracting firm (tile, hardwood flooring, and carpeting) catering to upscale construction trade.

Project Manager / Designer (functioning as Operations Manager/Business Developer)
Worked full-time while attending college (GPA 3.8). Promoted to Operations Management in 2001, and supervise 12 F/T and 8 P/T employees. Work in tandem with owner, branding and guiding thriving business.

- **Sales Growth.** Key player in propelling business within 7 years from $80,000 to $2.5 million. Initiated direct marketing cold calls with new-home general contractors, growing major contractor accounts from 3 to 10 (single-family home and condo projects increased from 30 in 1998 to 150 projects in 2004).

- **Customer Relationship Management.** Collaborate with homeowners and contractors to design and develop elaborate layouts, becoming trusted project advisor. Utilize solution-selling techniques and creative design skills to create added value and extend relationships, cross selling and up-selling to generate additional revenues and solidify account penetration.

- **Training & Team Motivation.** Develop, schedule and motivate 4-6 work crews (3-5 laborers and mechanics each) for custom new-home flooring construction projects. Handpicked to train and supervise employees in new installation techniques, quality production, and top-notch customer service practices.

- **Leadership.** Chosen to run daily operations, including sales and business development, benchmarking streamlined operations processes and innovative marketing strategies to promote best-in-class services.

Analysis of Blackmore Resume

With his new degree in Communications, Kevin wanted to change careers from Project Manager in a construction trades firm to Marketing and Advertising. The challenge was to position this new graduate also as an experienced job seeker, with relevant accomplishments to marketing and sales, so that he might "jump on" the marketing career ladder a bit higher up than just entry-level (i.e., making a higher salary).

I positioned his objective clearly at the top in the header area so there could be no confusion about the career path he was pursuing and followed it with relevant bullets supporting that objective (included quantifiers for "proof"). I also positioned the relevant keyword table at optimum eye level in the resume.

Following the Summary section lead-in, I prominently display his up-to-date and relevant Education, selected coursework, and array of Technology skills particularly important to Marketing.

The contact info, Objective header, Summary section, and Education section occupy a bit more than the top half of the resume. The Professional Experience follows last (bottom half of the page). It details his promotion and level of functioning, including supervisory experience. Then I selectively displayed his relevant accomplishments with bullet points. I used keyword lead-in phrases highlighted in boldface that conveyed his background in Sales & Marketing, Customer Relationship Management, Training, Team Motivation, and Leadership (all potentially important to a Marketing position). The accomplishments conveyed the scope of his job, as well as many results that either drove revenue or cut costs.

Outcome: Kevin found a job after three months (he needed additional coaching on interviewing) as an Assistant Director of Marketing and Sales for a regional tourism center in southern New Jersey. I had to coach him on how to talk about **relevant** marketing and sales experiences from his job, rather than talking flooring construction!

Henry A. Peterson, MBA, CPA

713 Excelsior Drive
Madison, WI 55715
hankpeters@gmail.com

Home: 608.663.5881
Mobile: 610.713.9945
Fax: 608.721.1121

Date

Name and Title
Organization
Address
City, State, Zip Code

Dear *Recruiter Name,*

Do you have a client in need of a **Senior Executive (CEO / President / COO) – Healthcare Delivery System or Hospital** with proven results in competitive healthcare markets and a tough economy? Whether developing new strategic alliances and joint ventures, responding to market challenges, motivating teams, or controlling expenses and leveraging cash flow, my track record includes (see résumé enclosed):

☑ **Strategic Business Development and Revenue Generation.** Spearheaded strategic visioning, tactical planning, operations and financial management in boom and bust markets that grew revenues and differentiated Edgewood Health from its competition. Turned $1.0 million loss into record $17.0 million profit over last three years. Pioneered joint venture with two independent health systems to launch new patient care technology solution within next 12 months. Developed PHO with 225 physicians and managed-care contracting network of 72,000+ insured lives.

☑ **Market-Responsive Growth Initiatives.** Focused on niche "branding" opportunities that realized 20.8% orthopedic growth and 12% gastro-intestinal growth in last three years. Involved employees in strategic planning and goal setting, facilitating vision "buy-in" and ownership. Championed effort to adjust organizational culture to support achievement of new value propositions and strategies. Result: consumer confidence and brand differentiation jumped to record levels (2004 survey). Edgewood is now the market leader in cardiac surgery, orthopedic surgery, and general surgery.

☑ **Quality / Process Improvement.** Positioned Edgewood Health as a low cost/high quality hospital by standardizing processes, eliminating operational inefficiencies, and improving medical staff relations. Results: National awards won, including Solcient's 100 Top Hospitals designation. HMO Capitol City Health Plan became first NCQA-accredited HMO in Wisconsin and won recognition as #1 health plan in the U.S. for prevention and wellness (2002 and 2003).

☑ **Corporate Financial Management.** Initiated and led long-term plans for capital accumulation and capital deployment to support growth strategies. Led four major tax-exempt bond-financing transactions and saved $1.4 million in interest with remarketing transaction in 1993. Managed $53.0 million hospital redevelopment project and developed 16 high-ROI physician clinic sites.

After 19 years with Edgewood, I am ready for new challenges. My geographic preference centers on the Midwest states. Although paid well ($225,000+ annually), I am not tied to finding a position where I am paid more than my current compensation. While EVP and CFO for the last seven years, I have functioned as #2 senior executive, partnering with the CEO and Board in all executive strategies, operations, and finances.

Realizing it is people who deliver results, my focus has been on building relationships with staff, managers, vendors, customers, and strategic partners as a primary tool for business excellence. With executive experience and expertise, as well as enthusiasm, drive, and seasoned leadership, I would like the opportunity to guide your client's organization to new levels of success. Thank you for your consideration.

Sincerely,

Henry A. Peterson

Henry A. Peterson
Enclosure

Analysis of Peterson Cover Letter

This client spent 19 years at Edgewood Health building his career, believing that some day he would become CEO. In his last job he even functioned as the #2 senior executive. However, when the CEO stepped down, the Board decided they needed "fresh blood" and passed Henry by for the promotion. The challenge was how to convey he IS CEO material, even though it would be readily apparent to the recruiter that he was not "bumped up" to the CEO job.

This cover letter (to be sent to a recruiter in the Healthcare arena) highlights his high-level accomplishments in every area of the Edgewood Health organization by using bullet points that are check-marked boxes with boldface leader phrases.

The initial interest-grabber first sentence is a question and makes clear (via boldface) the type of position he's seeking and in what industry (makes it quick for the recruiter to determine at first glance).

The first paragraph describes the value he can bring to an organization.

His salary and geographic requirements (essential for a recruiter to know) are listed in the next to last paragraph, and show that he is flexible.

The last paragraph speaks to his executive management philosophy and definitive characteristics. No pushy ending about calling – recruiters hate that approach!

Outcome: Within two months he was tapped to fill the CEO position at a major hospital in Middleton, Wisconsin.

Henry A. Peterson, MBA, CPA

713 Excelsior Drive
Madison, WI 55715
hankpeters@gmail.com

Home: 608.663.5881
Mobile: 610.713.9945
Fax: 608.721.1121

CEO / PRESIDENT / COO
Healthcare Management / Hospital Administration

- **Senior Executive with MBA in Healthcare Administration and proven expertise** in change management providing visionary leadership, strategic insight, and competitive plans during challenging economic periods. Track record of increasing revenues, improving quality and productivity, leading brand differentiation, executing business strategy, and directing turnarounds and transitions in tough markets.

- **Positive leadership style,** eliciting high levels of respect and loyalty from employees. Successful in building and empowering productive, quality teams who "see the vision" and own it. **Consultative business partner** integrating financial, operations, and administrative know-how to achieve objectives.

- **Well-honed executive presentation and communication skills,** with ability to connect benefits and value of recommendations to stakeholders' needs. Combine strategic and tactical financial expertise with strong foundation of general management, quality and process improvement, transaction structuring and negotiations, and proactive Board and staff relations to maintain environment of positive accountability.

AREAS OF EXPERTISE

- Leadership / Strategic Planning
- Quality / Process Improvement
- Corporate Financial Leadership
- Risk Management / Compliance

- Operations Management
- Corporate Development
- Turnaround Management
- Managed Care Contracting

- Executive Negotiations
- Medical Staff Relations
- Team Building / Motivation
- Cost Savings / Reductions

PROFESSIONAL EXPERIENCE

EDGEWOOD HEALTH, INC., Madison, WI   **1986 to present**
Leading multidiscipline healthcare delivery system (20 locations) in south central Wisconsin with 2,260 employees and net revenues of $224 million (2004). Consists of 170-bed inpatient and outpatient acute care hospital, 56-bed inpatient and outpatient psychiatric hospital, 100-physician primary care medical group, 187-member physician hospital organization (PHO), and managed care company, with associated ancillary subsidiaries and joint ventures.

Executive Vice President (EVP) and Chief Financial Officer (CFO) – 1998 to present
Partner with CEO and Board of Directors in all operations and strategic direction. Oversee managed care contracting and business customer relationships, PHO governance and direction, medical staff relations and recruitment, business growth strategies, and all financial matters. Full P&L for $216 million annual operating budget, $27 million capital budget, and $98 million in payroll. Manage 7 direct and 1,200 indirect reports.

- **Leadership / Competitive Differential Advantage.** Spearheaded strategic vision initiatives and plans that produced growth and record profitability despite competitive marketplace. Facilitated employee buy-in of vision, value proposition and strategies, including 21 high-level measures of progress. Employee retention rate at 90% (all-time high) and consumer surveys indicate improved brand differentiation.

- **Corporate Financial Leadership.** Established for-profit managed care company Partners in Health, Inc. in 1998 and negotiated ownership of HMO Capitol City Health Plan. Subsequent operations increased Edgewood's market share by 13%. Leveraged multi-million dollar gain on sale of HMO in 2004 to independent insurance company, yielding 100% ROI for shareholders.

- **Quality Improvement and Awards.** Co-led physician performance improvement plan regarding NCQA health initiatives. Result: HMO Capitol City Health Plan became first NCQA accredited HMO in Wisconsin and, in 2002 and 2003, achieved recognition as number one health plan in U.S. for prevention and wellness. Four-time recipient of Solcient's 100 Top Hospitals designation. Award of distinction for customer service (JD Power Associates) and recognition as distinguished hospital for clinical quality (Health Grades).

Henry A. Peterson | Home: 608.663.5881 | hankpeters@gmail.com | **Page 2**

- **Strategic Turnaround.** Partnered with senior leadership in creating $11 million annual waste reduction initiative (2001), as well as selected service growth strategies, that reversed $1.0 million operating loss in 2002 and led to $17.5 million profit in 2004 (most successful year in Edgewood's history).

- **PHO Development.** Recruited and developed first-class Physician Hospital Organization (PHO) of 225 physicians. Established corporate structure and worked with executive director to determine revenue sourcing, member dues, and service benefits, such as group supply and employee benefits purchasing. Enhanced PHO with managed-care contracting network strategy with more than 72.000 insured lives in contracting network.

- **Technology Development.** Created technology-solution joint venture (first ever in U.S.) with 2 independent healthcare systems in southern Wisconsin to launch electronic intensive care patient monitoring system (e-ICU) within next 12 months. Key team player in transition to new information system solutions, such as patient record automation and digital archiving of diagnostic images.

- **Process Improvements.** Introduced streamlined processes that enhanced reliability and contributed to Edgewood's current position as low cost producer of health care services in regional marketplace (10%-25% less than nearest competitors). Championed principles of "lean" thinking for all projects, such as patient registration simplification, which netted $200,000 in labor savings and patient goodwill.

- **Market Share Positioning.** Conceptualized and created "brand teams" to repackage service offerings into consumer-friendly, value-added products as response to new competitor entry in market (2001). Result: orthopedic volume level grew 20.8% and gastro-intestinal by 12% within last 3 years, positioning Edgewood as dominant market leader in cardiac surgery, orthopedic surgery, and general surgery.

- **Financial Management.** Partnered with investment banker in remarketing transaction of 1993 bond financing, saving $1.4 million in interest. Long-term financial planning has yielded $62 million in cash reserves, with all key ratios at or better than industry averages. Lead executive in 4 major tax-exempt bond financing transactions (1989, 1993, 2001, and 2003).

- **Cost Reductions.** Introduced new health benefit change incorporating financial and behavioral incentives that dropped average cost per plan employee by 24%-29% over past two years ($6.4 million saved), while improving average health assessment score for high risk and chronic group by 26.1%. Revised physician compensation to single model with uniform contract terms, saving $750,000 annually.

- **Redevelopment and Expansion.** Managed $53.0 million hospital redevelopment project and led development of 16 physician clinic sites over last 12 years. Clinic referrals constitute major component of increased market share to current 42%, and contribute $3.5 million net income annually. Collaborated with legal counsel in creating 8 out of 9 joint ventures, including JV with key cardiology physician group.

Chief Operating Officer (COO) and CFO – 1994 to 1998
Entrusted with oversight of business operations, financial affairs, and clinical quality while holding dual role. Managed 9 direct and 1,100 indirect reports (hospital clinical, support, and business staff). Reported to CEO.

- **Strategic Visioning.** Introduced strategic visioning, as well as short-, middle-, and long-range goals, at all department levels for clinical, support, and business areas, enabling steady growth in market share.

- **Change Management Initiatives.** Spearheaded far-reaching patient and employee safety improvements, reduced medication variances by 33%, and instituted latex-free environment. Resulted in workers compensation modification factor dropping below 0.70 (industry standard in excess of 1.00).

- **Organizational Realignment.** Led team that evaluated and reconfigured job descriptions, which eliminated multiple layers of hierarchy and reduced annual labor cost by $7 million. Boosted nurse satisfaction and retention rates to all-time high of 90%.

- **Take-over Threat Met Head-On.** Fended off adversarial take-over bid in 1997 by large competitor, which ended in favorable litigation outcome, maintaining Edgewood's independent status.

Henry A. Peterson | Home: 608.663.5881 | hankpeters@gmail.com | **Page 3**

Vice President of Finance (CFO role) – 1990 to 1994
Promoted to administer all financial affairs for system. Supervised five direct and 180 indirect reports.

- **Turnaround Leadership.** Oversaw turnaround of financially challenged 86-bed psychiatric hospital, which faced head-on competition in first three years of operation. Recouped initial start-up losses, with 2004 accumulated profit of $6.7 million. Outlasted for-profit competitor and negotiated favorable purchase of their more-efficient, one-story facility for psychiatric inpatient and outpatient services.

- **Cost Reduction Initiatives.** Led plan to reduce annual operating costs by $6.0 million during economic downturn (1991-1992). Restructured compensation strategies, eliminated inefficient spending, and standardized medical supply and pharmaceutical consumption which facilitated favorable vendor pricing.

- **Risk Management/Compliance.** Spearheaded first coordinated risk management program to ensure compliance with accreditation criteria. Formulated broad plan (still in existence with enhancements) to identify and ameliorate areas of high risk, safeguard assets, and provide safety for all staff and patients.

- **Capital Project Management.** Key player in major capital construction ($10 million project) of new surgical area, still considered state-of-the-art by surgeons, within Edgewood Hospital.

Controller – 1986 to 1990
Oversaw financial accounting/reporting, billing and collections, corporate banking, and cash management. Supervised 80 staff in Accounting, Billing, Medical Records, and Patient Admissions. Reported to CFO.

- **Financial Technology Introduction.** Challenged to implement decision support/cost accounting system that would accommodate 3,500+ billing/procedural elements in charge master. Completed new technology implementation within one year, including staff training related to software and financial reporting. Achieved model-site status with software vendor due to Edgewood's success with program.

- **Financial Reporting Expansion.** Revised rudimentary chart of accounts to provide more detail on expense reporting and resource allocation, enabling more accurate projections for annual budget.

- **Turnaround Leadership.** Brought struggling durable medical equipment subsidiary from $150,000 annual loss position to sustained profitability within two years. Scaled down product offerings, improved inventory controls, shortened billing and collection cycle, and eliminated redundant staff. Assisted VP of Finance in business downsizing Edgewood Hospital, restoring profitability for two consecutive years.

- **Cash Management Initiatives.** Reduced billing cycle time by 15 days by simplifying billing process and improving credit/collection policies and procedures. Yielded $3.0 million in positive cash flow.

ANDERSON, STONICKER & JONES, LLP, Milwaukee, WI   1980-1986
Financial consulting services CPA firm (accounting, auditing, and tax preparation) with 200 employees.

- **Audit Manager.** Promoted to Audit Manager within six years. Team participant in $250 million corporate acquisition transaction. Highly sought-after auditor for staffing client engagements.

EDUCATION & TRAINING

MBA, Health Care Administration (GPA 3.98), University of Wisconsin, Madison, WI – 2001
BBA, Accounting (Cum Laude), Carthage College, Kenosha, WI – 1979
Certification: Certified Public Accountant (CPA)

Recent Professional Development:
United States/United Kingdom Exchange, Health Care Management Association – 2004 and 2005

Institute for Health Care Management Improvement – 2003 and 2004

Managed Care Congress (Washington, D.C.) – 2003

Annual National Institute, Health Care Management Association – 1997

Henry A. Peterson | Home: 608.663.5881 | hankpeters@gmail.com | **Page 4**

PROFESSIONAL AFFILIATIONS

Health Care Management Association, Wisconsin Chapter – 1988 to present
President 1995-1996, President Elect 1994-1995, Treasurer 1993-1994, Board of Directors 1990-1993

American College of Health Care Professionals & Managers – 1995 to present

Wisconsin Healthcare Managers Association, Council on Finance – 1993 to present
President of Southern Region District 1998

COMMITTEES & DIRECTORSHIPS

Planning Committee, Edgewood Health, Inc. – Administrative Lead 2000 to present
Corporate Compliance Committee, Edgewood Health, Inc. – 1998 to present
Finance Committee, Edgewood Health, Inc. – Administrative Lead 1990 to present
Board of Directors, Capitol City Health Plan, Inc., Kenosha, WI – 1999 to present
Finance Committee, Michigan Shores Healthcare, Milwaukee, WI – 1999 to present
Board of Directors, Edgewood Physicians Group, LLC – 1998 to present
Board of Directors, Partners in Health, Madison, WI – 1997 to present
Governing Council, Shore Drive Hospice, Madison, WI – 1993 to present
Board of Directors, Edgewood Health Investments – 1990 to present

PRESENTATIONS

Edgewood Health, Leadership Development Classes, Madison, WI – 1994 to present
Developed curriculum and delivered leadership training to 300+ mid-level and senior-management professionals (four sessions over four weeks) employing interactive methods in small group settings. Curriculum supports organizational culture transformation, key to sustaining growth, change, and profitability.

Institute for Health Care Management Improvement, "Encouraging Community Involvement in Healthcare Development Strategies – A Survey," Washington, DC – December 1997

University of Wisconsin-Madison, Healthcare Leadership Forum, "The Upcoming Trends in Healthcare Management and Why You Should Care," Madison, WI – 1995, 1996, and 1997

Healthcare Management Association-Wisconsin Chapter, "Strategic Planning and Succession Management for Healthcare Institutions," Kenosha, WI – 1996

COMMUNITY INVOLVEMENT

Downtown Madison Rotary – 2003 to present

St. Mark Lutheran Church – 2002 to present
Congregation President 2004 to present, Chairman of Strategic Planning Committee 2002 to 2004

First Lutheran Church – 1986 to 2002
Congregation President, Board of Finance, Board of Elders

Leadership Madison Graduate, Madison Chamber of Commerce – 1989

Open to travel and relocation within U.S.

Analysis of Peterson Resume

This client spent 19 years at Edgewood Health building his career, believing that some day he would become CEO. In his last job he even functioned as the #2 senior executive. However, when the CEO stepped down, the Board decided they needed "fresh blood" and passed Henry by for the promotion. The challenge was how to convey he is CEO material, even though it would be readily apparent to the recruiter that he was not "bumped up" to the CEO job.

This executive resume needed to be more than two pages – Henry had accomplished a lot in various functional areas over his 19 years at Edgewood. The "meat" of the resume is the first two pages which cover 10 years of career history. Page three covers his previous career history with significant achievements as he climbed the career ladder at Edgewood, as well as his Education background. The final page is for the selected categories (Professional Affiliations, Committees & Directorships, Presentations, and Community Involvement) that would be expected on an executive resume. These categories underpin his leadership experiences and abilities, including executive-level communications.

Clear target is identified in the Header by position and industry.

Used a reverse-chronological format, with the most recent 10 years highlighted. Prior experience was condensed. Used bullets for accomplishments only (duties and responsibilities presented in paragraph style) and identified each accomplishment with a keyword lead-in phrase.

Created Summary of Qualifications with first bullet point a statement addressing the needs and expectations of a healthcare organization in today's economy for a high-level CEO. Remaining bullets in Summary address executive characteristics and "philosophy." Summary closely followed by Areas of Expertise (keyword summary).

Set the context for the company by explaining its services, scope, and ranking, and for each position by relating the scope and depth of the position. Accomplishments show results that are qualified and quantified, and that demonstrate high-level executive functioning and strategic thinking. Kept accomplishments succinct (two to four lines) while being descriptive in terms of challenge, actions, and results.

Outcome: Within two months he was tapped to fill the CEO position at a major hospital in Middleton, Wisconsin.

Jeffrey C. Smithson

| 111 Valley Road | Home: 975-618-0337
| Caldwell, NJ 07006 | jeffcsmithson@newgrads.com

SALES REPRESENTATIVE / SALES TRAINEE

- **Bachelor's Degree graduate** with experience in sales and marketing, project management, client relationship management, and teamwork in commercial (B2B) and consumer (B2C) marketplaces. Calm demeanor under stress and cooperative attitude contribute to team success. Passionate about excelling.

- **Solid customer relationship management and communication skills,** with ability to build on credibility and gain customers' respect and trust quickly. Motivated team player willing to "go the extra mile." Experienced in identifying needs, communicating creatively, and delivering on-target solutions.

- **Technology Summary:** Windows XP/2000, Microsoft Office Suite 2003, MS Word, MS Excel, MS Outlook, MS PowerPoint, SPSS, ACT, all Lotus systems, Internet, email.

EDUCATION & TRAINING

Master's Certificate: Miller Heiman Sales Masters Program   September 2005
Sales development (4 courses): Strategic Selling, Conceptual Selling, Negotiate Success, Executive Impact

B.S., Business Administration (Marketing major), Caldwell College, Caldwell, NJ   May 2005
Study Abroad Program (Humanities & Business), Queens College, London, England   Fall 2004

Related Coursework: Marketing Channels, Retailing, Strategic Marketing Management, Services Marketing, Consumer Behavior, International Marketing, Principles of Marketing, Sales Force Management, Public Speaking

RELATED EXPERIENCE

Pharmaceutical Solutions, Inc. (PSI), – Caldwell, NJ   Summer 2004
Global leader and supplier of custom formulation solutions for pharmaceutical and neutraeutical manufacturers.

Sales & Marketing Intern
- **Sales and Marketing Support.** Assisted Vice President of Marketing with special marketing projects, as well as daily duties. Generated follow-up phone calls to trade show attendees, capturing 22 new B2B client accounts. Supported 9 field sales representatives (via phone and email), as well as inside sales position. Used ACT database to retrieve client information and status of order fulfillment in real time.

- **Database Management.** Researched and created 4,00-file, cross-indexed database of competitive market intelligence for management's use in strategic decision making for upcoming fiscal year. Designed database to capture marketplace information regarding PSI's end-use customers for market research, market positioning and development, and new product development.

ADDITIONAL WORK EXPERIENCE

Edison Heights Country Club, Edison Heights, NJ   November 2003-August 2004
The Top of the Club Restaurant, Edison, NJ   March 1997-December 2003
Inspirations Restaurant, West Caldwell, NJ   May 2001-September 2002

Catered Event Coordinator & Waiter – Worked overlapping part-time jobs while attending school full ime.
- **Sales & Customer Service.** Served discriminating diners in popular, upscale restaurants, exceeding their expectations in highly service-oriented role. Developed and delivered persuasive sales presentations of nightly specials, and responded to unique customer needs, generating increased sales and customer satisfaction. Received recognition for top-notch customer service and positive attitude.

- **Project Management.** Chosen by country club management to coordinate, set up and supervise 100+ catered events (e.g., high-profile weddings, business conferences) in main banquet hall and off-site.

HONORS & AFFILIATIONS

Honors: Chosen (4 out of 40 applicants) to attend American Marketing Association's National Conference in Washington, DC (2005). Received All Academic Athletic Award from NCAA for Men's Swim Team efforts.

Affiliations (Caldwell College): American Marketing Association, Study Abroad Club, Men's Swim Team

Analysis of Smithson Resume

Jeff is a typical recent graduate in that he has worked several part-time restaurant jobs while attending college and had a short summer internship in his major field of study (marketing). Trying to make the most of those limited experience opportunities was a challenge. Luckily, Jeff also had some special "assets" to call upon for further proof of his abilities.

I formatted this resume to have impact visually, using bold graphic lines and a more contemporary typeface (Arial). Graphics elements separated the content into digestible chunks.

A clear objective sets the reader's expectations for what's to follow. Bulleted "proof" points summarize his relevant transferable skills (many keywords), education (including courses which were also keywords) and technology skills (again, many relevant keywords).

The Education & Training area starts with his specific sales training (Miller Heiman training is very well known and respected in the sales world). I put this **before** his Bachelor's Degree because of its high relevancy. I also indicated specific courses taken to show relevancy and keywords. Under his Bachelor's Degree I showed his internship abroad in London at Queens College (very well known for Business Administration program) as evidence that while he is a recent grad he also has international experience.

His experience is broken into "Related Experience" – his summer internship as a Sales & Marketing Intern (highly relevant to his objective) – and "Additional Work Experience" (his restaurant jobs). Under his internship I showed his Sales and Marketing experience first, followed by his DBM experience. I used functional lead-in phrases, bulleted points and quantifiers to show the scope of his job and accomplishments. All of his restaurant jobs were combined into a grouping, because all of the duties were the same. I showed separate accomplishment for country club under Project Management lead-in phrase.

Honors & Affiliations end the resume with items relevant to his objective, demonstrating his leadership and desire to excel. Affiliations show his membership in the American Marketing Association (highly relevant).

Outcome: Jeff obtained several offers from this resume within three months, but chose a Sales Rep job with a pharmaceutical company based out of northern New Jersey.

Elizabeth M. Hechinger

2721 Chesney Drive, West Long Branch, NJ 07764
(732) 571-9711 Home • elizahech@vpatmedia.net

September 18, 2005   Email Transmittal: jkrause@verticom.com
                                          Re: Project Manager position

John Krause
Managing Director, Learning Solutions
Verticom Corporation
212 Little Patuxent Parkway, Suite 331
Columbia, MD 21045

Dear Mr. Krause,

Verticom is on the path to exponential growth – and I'm poised and ready to help you achieve that goal. Creating effective, exciting solutions to operations and project-management challenges is what I do best. In fact, I am known as a "Make-It-Happen" person (my references are eager to validate that for you).

Whether working on corporate projects for start-up or early-growth-stage companies, or delivering on PR and fundraising goals for not-for-profit enterprises, I am committed to building relationships and parlaying the strengths of all stakeholders to achieve on-target, revenue-enhancing results, such as:

- Initiated dramatic changes in first weeks as Project Manager at Pharma Solutions Marketing (PSM) yielding cost reductions, faster project implementation, and higher quality (error rates slashed by 75%). Within first 2 months reconciled 6 problematic budgets ($100,000 each).

- Enhanced organizational performance at PSM, streamlining operations and building cross-divisional cooperation, to deliver 40 projects within 6 months (controlled budgets up to $2 million). Within first 2 weeks of hire, built team consensus, which had been stalled, on $2.5 million project. Restructured day-long project status meetings into 30-minute sessions that "cut-to-the-chase."

- Secured national publicity for American Standard Poodle Club from NBC Today Show and other media outlets, which resulted in highest fundraising year to date. Spearheading 2006 National Convention management with high-profile speakers (such as Dr. Jane Goodall) and international coverage. Centralized convention management to ensure continuity of sponsor and guest-speaker relationships, as well as optimizing efficiency of operations, logistics, marketing, and PR.

In addition, my "fit" with Verticom's culture and industry can be summed up in two words: values and experience. My values-driven personal credo aligns with your socially responsible mission and vision, and my experience meshes with your target clients: background in life sciences (degree in Food & Nutrition), early experience in the healthcare industry, and current business contacts in the healthcare, medical research, and pharmaceutical industries (such as Bristol-Myers Squibb, Johnson & Johnson, Robert Wood Johnson University Hospital, Interactive Health, and Ventiv Health).

If you are interested in improving the effectiveness and reach of your projects, as well as increasing the growth-generating trust of your clients, then I would like to share with you how I have done that in my previous roles...and how I believe I can do that for you. May we talk soon?

Sincerely,

Elizabeth M. Hechinger

Attachment: Résumé

Analysis of Hechinger Letter

Elizabeth had targeted Verticom as one of her "A" list companies and had cold-called the Managing Director of Learning Solutions. Due to her outgoing personality and tactful request, he agreed to look at her resume if she would e-mail it to him **and** send him a letter persuading him why he should read it. The challenge was how to convey her enthusiasm, relevant experience, and knowledge of Verticom to Mr. Krause (apparently he gets bombarded with hundreds of resumes daily from applicants when Verticom hasn't even posted job openings!) However, he did let slip in his conversation with Elizabeth that there was indeed a Project Management slot opening up.

This cover letter reflects Elizabeth's "voice" and outgoing personality combined with discreet professionalism (I used an unusual font, Gill Sans MT, rather than the standard Times Roman or Arial). The letter shows in the first and third paragraph that she had done her research about Verticom, and that she is a good "fit" for the company and a Project Management position within the company.

The selected bullet points show her strong project management accomplishments (including quantifiers and "name dropping") in both the business aspect of her life, as well as her avocational life (American Standard Poodle Club). This was done because her "formal" job as a Project Manager (last position held) only lasted six months due to a downsizing...so I wanted to show she really had more project management experience than just those six months.

Ended the letter by appealing to **his** interests ("improving the effectiveness and reach of your projects," "increasing growth-generating trust of your clients") and asking him (puts the power in his control) for a meeting.

The bulk of the letter is bulleted "proof" of her accomplishments, as well as a solid paragraph demonstrating her unusual "fit" with the organization – all communicated in a professional, non-pushy way that shows her genuine interest and excitement.

Elizabeth M. Hechinger

2721 Chesney Drive, West Long Branch, NJ 07764
(732) 571-9711 Home • elizahech@vpatmedia.net

Project Manager / Operations Manager
Project Facilitation ▪ Product Management ▪ Sales and Marketing ▪ PR

Proactive Project Manager with 20 years of progressive experience and expertise in project/ operations leadership and problem-solving roles for start-up, early-stage growth, and Fortune 500 companies. Leader in introducing systems methodologies and processes that streamline operations, increase revenues and profits, and achieve quality, production, and cost. Proven expertise in:

☑ Project Ownership / Leadership	☑ Vendor Management & Negotiation	☑ Project Development
☑ Strategic Product Launches	☑ New Product Planning & Marketing	☑ Budget Management
☑ Innovative Strategy Development	☑ Life Cycle Planning & Management	☑ Cost Avoidance

Keen understanding of commercial business priorities...a genuine team player committed to managing operations and projects while contributing to business development and revenue-producing activities. Cross-functional communications and interpersonal skills. Easily interface with high-profile business clients, manufacturers, distributors, consultants, staff, vendors, governmental agencies, media, and others.

PROFESSIONAL EXPERIENCE

PHARMA SOLUTIONS MARKETING, INC. (PSM), West Long Branch, NJ   January – June 2005
Leading consumer pharmaceutical marketing services firm specializing in patient relationship marketing. PSM markets 4 of top 10 best-selling drugs in world. Fortune 500 clients such as Pfizer, Wyeth, and J&J.

Project Manager
Recruited to direct cross-departmental project management for 6 divisions. Reported to President and CTO.

Project Management / Operations Management
- Managed multiple overlapping projects (40 within 6 months) from launch through client delivery for 12 Fortune 500 clients. Directed and monitored operations and admin-istrative logistics (controlled budgets up to $2 million) keeping projects on schedule and within or under budget. Pinpointed and eliminated bottlenecks, including project realignments involving changing client demands and vendor constraints.

- Led 12-member cross-divisional team through project management cycle for million-dollar-plus projects lasting 3-4 months. Within first 2 weeks of hire, built team consensus on $2.5 million project. Created collaborative team environment with focus on quality, customer service, and cost-effectiveness.

- Introduced continuous process improvements (e.g., workflow optimization, systems upgrades, and resource leveling) which increased efficiency by 10%, slashed error rate by 75%, and accelerated client satisfaction. Developed and maintained up-to-date project status reports/files (computerized and manual).

- Transitioned weekly 14-member project status meetings, comprised of executive board and department heads, from day-long events to 30-minute highly targeted sessions, saving them 112 hours per month. Led using top-notch organizational and time-management skills to juggle diverse expectations and topics.

Budget Management / Cost Avoidance / Revenue Generation
- Within first 2 months of hire, successfully reconciled 6 inherited problematic budgets ($100,000 each). Initiated financial systems technology improvements (computerized project tracking and vendor database) to facilitate seamless integration of personnel, technology, resources, production, and project reporting.

- Captured revenues through stringent vendor management (15 vendors, 10 freelancers, 8 consultants), re-negotiating cost estimates and contracts that saved $5,000 per project. Facilitated logistics and upgraded marketing materials (under tight budget) for 2 trade shows that won additional client business.

INNOVATIVE PRODUCTS, LLC, Jersey City, NJ   1997 – 2004
Operations Manager / Business Development
- Promoted to start-up international product development and licensing business (spin-off from Engineering Technologies). Key player in building business (ranked #3 nationally in home care appliances) through role in product planning and design, off-shore manufacturing and distribution channels, operations, marketing and sales, new product launches, client relationship management, and media/PR.

- Spearheaded and maintained administrative and legal structure for this international business. Developed and transitioned manual financial record keeping system to computerized financial systems.

- Developed initial product offering in less than 10 months, which represented 100% of revenues for first 2 years and continued to generate revenues thereafter. Played instrumental role in bringing 5 products to market in 5 years, capturing Revlon as key national account.

- Saved 2 production days per month and $4,000 in monthly expenses by changing from out-of-town to local attorneys. Realized 20% savings in annual corporate income taxes by sourcing new CPA.

ENGINEERING TECHNOLOGIES, INC., Jersey City, NJ   1988 – 1997
Operations Manager
- Contributed to rapid growth of engineering consulting group, which specialized in technology transfer and development, and litigation support. Reorganized chaotic office management systems, authored SOP manual, and introduced standardized tracking systems for cash flow, revenues, and operating expenses.

- Initiated and project managed transition from manual to computerized record-keeping system, which increased operations efficiency by 80% and eliminated need for 3 full-time employees.

Elizabeth M. Hechinger
(732) 571-9711 • elizahech@patmedia.net   Page 3

- Developed and managed effective PR and CRM strategies, which laid groundwork for securing and retaining major government, entertainment-industry, and international contracts.

NEW YORK STATE BROKER ASSOCIATES, New York, NY   1985 – 1987
Supervisor, Insurance Licensing Department
- Oversaw daily operations of mission-critical department for #2 stock brokerage NY headquarters and 43 domestic branch offices, maintaining 9,200 state licenses for 800 account executives. Managed staff of 12. Streamlined licensing process from 3 months to 3 weeks, which enabled 50% reduction in staff.

THE HELLERMAN GROUP, San Francisco, CA   1982 – 1985
Insurance Licensing Administrator
- Promoted from Account Executive to key administrative management role in corporate office. Established and managed Licensing Department for home office and 4 branch offices, representing 600 agent and broker licenses in 50 states. Restructured and streamlined complex licensing procedures.

EDUCATION

Bachelor of Science, Montclair State University, Upper Montclair, NJ
Continuing Education: Certificates in Project Management and Human Resources from the American Management Association and Zenger – Miller Frontline Leadership Program.

PROFESSIONAL AFFILIATIONS

Project Management Institute (PMI) – Professional Member
Edison Chapter of ACM / IEEE Computer Society – Board Member
American Standard Poodle Club – PR and Fundraising Manager

COMPUTER SKILLS

Windows XP, MS Office 2003, MS Project, Word, Excel, PowerPoint, Access, Outlook, Internet Explorer

Analysis of Hechinger Resume

Until recently Elizabeth had been in Operations Management for 16 years. She decided to make a career switch to Project Management and did secure a job with Pharma Solutions Marketing in West Long Branch, NJ. However, it only lasted six months before her position was downsized. The challenge was to show she had significant project management experience, even though her job only lasted six months.

I formatted this resume using bold design graphics and contemporary typeface (Gill Sans MT). It's two pages long – the first page starts with a Summary Section, showing her career target area (Project Management / Operations Management) along with a keyword-rich description and bulleted table of relevant keyword functional areas. The rest of the first page covers her most recent job in Project Management, with headers emphasizing Project Management/Operations Management (her target) and Budget Management/Cost Avoidance/Revenue Generation (all benefits to the employers).

The selected bullet points on the first page show her strong project management accomplishments (including quantifiers) in what was a relatively short time on the job. The second page continues to show her Operations Management achievements in her last positions over the past 20 years. I included her earliest jobs to show that she was even doing project and administrative management then, and at high-profile employers (e.g., #2 stock brokerage in New York).

I capped off the resume with her Education, listing her Bachelor's Degree, Project Management and HR Certificates, and Zenger-Miller Frontline Leadership Training (all relevant and high-powered credentials) and her Professional Affiliations. At my insistence, Elizabeth joined the Project Management Institute where she is actively pursuing more project management training and member networking.

Finally, the Technology section shows that while she has 20 years' experience in Project Management/Operations Management, she is **not** an "old fogey." She is quite up-to-date with MS Office programs, including MS Project.

Outcome: Elizabeth is currently, as she says, "fielding interviews bumper-to-bumper" and looking for just the right opportunity. Since it is still early in her job search, she feels certain she will land her "dream job" within the next three to six months. I'm inclined to agree; Elizabeth is an avid networker and has a vast array of folks mining for job leads.

June Ellen Berringer

135 Killdeer Road, Apt. 721, Ewing, NJ 08628
(609) 771-7665 Residence Phone / Fax ▪ juneberringer21@yahoo.com

Medical Billing / Medical Records Technician

Dedicated, experienced professional with recent training in medical billing, medical terminology, and ICD-9-CM coding. Strong organizational, communications, and project management skills. Calm demeanor under stress; cooperative team leader. Proven multi-tasking / operations support skills. Adept in:

☑ Client Relationship Management	☑ Medical Records Terminology	☑ Budget Controls
☑ Customer Needs Management	☑ Administrative Support	☑ Project Coordination

KEY SUPPORTING SKILLS

- **Administration:** Diverse administrative expertise includes directing nationwide CHART (California Hospital Association Review Team) Program for American Hospital Association, managing seven-county sales territory in south central California, and maintaining large, upscale apartment complexes.

- **Time Management:** Demonstrate top-notch organizational skills, with ability to prioritize and multi-task. Developed records management systems to expedite back-office operations for sales generation, residential and retail property management, and meeting and event planning.

- **Communications:** Employ proactive problem-solving communications skills to generate "win-win" scenarios. Effectively communicated special situations and potential problem areas to management.

- **Personal Strengths:** Conscientious in following through on commitments and deadlines. Mature, discreet team player with experience interfacing with high-level executives and corporate clients.

EDUCATION

Medical Records Technician Program, The College of New Jersey, Ewing, NJ – 2005
Courses: Medical Terminology, Advanced Medical Terminology, Medical Billing, ICD-9-CM Coding
Associate of Arts Degree, San Diego Community College, San Diego, CA

PROFESSIONAL EXPERIENCE

Estate and Health Care Management, Princeton, NJ   2003 – 2005
✓ **Administrative Management.** Acted as prime interface with 60+ physicians, nurses, hospice, attorneys, CPA, stockbroker and insurance companies for elderly parents with progressive, debilitating illnesses. Managed health care appointments and treatment, as well as daily living arrangements onsite.

✓ **Records Management.** Submitted insurance claims and tracked insurance reimbursements. Oversaw distribution of $1 million estate. Arranged sale of house and distribution of all household goods.

Manufacturer's Representative   2001 – 2003
Pacific Printing, San Diego, CA and Elegant Communications, Inc., San Francisco, CA
Independent contractor representing fine gift, paper/stationary, and greeting card lines for two businesses.

✓ **Account Management.** Grew accounts by 45% (from 175 to 250) and increased sales by 20% in seven-county south central California territory. Generated 25 new key accounts (such as Yellowstone Park gift shops) through thorough market research, competitive market analysis and persuasive prospect interaction. Provided personalized customer service that generated 100% customer retention.

✓ **Customer Relationship Management.** Developed strong client communications networks, building relationships with 250 buyers for retail stores, museums, hospital gift shops, and nurseries. Educated buyers in 60+ lines of merchandise, updating them on retail trends and demographics-driven marketing.

June Ellen Berringer
(609) 771-7665 Residence Phone / Fax ▪ juneberringer21@yahoo.com   Page 2

PROFESSIONAL EXPERIENCE (continued)

Residential Property Management   1999 – 2001
Excelsior Properties, San Raphael, CA (1999-2000), and Seaside Views, San Diego, CA (2001)

✓ **Administrative Management.** Managed two upscale apartment communities (up to 516 units), with monthly rent collections of $432,000. Supervised on-site leasing, as well as 18 maintenance and grounds staff. Closely controlled $2,500 per month expense budget, monitoring five vendor services. Oversaw renovation of 35 apartment units, coordinating workflow and scheduling of carpet, flooring, paint, and fixture vendors with tenants.

✓ **Customer Service.** Maintained 92% residency rate and achieved 98% on-time rent collection by developing proactive tenant relationships programs. Initiated educational newsletter for tenants, as well as open-door policy for tenant complaints. Credited with stabilizing the tenant community through lawful evictions of known drug dealers.

Retail Property Management   1994 – 1999
Townsend Group Companies, San Diego and San Francisco, CA

✓ **Administrative Management.** Initiated and developed specialty leasing programs for three major developers (12 regional shopping centers) in high-profile metropolitan areas. Maintained high occupancy rates (95%) by actively recruiting retailers for year-round common area, as well as developing long-term, favorable leases for in-line sales operations.

✓ **Program Management.** Conceptualized and supervised design projects for kiosks and store décor, as well as for marketing communications (brochures, print advertising, and directories). Developed and met program budgets, generating in excess of $500,000 for each shopping center annually.

Meeting and Event Management   1993 – 1994
California Hospital Association, San Diego, CA

✓ **Program Management.** Served as Director of CHART (California Hospital Association Review Team) Program. Traveled statewide conducting peer review meetings for 8 to 10 state hospitals. Wrote reports based on participant feedback and critical observations and analysis of policies and procedures. Recommended policy and methodology changes, 90% of which were implemented by the Boards of the state hospitals.

✓ **Customer Service.** Facilitated in-house discussions on-site of hospital personnel and management at all levels to increase quality assurance, strengthen employee relations, improve customer service, and streamline processes and procedures. Initiated and encouraged constructive dialogues among groups that had a history of communication breakdowns.

COMPUTER SKILLS

☑ Training in Medical Billing software, Medical Records databases, and ICD-9-CM coding.
☑ Experienced in composing and editing letters, memos, marketing communications and reports.
☑ Utilize Windows XP, MS Office 2003 – Word, Excel, PowerPoint, Access, Internet Explorer, email.

Analysis of Berringer Resume

The challenge of re-entry after two years out of the workforce, combined with a career change, made this a particularly difficult resume to strategize and write. June Ellen had jumped around in her career (from Meeting and Event Management to Residential Property Management to Manufacturers Rep to the latest incarnation, Medical Records Technician.

I formatted the resume using a conservative font (Times New Roman) and traditional reverse-chronological layout. However, I started with a Summary area highlighting her new career target area and supported with relevant new training, transferable skills, and desired attributes along with a keyword table positioned to "show off" her primary assets.

Then I followed that with a segment highlighting her Key Supporting Skills, trying to "weave together" the diverse types of jobs into coherent functional areas. I felt this was necessary because her work history was so diverse. I mentioned her work with CHART first in this area, although chronologically it is last in her series of jobs. All of these key supporting skills relate to her career objective.

Positioned her Education next at mid-page before her Experience to highlight her recent Medical Records Technician Certificate and coursework (includes many keywords). Her Associate's Degree (her only college degree) was quite old, so I did not list the date.

The first thing I listed under Experience dealt with her most recent two years taking care of her two elderly parents and then their estate in New Jersey after they passed away. I used functional headers to show that she was using transferable skills relevant to her objective even during this period of "unemployment" and had extensive dealings with medical staff and management. Also, clearly during this period she also went to The College of New Jersey to get her certificate in Medical Records. So this period of time was accounted for constructively.

Then for each of her previous jobs, I unified them thematically by using consistent functional skill headers (Account Management, Administrative Management, Program Management, and Customer Service). This was done to show that while these were different types of jobs, she was using the **same** type of functional skills repeatedly – the same type of skills she would need in Medical Records management. Her accomplishments (bulleted) were laced with quantifiers and demonstrated that she is a real go-getter and take-charge person, as well as being extremely adaptable and producing outstanding results no matter what situation she lands in.

Finally, her bulleted list of Computer Skills again repeats her Medical Records technical training, as well as general administrative technology skills, and a listing of up-to-date computer skills.

Outcome: June Ellen landed a Medical Records Technician/Medical Billing job within 6 weeks with a large dental group practice in California.

SHARON C. CLEMENTS
2721 Abernathy Drive, Columbia, MD 21044
(410) 997-7521 Home ▪ (703) 771-8113 Mobile ▪ sharonclem@newmedia.com

---

Operations & Management Executive
Area Director / Regional Director ▪ **General Manager** ▪ **Operations Manager**

General/Operations Management professional with creative vision and flawless execution. Proven expertise in expanding product/program lines, increasing revenue streams, and capturing market share in highly competitive Health and Fitness industry. Leadership role in health and fitness clubs expansion (15 greenfields and 10 acquisitions). Key contributor to market dominance on East Coast.

Hands-on P&L role in strategic planning and initiative management, multi-site operations, recruitment and training (60 management and 1,000 line staff), team building, and project management. Met or exceeded revenue/development expectations for 20+ years. Experienced in:

☑ Revenue & Market Expansion	☑ Change Management	☑ Start-ups & Acquisitions
☑ Staff & Management Development	☑ Sales & Marketing	☑ Business Development
☑ Budget & Financial Performance	☑ HR Management	☑ Branding & Technology

---

PROFESSIONAL EXPERIENCE

FITNESS CLUBS INTERNATIONAL, Washington, DC (corporate headquarters)   1984 – 2005
Leader in Health & Fitness Industry, ranked 2nd in U.S. and 7th worldwide (based on revenues) with 365,000 members at 132 clubs and 7,200 employees.

General Manager – Columbia Fitness Club (CFC), Columbia, MD (2003-2005)
Full P&L responsibility for sports club ranked 1st in suburban-DC market. Managed 20,000 SF club with 2,000 members, and supervised 40 management and line staff. Key player in strategic planning, business development, operations, sales and marketing, brand building, PR and community relations, customer service/retention, human resources, administration, and technology performance.

ACCOMPLISHMENTS
Challenged in company restructure and brand-building initiative to deliver smooth-running, profitable operations and sales in high-profile fitness club facility. By 2004 voted "Best Health Club" in DC-Metro area. Introduced new product and service lines, negotiated cost reductions (from 10% to cost of item) with vendors, collaborated in succession planning and team building, and led major revenue and profitability increases (demonstrated by financial metrics below):

Per Cent Growth 2004 v. 2003

PT Revenues
Gross Revenues
Membership
Desk Revenues

0%   50%   100%   150%   200%

2004 v. 2003
PT Revenues: $509,136 v. $197,225
Gross Revenues: $1,863,790 v. $881,506
Membership Income: $1,544,748 v. $768,564
Desk Revenues: $27,541 v. $18,774

SHARON C. CLEMENTS   Page 2
(410) 997-7521 Home ▪ (703) 771-8113 Mobile ▪ sharonclem@newmedia.com

Area Manager – CFC, Columbia, MD (1999-2003)
Oversaw operations and explosive growth of suburban-DC clubs. Full P&L responsibility for Sales and Marketing, Systems, Finance, SOP, Customer Service, Multi-Unit Management, HR, Initiative Management, Succession Planning, Recruiting, Training and Management Development.

- **Start-up and Acquisition Leader.** Delivered strong revenues and development results in soft market: spearheaded growth from 1 club with 500 members (starting revenues of $1.4M) to 6 clubs with 13,200 members and annual revenues of $14.5M (2003). Clubs ranged in size from 20,000 SF to 200,000 SF on 23 acres. Managed and motivated team that grew to 550 employees. Chosen as member of Washington, DC Mayor's Health & Fitness Council Committee in 2003.

- **Technology Improvements.** Played key team role in 2002-2003 rollout of Club Networks, integrated enterprise software solution for sales reporting with online point-of-sale/real-time sales, tracking, financial, and reporting capability. In 2000 successfully launched automated Fitness Database, as well as online direct payroll processing IT system (Kronos).

General Manager – Washington, DC Fitness Club (DCFC), Washington, DC (1990-1999)
Directed operations of largest sports club in DC market (8 locations), with full P&L responsibility. Supervised 30-60 management and line staff, including recruitment, training, and staff development.

- **Acquisitions and Revitalization.** Designated Lead Management Trainer for new Manager Orientation, including Senior Management. Initiated Employee Cross-Training Programs, New Employee and Customer Service seminars, monthly performance incentives, and SOP guidelines for training, operations, maintenance, tracking and production. Negotiated cost-saving contracts with outside vendors. Oversaw multi-million-dollar club renovations.

- **New Technology and Products.** In 1997 transitioned club from manual to computerized system for sales tracking (Sales, Leads and Management System software), increasing accuracy and turnaround time for sales reporting. First to introduce electronic funds transfer.

Previous FCI Career History:
Progressive promotions from Sales Consultant through Sales Supervisor to Area Membership Supervisor (supervised 36) as company grew from 3 to 9 locations. Set year-over-year (YOY) sales records, pre-sold and assisted in opening 7 clubs, and initiated performance improvement processes.

EDUCATION & AWARDS

Bachelor's Degree Program, University of Maryland, College Park, MD
Certificate, Managing Performance, American Management Association (AMA) 1999
Certificate, The Manager's Role in Professional Management, AMA 1998
International Racquet Sports Association (IRSA) Conventions & Seminars, 1986-1998

Fitness Clubs International (FCI) Management & Sales Awards
Service Recognition Award for Outstanding Achievement in Sales & Marketing, 1999
Certificate of Achievement "Employee Primer" Award, 1997
Certificate of Achievement for "greatest drop in cancellation percentage," 1996

Analysis of Clements Resume

The challenge here was that Sharon had been with Fitness Clubs International (FCI) all of her career life (21 years) with no other previous employers. While she was progressively promoted and reached General Manager and Area Manager levels, her experience was extremely niched in the fitness industry. Also, while she had attended college in a Bachelor's degree program, she had not graduated (too many years ago to pick up the credits any longer).

I used conservative fonts and bold graphic lines, as well as an eye-catching chart and graph at the bottom of page 1, to capture attention while also being consistent with the level of her position and industry.

The first page is broken into two main sections: Summary section and Professional Experience focusing on her most recent two years with TSI. The Summary begins with a header delineating the types of positions she is qualified for and is seeking (all keywords) followed by an overview of her qualifications. The first paragraph concentrates on benefits to the employer, as well as a "taste" of her accomplishments. The second paragraph summarizes her primary functional skills and scope of accomplishments, followed by a table grid using check marks for bullets showing relevant keyword areas of experience.

Professional Experience is laid out in reverse-chronological style with her most recent two years on the first page. I defined FCI's company background in a short paragraph, followed by Sharon's most recent job title and duration, as well as a paragraph defining the scope of her responsibilities and duties. A strong paragraph with a graphic demonstrating her most recent accomplishments driving revenue ends the page in such a way that the reader is compelled to turn to the second page to see more!

Her two major positions (going back 15 years) are detailed with functional header phrases in boldface to capture attention and show her leadership in revenue growth and technology acquisition. Many quantifiers are used to show the scope of her duties, as well as her achievements (bullet points reserved for accomplishments only). I then summarized her previous six years with FCI in a brief paragraph (Previous FCI Career History) demonstrating her progressive promotion and accomplishments.

I combined the categories of Education and Awards since Sharon's education background was lacking a college degree. The Awards section mitigates that lack by clearly showing her excellence in sales and marketing, training, and client relationship management.

Outcome: After five months of intensive job search efforts and coaching, Sharon landed a position with an international fitness equipment distributorship as Operations Manager of the North American Division.

Deborah B. Monforth
1711 Lincoln Street, Princeton, NJ 08540
(609) 973-1331 Home ▪ (510) 259-7599 Mobile ▪ debbmon@patmedia.com

Application Support Administrator / Technical Support Specialist / Desktop Support

Technologically sophisticated, bilingual (Spanish/English) IT Support/Training Specialist with hands-on experience in project lifecycle management for technical and intranet applications, website development, workgroup support, and desktop and network troubleshooting. Certificate in Computer Programming. Skilled in:

☑ Help Desk & Hardware Support	☑ First-Level PC Support	☑ Project Management
☑ System Upgrades / Conversions	☑ LAN / WAN Architecture	☑ Escalation Resolution
☑ Peer-to-Peer User Groups	☑ Web Content Upgrades	☑ Customer Service

TECHNOLOGY SUMMARY

Networking – LAN / WAN, Windows 2000 / NT 4.0 Server, Windows 95 Server, TCP/IP, SQL Server

Operating Systems - Windows 95 / 98 / 2000 / XP, Windows 2000 / NT 4.0 Server, DOS 6.0

Applications - MS Office Suite 97/2000/2002 (Word, Access, Excel, PowerPoint), MS FrontPage 2000, Macromedia Dream Weaver 3.0, Adobe Acrobat 5 and PDF, Flash 4.0, Novell GroupWise 5.5, Adobe Pagemill 3, Lotus Suite 96, Corel Suite 96, Corel 9, Adobe PhotoShop, Kodak digital software, Symantec pcAnywhere 32, Internet Explorer, Netscape Communicator, and WinZip

Programming – HTML code, CGI, Java, JavaScript, C Programming, RPG 400, SQL, Visual Basic 5.0, Visual InterDev 6.0, AS/400, ASP code

PROFESSIONAL EXPERIENCE

STATE OF PENNSYLVANIA, TREASURY DEPT., DIV. OF TAXATION, Philadelphia, PA   1995 – present
Senior Technician, MIS – Technical Support Activity (2001 – present)
Promoted to provide help desk support for 2,000+ end-users (including remote users) in 9 locations throughout Pennsylvania, as well as project management team leadership for special technical assignments. First-point-of-contact (Tier 1 Help Desk Technician) for support incidents, as well as end-user training.

- **Help Desk.** Ensure effective 24-hour "one-stop" technical support for mainframe, WAN, LAN, and remote system. Install and update software. Set up, configure, and troubleshoot Technology Center equipment. Track and de-escalate technology and workflow problems, collaborating with 10 cross-functional IT groups.

- **Website Development.** Project-managed Division of Taxation's website redesign to text-only version, enabling fast and easy access for all users, including vision impaired. Supervised staff of 8.

- **Intranet Development.** Key player in creation, launch, and maintenance of Division of Taxation intranet site, providing management with easily retrievable, up-to-date information for operations decisions. Initiated, created, and maintain Access users group intranet to facilitate information sharing and learning.

- **Project Management.** Led PAX CD-ROM project for 2 years, delivering interactive CD-ROMs with 1,000+ tax-law-verified documents for simplified tax preparation (tax years 2001 & 2002) on schedule.

- **ASP Development.** Played pivotal role in beta-test programming and development of causal sales application (upgraded Alpha 4 database into back-end of Access 2000 and SQL Server, front-end into Internet Explorer via ASP programming).

- **End-User Training.** Expanded Technology Center offerings by designing, developing, and delivering advanced programs and manuals for MS Office, GroupWise, Novell Network, and Internet, increasing usability. Currently manage 12 Access courses, training and supervising 5 adjunct team instructors.

Deborah B. Monforth

(609) 973-1331 Home ▪ (510) 259-7599 Mobile ▪ debbmon@paatmedia.com   Page 2

STATE OF PENNSYLVANIA – continued

Technical Assistant, MIS – Technical Support Activity (1999 – 2001)
First-level technical support for software installation, as well as setup and configuration of new equipment used in Division of Taxation (PCs, laptops, printers, scanners, projectors, digital & video).

- **IT Software Training.** Designed curriculum and materials, and delivered technical training, for introductory programs in Microsoft Office Suite (Word, Excel, Access), as well as Windows 95, keeping staff motivated and focused while improving job satisfaction and productivity. Personally trained more than 800 end-users.

- **Website Support.** Functioned as Web Editor for Division of Taxation's Internet/Intranet website, proofing and updating website information on a daily basis (fastest turnaround time of any PA State department).

- **Database Maintenance.** Upgraded and maintained link-shared employee Access database with Chief of Staff's office, ensuring data integrity for training. Created database reports for management evaluation.

- **Technical Development Project.** Pioneered development and implementation of storage, archive, and retrieval system for 500+ electronic presentations used throughout Division of Taxation.

Principal Clerk – Technical Education (1997 – 1999)
Promoted to provide installation, configuration, and troubleshooting support for new equipment and software in Technology Center, as well as evaluation and modification of skills assessment.

- **Training Center Database.** Initiated and implemented Access-based data gathering system to compile, store, and retrieve statistics on computer training classes. Researched and wrote monthly reports used to evaluate training trends and staff training needs.

- **NJ Saver Rebate Program.** Key team player in initial, large-scale data compilation for PA Saver Rebate Program, including retrieval, distribution, quality control, and storage of tens of thousands of data files.

Senior Clerk Typist, Clerk Typist – Corporation Business Tax (1995 – 1997)
Assisted 8 auditors by researching taxpayer information on mainframe, ordered work files for Supervising Auditor using HLLAPI information system, and prepared report statistics using Excel spreadsheets.

STATE OF PENNSYLVANIA, DEPT. OF BANKING, Philadelphia, PA (temp contract)   1994 – 1995
Data Entry Specialist / Legal Secretary
Front office support for 5 attorneys and 3 accountants: records management, legal document preparation, purchasing, and equipment maintenance. Used IS software for research and to process taxpayer complaints.

AMERICAN COMMERCIAL BANK, Edison, NJ   1990 – 1993
Customer Service Representative / Supervisor Teller
Instructed 35 employees in use of computerized banking systems and procedures. Verified and audited financial reports and balance sheets. Cash management responsibility exceeded $100,000.

EDUCATION

Instructor Certification, HRDI, Philadelphia, PA – 2000
Courses: Curriculum Design, Performance Consulting, Training Presentations, Design Surveys and Questions, Determining Training Needs, and Active Techniques for Teaching.

Certificate in Computer Programming, DeVry Institute, New Brunswick, NJ – 1999
Courses: HTML, CGI, Java Programming, JavaScript Programming, RPG 400, C Programming, SQL, Visual Basic 5.0, AS/400 Subfiles & Common Language Queries, MS Office, Windows NT 4.0

Ongoing Professional and Technical Development in-house and at vendor locations (1995 – present)

Analysis of Monforth Resume

This client spent 10 years at the State of Pennsylvania, moving up from a Clerk Typist position to the highest level of technician in the MIS department. She wanted a higher salary and discovered she could make a lot more money in the corporate sector. The challenge was in conveying accomplishments – initially she said she had none and she did not have a college degree.

Began with Summary of Qualifications area and header that makes clear the career target. Highlighted her bilingual ability. Included keyword table using check-marked bullets for visual appeal, as well as strong horizontal lines to separate the areas of the resume.

Positioned Technology Summary at mid-view point of first page for optimum placement. Separated the different technical areas (Networking, Operating Systems, Applications, and Programming).

Positioned Education after Professional Experience (extensive relevant Experience more important and wanted to downplay Education category since she did not receive a college degree). Identified names of courses in each certificate area (many of these course names are keywords).

Showcased accomplishments with bullet points (duties were stated in brief paragraphs after each job title) and with boldface lead-in keyword phrases. Quantified scope of her positions, as well as many of the accomplishments. Showed she had initiated and upgraded many systems and programs in the last 8 years working independently, as well as collaboratively.

Outcome: Within six weeks Debbie was hired by the largest Spanish-language radio station in New Jersey as Associate Director of Technical Support and signed on with a 50% increase in salary! This was a much higher-level position than she or I had anticipated – her ability to translate tech-speak into user-friendly language and training programs **and** her bilingual abilities cinched the job for her.

MARLA C. COSSICH
9321 Pinecrest Avenue, Rochester, MN 48309
248-370-5555 Home ▪ Marlacossich@popmail.com

OBJECTIVE: Academic Admissions / Program Coordination / Event Planning

Experienced Administrative professional with background in Academic Admissions and Special Events Program Coordination. Highly organized, mature and cooperative team player with proven strengths in communications and interpersonal relations. MS Office 2003 (Word, Excel, PowerPoint, Outlook), Windows XP, Internet and email.

EDUCATION
Master of Arts (MA), History of Art – Oakland University, Rochester, MN
Bachelor of Arts (BA), English Literature – University of Wisconsin, Madison, WI

PROFESSIONAL EXPERIENCE

UNIVERSITY OF MINNESOTA-TWIN CITIES, Minneapolis, MN
Senior Admissions Officer – 2 years

- Recruited freshman students, providing information and counseling to prospective undergraduate students and their families regarding academic requirements, educational facilities and activities, and student life.

- Represented the University at outreach recruitment activities (college fairs and school visits), requiring contact with the public and education officials.

- Screened and evaluated potential students, transcripts, and applications, making independent decisions based on enrollment goals and admissions requirements.

- Selected as liaison to 12-member admissions committee reviewing special admissions cases. Investigated and made decisions on legal residence cases.

OAKLAND UNIVERSITY, Rochester, MN
Coordinator for Special Events (Performing Arts) – 2 years

- Coordinated and ensured smooth delivery of multiple-event performing arts series ($80,000 annual budget), as well as University-sponsored lecture / recital series. Supervised and provided effective team leadership for office support staff.

- Independently oversaw promotions and marketing, box office management, budget analysis and preparation, financial record keeping and reports, contract negotiations, and production supervision for these well-attended special events.

- Wrote series marketing plans and promotions, PR and marketing communications, which contributed to series success ($250,000 in gross revenues over 2 years).

Lecturer & Teaching Assistant (Art History) – 5 years

- Taught undergraduate-level art history survey course each semester. Developed curriculum, led discussions, and generated a high level of student participation.

COMMUNITY SERVICE

☑ Special Education Advisory Committee, Hightop Valley Regional School District Active Member and Committee's Representative to the District Parent Council
☑ Founding Member of DASH Group (Disabled Animals Support & Hope Group)

Analysis of Cossich Resume

Marla had been a stay-at-home mom, with very little work history. She had worked in University Admissions more than 15 years ago, with other academic employment previous to that, for a total work history of nine years. I eliminated actual dates and instead indicated periods of employment, along with quantifiable achievements wherever possible, to overcome her lack of recent employment.

Outcome: Marla was able to obtain a Program Coordinator position within a local university after three months of job search.

Mark W. Massingill

1711 Crestview Road, Manhattan, KS 66506
785-532-5555 Home ▪ markmass@popmail.com

OBJECTIVE	**Help Desk / Computer Support Technician** position

PROFILE

☑ Recent computer center graduate with **proven organization abilities**.
☑ Demonstrated track record of achieving goals in a team environment.
☑ Highly motivated and dependable – able to take responsibility for projects.
☑ Proven skills in problem solving, team leading, and customer relations.

EDUCATION

Tri-State Computer Learning Center, Topeka, KS   2004 - 2005
Computer Courses completed in:
✓ Networking Essentials
✓ Beginning Windows NT

✓ A+ Certification
✓ Administering Windows NT

✓ Intermediate Word 2003
✓ Windows NT Core Technologies

✓ Beginning Word 2003
✓ Windows NT Support By Enterprise

✓ Beginning Access 2003
✓ Beginning Business on the Internet

✓ TCP / IP protocol
✓ Beginning FrontPage 2003

University of Kansas, Manhattan, KS   2002 – 2003
General first-year coursework in Bachelor's Degree program.

EMPLOYMENT

A Cut Above, Topeka, KS   2004 - 2005
Receptionist/Cashier

▪ Successfully handled front desk and three incoming telephone lines for busy, upscale hair salon. Greeted and logged in steady stream of customers, coordinating appointments with hairdresser availability.

▪ Developed cooperative, team-oriented working relationships with owners and co-workers in this 8-station salon.

▪ Managed customer problems and complaints with tact and attention to prompt customer service.

▪ Experience gained in opening and closing procedures, cash register receipts, counter sales, light bookkeeping, and telephone follow-up.

Plains Soccer Camp, Manhattan, KS   2002, 2003 Summers
Trainer / Coach

- Assisted Woman's Soccer Coach in 200-participant soccer camp. Worked with individuals, as well as teams, to improve their attitude and resulting soccer performance.

ACTIVITIES & AWARDS

Kansas Cowboys Soccer Semi-Pro Team – Center Half   2000 - 2004
✓ Team consistently ranked in top 10 semi-pro teams in the nation.

Manhattan High School Soccer Team   1999 - 2002
✓ Captain of team that won the State Soccer Title in 2001
✓ Recognized as one of the top two mid-fielders in the state 2002

Analysis of Massingill Resume

Mark's challenge was in not finishing college (he barely got through two semesters) and minimal work experience. Mark was engrossed playing soccer – first, in high school and then on a semi-pro soccer team. His work history includes coaching soccer and a receptionist job at a hair salon. Mark discovered a love for computers and went on to a computer training center where hands-on learning suited him. I positioned his recent computer training (including coursework) for maximum exposure, along with a Profile that highlighted his computer training and goals orientation, along with other desirable transferable skills.

Outcome: Within two months of marketing himself with this resume he landed a help desk position with a start-up company in Topeka.

DEBORAH M. MACE

543 Pacific Highway, Corvallis, OR 97331
541-737-5555 Home ▪ debmace@popmail.com

MARKETING / MARKETING MANAGEMENT / ADVERTISING & PROMOTIONS

SUMMARY OF QUALIFICATIONS

Marketing Director with 17 years' experience in marketing communications (marcomm), marketing management, project management, and sales. Proven information management and analytical skills combined with a natural talent for strategic market planning and team building. Experience across broad industries in consumer products and services. Fluent in Spanish. Expertise in:

☑ Multiple Project Management	☑ Market Development	☑ Strategic Marketing
☑ Client Relationship Management	☑ Key Account Management	☑ Competitive Analysis
☑ Competitive Market Intelligence	☑ Training & Development	☑ Presentations

PROFESSIONAL EXPERIENCE

PACIFIC COAST SPA, Corvallis, OR   2001 – present
Marketing Director / General Manager
Recruited to increase market optimization for $3M full-line beauty and rejuvenation spa. Promoted to General Manager concurrent with Marketing position. Oversee business development initiatives, as well as marketing, advertising, and promotions. Supervise 6 direct reports (Managers), as well as 86 indirect reports (front- and back-of-house operations) in 2 shifts, including weekends.

MARKETING, ADVERTISING & PROMOTIONS
- Manage advertising, strategic, and tactical marketing to support sales, promotions, and special events. **Results:** Year-over-year ROI consistently top-notch: first year – 48% increase in sales, second year revenue growth of 57%, and third year sales increase projected to be 73%.

- Spearheaded innovative and successful multi-media advertising and marketing programs:
  - initiated cost-saving Gift Certificate promotion aligned with radio stations' holiday promotions
  - developed 60-second video, including scripting and choreography, aired by local cable stations
  - introduced voice advertisement on hold line, which increased bookings and direct sales by 34%
  - designed/launched billboard advertisement for local traffic increasing public awareness by 68%.

ACCOUNT DEVELOPMENT
- Formulated strategic new market development initiatives, including aggressive corporate plan for Account Executives. Originated new business development concepts and profit streams, such as medical accounts (promoted stress-free monthly meetings/seminars/executive retreats). **Result:** Yielded substantial increase of standing clientele (27%).

INFORMATION SYSTEMS & REPORTING
- Designed, developed, and project managed installation of 9-workstation computer system. Ensured efficient and compatible systems integration of product and services inventory and passwords. Collaborated with software provider to develop accurate market-analysis reports.

MANAGEMENT & TRAINING
- Secured cost-effective contract negotiations with 10 vendors (saved $18K/week). Deliver favorable vendor and supplier management programs obtaining maximum value.

- Developed protocol for customer service training. Mentored Customer Service Manager in coaching and proven customer satisfaction techniques. Delivered both software applications training, as well as high-impact platform presentations (sales / motivation) to staff.

DEBORAH M. MACE

541-737-5555 Home ▪ debmace@popmail.com   Page 2

SALON EFFECTS – ESTEE LAUDER, Portland, OR   2000 – 2001
Sales Account Executive
Complete account development and account management for 32 establishments within Pacific, Central, Washington, and Columbia counties in Oregon.

- Developed and implemented key programs in marketing and sales management, such as promotions and special events, product education, and sales strategies programs.

- Provided mentoring leadership and management development for 3 account executives, in conjunction with Regional Manager, increasing their product knowledge, sales effectiveness, and sales forecasting abilities. **Result:** Increased product sales by 50% overall within one year.

CAFÉ PACIFICA, Portland, OR   1995 – 2000
Proprietor – Marketing / Sales / Advertising
- Established successful coffee distributorship, culminating in 33 corporate and small business accounts with consistent track record of customer loyalty (100%) and referrals (35%). Initiated full-service coffee product, increasing customer convenience and value.

- Spearheaded new account development by creating and implementing direct marketing campaign targeting corporations, professional offices, and bakeries. Led brand management and customer relationship management initiatives, gaining local market penetration.

VERVE RECORDS, Portland, OR   1992 – 1995
Advertising Executive – Marketing Division
- Developed, promoted, and implemented special events for employee relations, as well as client relationship management for 100+ Verve artists (including the status of royalties). Coordinated logistics for well-received events, which increased employee productivity and morale.

KODAK CAMERA CORPORATION, Seattle, WA   1988 – 1992
Marketing and Communications Assistant
- Key player in project management of new product introduction for Panorama camera, including marketing communications, branding integrity, advertising, promotions, and merchandising (fashion and apparel) in Bloomingdale's, Saks, and Macy's. **Result:** Drove $3K in sales/month.

EDUCATION
2005 – present University of Oregon, School of Business – Bachelor's Degree (in progress)
2004 – 2005 E-Myth Management Coaching, Dale Carnegie Seminar
2003 – 2004 Sales Presentations and Communications Skills, Dale Carnegie Seminar

COMPUTER SKILLS
Windows 2003, MS Office 2003 - Word, Excel, Access, PowerPoint, MS Outlook, MS Works, MS Publisher 2003, Quicken, QuickBooks, Internet Explorer.

LANGUAGE SKILLS
Spanish - fluent

PROFESSIONAL ASSOCIATIONS
American Marketing Association
Beauty.com

Analysis of Mace Resume

Deb's big handicap was the lack of a college degree. While she had extensive management experience, her lack of a Bachelor's Degree was holding her back. I advised her to enroll in a Bachelor's Degree program and begin taking courses (one per semester to start) so we could list her degree in progress.

Outcome: This strategy, along with her accomplishments and experience in Marketing Management, won her a Marketing Management slot with the Estee Lauder organization (she had worked as an Account Rep with them in 2000-2001 and had left on good terms).

Louise Garver

MA, CMP, CPRW, CEIP, MCDP, JCTC
Career Directions LLC
Website: www.CareerDirectionsLLC.com
E-mail: CareerPro@cox.net
Tel. 860-623-9476
Fax 860-623-9473

Louise is an award-winning, professional resume writer and certified career coach with a 20-year record in effectively positioning executives and managers to achieve their next career move. She specializes in creating strategic resumes that showcase each client's unique value proposition, as well as in building a successful job search campaign from self-presentation to interview and negotiation coaching to win the right offer. A career expert on TheLadders.com, AFPOnline.org, GoingGlobal.com, and other websites, her articles and sample documents have appeared in numerous resume, cover letter, and other publications.

The following resumes incorporate several compelling elements and highlight Louise's different approaches to different clients. In addition to Objectives, Louise incorporates "Core Competencies" and key break-out elements (Challenge/Actions/Results) under Professional Experience in the Susan B. Almann example on pages 288-289. The Elaine Erickson example on page 292-293 incorporates separate "Accomplishments" statements and a supervisor's evaluation comments under the Experience section. The Paula Martin example on page 295 includes a graphic element to illustrate the candidate's career focus.

SUSAN B. ALMANN

589 Brighton View
Croton, NY 10520

914.555.8977   almann@protypeltd.com

CAREER OBJECTIVE

Human Resources Executive and member of the senior
leadership team using proven expertise in guiding the design
and execution of performance-based HR initiatives that
achieve business objectives.

Provided vision and counsel in steering organizations through
accelerated growth as well as in turning around underperforming
businesses in both union and non-union environments. Diverse
background includes multinational corporations in healthcare and
manufacturing industries.

Core Competencies

- Long-Range Planning
- Recruitment & Staffing
- Employee Relations
- Leadership Development
- Succession Planning
- Compensation Design
- Culture Change
- M&A Integration
- HR Policies & Procedures
- Expatriate Programs

PROFESSIONAL EXPERIENCE

MARCON MANUFACTURING COMPANY, Peekskill, NY
Director, Human Resources (1996–Present)

Challenge: Recruited to create HR infrastructure to support business growth at a $30 million
global manufacturing company with underachieving sales, exceedingly high turnover,
and lack of cohesive management processes among business entities in U.S. and Asia.

Actions: Partnered with the President and Board of Directors to reorganize company, reduce
overhead expenses, rebuild sales, and institute solid management infrastructure.

Results: ♦ Established HR with staff of 5, including development of policies and procedures;
renegotiated cost-effective benefit programs that saved company $1.5 million
annually.
♦ Reorganized operations and facilitated seamless integration of 150 employees from
2 new acquisitions within parent company.
♦ Reduced sales force turnover to nearly nonexistent, upgraded quality of candidates
hired by implementing interview skills training and management development
programs. Results led to improved sales performance.
♦ Recruited all management personnel; developed HR policies, procedures, and
plans; and fostered team culture at newly built Malaysian plant with 125
employees.
♦ Initiated business reorganization plan, resulting in consolidation of New York and
Virginia operations and $6.5 million in cost reductions.

BINGHAMTON COMPANY, New York, NY
Director, Human Resources & Administration (1993–1996)

Challenge: Lead HR and Administration function supporting 1,600 employees at $500 million
manufacturer of medical equipment. Support company's turnaround efforts, business
unit consolidations. and transition to consumer products focus.

Actions: Established cross-functional teams from each site and provided training in team
building to coordinate product development efforts, implement new manufacturing
processes, and speed products to market. Identified cost reduction opportunities;
instrumental in reorganization initiatives that included closing union plant in Texas
and building new plant in North Carolina. Managed HR staff of 12.

SUSAN B. ALMANN • Page 2

Director, Human Resources & Administration continued...

Results:
- Instituted worldwide cross-functional team culture that provided the foundation for successful new product launches and recapture of company's leading edge despite intense competition.
- Led flawless integration of 2 operations into single, cohesive European business unit, resulting in profitable business turnaround.
- Restructured and positioned HR organization in the German business unit as customer-focused partner to support European sales and marketing units.
- Initiated major benefit cost reductions of $3 million in year one and $1 million annually while gaining employee acceptance through concerted education and communications efforts.

ARCAMED CORPORATION, New York, NY
Manager, Human Resources (1989–1993)

Challenge: HR support to corporate office and field units of an $800 million organization with 150 global operations employing 4,500 people.

Actions: Promoted from Assistant Manager to lead staff of 10 in all HR and labor relations functions. Established separate international recruitment function and designed staffing plan to accommodate rapid business growth. Negotiated cost-effective benefits contracts for union and non-union employees.

Results:
- Oversaw successful UAW, Teamsters, and labor contract negotiations.
- Established and staffed HR function for major contract award with U.S. government agency.
- Introduced incentive plans for field unit managers and an expatriate program that attracted both internal and external candidates for international assignments in the Middle East.
- Managed HR issues associated with 2 business acquisitions while accomplishing a smooth transition and retention of all key personnel.
- Restructured HR function with no service disruption to the business while saving $500,000 annually.

EDUCATION / AFFILIATIONS

M.B.A., Cornell University, New York, NY
B.A., Business Administration, Amherst College, Amherst, MA

Society for Human Resource Management
Human Resource Council of Albany

MARY ANN BURROWS
123 Randolph Street
Ithaca, New York 11923
(914) 644–6653

OBJECTIVE

CERTIFIED MEDICAL ASSISTANT seeks opportunity to apply qualifications in clinical medical assisting, including performing basic laboratory procedures, assisting with medical/emergency procedures, and taking medical histories. Thorough and accurate in completion of insurance forms and patient documentation. Demonstrate a sensitive, caring approach to patient care along with the ability to work cooperatively with all members of the health care team. Excellent interpersonal, organizational, problem solving, and communication skills. Computer proficient.

EDUCATIONAL BACKGROUND

Certificate - Medical Assistant Program, Clinical Specialty
Westchester Community College, Valhalla, New York (2003)

Certifications

Registered Medical Assistant, 2005 (#567834) - American Registry of Medical Assistants
Phlebotomy Technician • EKG Technician • CPR Certified
Level III Collection Services Technician • Psychemedics Sample Collection

CLINICAL and MEDICAL OFFICE SKILLS

Skin/Venipuncture ... Specimen Collections (Urinalysis, Hematology, & Psychemedics)
Medical Histories ... Lab Procedures ... Vital Signs ... EKGs ... Emergency Treatment
Assisting with Physical Examinations ... Medical Terminology ... Biohazardous Materials Disposal

HIGHLIGHTS of EXPERIENCE

♦ Conducted examinations involving complete patient medical histories, blood pressure readings, urine and blood sample collections, and drug screening for company serving the insurance industry. Frequently assigned to handle difficult clients and recaptured key accounts by ensuring timely service.

♦ Provided ongoing care to private, elderly patients. Took vital signs, administered medications and supplemental nourishment through IV therapy, and assisted patients with activities of daily living.

♦ Performed emergency services rotations at Memorial Hospital, assisting medical team in providing treatment at accidents and other emergency situations.

♦ Taught several courses in Medical Assistant Training Program at Health Education Centers, including anatomy, physiology, medical assisting, EKG, phlebotomy, and medical laboratory testing.

PROFESSIONAL EMPLOYMENT

Paramedical Insurance Examiner • INSURANCE SERVICES, INC., White Plains, New York • 1996-2005
Instructor - Medical Assisting • HEALTH EDUCATION CENTERS, White Plains, New York • 1994-1996

PRIOR EXPERIENCE

Office Manager • SCOPE COMMUNICATIONS, White Plains, New York • 1993-1994
Customer Service Representative • BOWEN CORPORATION, White Plains, New York • 1991-1993

LYN CHEN
(703) 555–4478

443 Nestor Road
Alexandria, VA 22003
lchen@protypeltd.com

■ OBJECTIVE

Seeking to apply solid experience in e-business, e-government, and telecommunications markets for a management consulting organization in the Asian-Pacific Region. Project management, market research, and cross-cultural communication skills (Western and Asian) combine with diverse business background. Bilingual in Chinese (Mandarin and Shanghai Dialect) and English.

■ EDUCATION

M.B.A. with concentration in e-Commerce Marketing, 2004
AMERICAN UNIVERSITY, SCHOOL OF BUSINESS, Washington, D.C.

Management Consulting Projects

- **Redman, Brotter & Williams Communications, Washington, D.C.**—Assessed business practices of the Washington DC-based public relations firm. Designed a detailed e-business plan for focusing on process improvement and communication strategies, integrating order fulfillment, service delivery, and customer relationship management, resulting in significant reduction in daily operating costs.

- **ADI Management Institute, Alexandria, VA**—Conducted an on-site analysis of the organization's management information systems requirements and designed procurement system that integrated contracting, accounting, and receiving processes, resulting in more responsive, user-friendly system with real-time trackable data.

- **PacSystems Inc., Arlington, VA**—Analyzed existing business model and global expansion opportunities for a B2B e-marketplace serving the U.S. packaging industry. Conducted extensive research of major international packaging markets in Asia and Europe. Designed and presented to senior executives the region-specific sales/marketing for effective market positioning and entry. Commended on research depth and dynamic presentation style.

Awards

- **Case competition winner out of 10 teams** in the Managers in International Economy class on Steinway's entry strategy to the China market. Professor's comment: *"You delivered the most compelling presentation; no one else was even close."*

B.S. in Communications, graduated summa cum laude, 2002
UNIVERSITY OF NORTH CAROLINA, Chapel Hill, NC

■ INTERNSHIPS

MYRON INTERNATIONAL, Washington, D.C. (2003-2004)
ELLISON CORPORATION, Washington, D.C. (2003-2004)

Intern—During the MBA program, completed internships related to business outreach, e-commerce marketing, and e-business/e-government analysis.

Client Engagement Projects

Myron International—Performed market-risk analysis on telecom, Internet, and e-commerce development throughout the Greater China Region (China, Hong Kong, and Taiwan) and identified global market trends, growth areas, and investment opportunities for Aster Technologies, a client of the international investment and consulting firm. Results were published for senior decision makers on Aster's Intranet.

Ellison Corporation—Evaluated e-business policy/leadership and e-government readiness in the China market for the global technology and policy consulting firm and clients, including Dunston-Patterson, Jones Smythe and Hamden. Contributed research and analysis to company publication, *"Risk E-Business: Seizing the Opportunity of Global E-Readiness."* Utilized contacts in China and acted as liaison between firm and Chinese Ministry of Industry Information that regulates Internet and telecommunications development.

ELAINE ERICKSON

Box 9004
APO AE 09220
011-972-4499-3267
Elaine_Erickson@net.com

CAREER FOCUS

Seeking position as a **Site Manager**, offering a bachelor's in Criminal Justice and 4 years of progressive military experience in security operations in hostile environments. Hold Secret Security Clearance - Protective Services Qualified.

✓ Solid qualifications in supervision and personnel training, contributing to operational readiness/success.
✓ U.S. citizen; born and raised in Russia; Russian Linguist; Scored 4/4 on Defense Language Proficiency Test.
✓ Recognized by supervisors as a highly self-motivated, efficient professional who delivers outstanding results through problem-solving, communications, and interpersonal strengths.
✓ Personal qualities include reliability, trustworthiness, sound judgment, and strong work ethic.

EXPERIENCE

U.S. NAVY COMMANDER FLEET, U.S. NAVAL CENTRAL COMMAND   2003 to Present
Protective Service Agent

Handpicked as the first woman to represent Naval Support Activity as a Protective Service Agent in the Gulf. Conducted more than 100 VIP movements without any incidents.

▪ Plan, coordinate and provide security, administrative, and logistics support to the Commander of the U.S. Fifth Fleet and visiting dignitaries who are high-risk targets of terrorism.

▪ Entrusted to coordinate monthly Motorcade Operations detail for the Commanders of Joint Chiefs of Staff and U.S. Naval Central Command.

▪ Range of experience includes protective service tactics, anti-ambush operations, counter surveillance operations, evasive driving techniques, and providing physical security.

▪ Execute and monitor force protection level training for the Command with an emphasis on crime prevention, port security, public relations, and language instruction.

▪ Train security staff in force protection, anti-terrorism, threat collection, information security, crisis management, terrorist and weapons of mass destruction response, mass casualty and physical security planning.

Accomplishments & Awards

• Liaised with numerous U.S. protection agencies and host nations, playing a key role in the successful protection of the Vice Admiral, 20+ visiting Flag Officers and dignitaries.
• Recognized for successful results in planning and coordinating physical fitness assessment program for 50 Central Command personnel.
• Earned the National Defense Service Medal, 2003; Armed Forces Expeditionary Medal, 2003; Navy and Marine Corps Achievement Medal, 2002; and Meritorious Unit Commendation, 2002.

Supervisor's Evaluation Comments: *"Elaine is a key member of the Commander's Executive Protection Detail. One of the go-to sailors when things need to get done. A self-starter who rapidly established herself as a leader in the work center; both junior and senior personnel look to her for direction. Her knowledge and drive have reinvigorated the Executive Protection Detail She is essential to its success."*

ELAINE ERICKSON - PAGE 2

NAVAL SECURITY FORCE
Training Officer   2003 to 2003

Promoted to Master-at-Arms Second Class and assigned to Protective Service Detail in Bahrain following closure of Roosevelt Roads Naval Base.

- Planned and coordinated bi-monthly training schedules for new Security Personnel in all aspects of force protection and security issues.
- Taught courses in Security Department operations and job duties, Crime Prevention, Search and Seizure, Jurisdiction, Public Relations, Uniform Code of Military Justice, Use of Force, Report Writing, Perimeter Searches, Interview and Interrogation, Crime Scenes and Preservation of Evidence, and CPR.

Accomplishments

- Trained and ensured that all personnel were properly trained and qualified in Search and Seizure procedures, vehicle and personnel searches, and detention and apprehension of suspects.
- Initiated the Naval Security Force Bahrain CPR Program, certifying over 150 security personnel and maintaining 300 records.

Patrol Officer / Training Coordinator   2001 to 2003

Supervised a team of 15 personnel on Vieques Island during quarterly military exercises. Scheduled work assignments/rotations and acted as liaison between military and local authorities.

- Evaluated daily operations of Force Protection and Physical Security. Analyzed and reviewed complex security issues. Recommended action steps to ensure appropriate implementation of security measures in response to threat assessment and intelligence.
- Acted as a liaison for the Naval Security Department with Marine Support Units and the Coast Guard for safeguarding the Live Impact Area during exercise operations.
- Ensured that Security Force personnel were properly equipped and briefed on threat level during protests.
- Performed additional responsibilities as Dispatcher, Incident Report Writer, DWI Patrol Officer, security and riot support, protective service volunteer, range support and base security.

Accomplishments

- Developed and coordinated security policy and procedures for assigned security programs.
- Trained over 300 Naval Security Force Personnel on all aspects of law enforcement and force protection, ensuring their qualification in Search and Seizure procedures, vehicle and personnel searches, detention and apprehension of suspects, CPR and weapons.
- Prepared and implemented automated presentations in classroom settings during the Department of Defense Joint Service Integrate Vulnerability Assessment briefings.
- Assisted in the safe removal of 16 anti-Navy protestors on the island, enabling Joint Forces and U.S. Naval Battle Groups to maintain operational readiness.

EDUCATION

B.A. in Criminal Justice, emphasis in Policing, Excelsior College (military distance learning program), 2004
Courses include: Criminal Investigation, Corrections, Deviant Behavior, Juvenile Delinquency, Forensic Science

MILITARY TRAINING

Naval Security Force Field Training Officer Academy, Protective Training and Antiterrorism Evasive Driver Course, Protective Service Detail School, Executive Protection Driver School, Naval Criminal Investigative Service Surveillance Course, Executive Protective Services, Emergency Medical Technician and Law Enforcement Apprentice Course.

DAVID A. JONES

85 Ellington Street • Groton, CT 06098 • (203) 437-6779

MAINTENANCE / MATERIALAS / OPERATIONS MANAGEMENT

Transportation ~ Shipping Industry

> *"David is an exceptional planner, organizer, and innovative problem solver who has succeeded where others have failed … he has exceptional operations expertise, strong leadership skills, and sound judgment."*
>
> Bertrand Fisher
> Commanding Officer

Management Professional offering 15 years of experience in electronics equipment maintenance, materials, operations and security.

- Promoted through increasingly responsible technical and supervisory positions based on expertise, demonstrated initiative, and contributions to operational efficiency.

- Effective trainer who develops and leads staff to peak performance.

- Expert in navigation and ship-handling operations and systems.

- Recipient of 15 achievement, commendation and distinguished service awards throughout naval career.

RELEVANT EXPERIENCE & ACCOMPLISHMENTS

Maintenance & Materials Management

- Improved operations through aggressive materials improvement and equipment refurbishment programs that were subsequently instituted throughout the organization.
- Supervised electronics technicians in maintenance/repair of various communications, radar, and other electronics systems, ensuring peak efficiency and reliability.
- Led implementation of efficient purchasing and JIT inventory management system.
- Oversaw hazardous cargo certification requirements, equipment maintenance and safety.

Operations Management

- Managed the daily planning, coordination, and supervision of 45 staff members, effectively ensuring stringent compliance with vessel safety standards.
- Developed and executed detailed operational review plans for command administrative inspection, resulting in timely problem identification and corrective actions.
- Recognized for instrumental role in achieving "excellent" ratings in all areas during plant inspections.

Staff Training & Management

- Trained more than 500 military and civilian personnel in maintenance procedures, navigation, fire fighting, damage control, security, and other areas.
- Turned around an under-performing division to rank #1 in productivity by improving the training curriculum.

CAREER HISTORY

United States Navy • 1989 to Present
Patrol Boat Captain • 1989 to 1990; Legal & Administrative Officer • 1988 to 1989
Assistant Operations & Electronics Material Officer • 1986 to 1988

EDUCATION

B.E., Electrical Engineering, Connecticut College • New London, CT
Additional Training: Electronics Material Management Training Program
Boat Group Management Training Program, Military Justice Legal Training Program

PAULA MARTIN
VETERINARY TECHNICIAN
pmartin@protypeltd.com

889 Westfield Street
Agawam, MA 06001
413.555.7644

CAREER FOCUS AND SUMMARY

Compassionate and competent **Veterinary Technician** with 5+ years of experience assisting veterinarians in medical and surgical procedures, ranging from routine to emergency and critical care. Recognized as efficient, skilled in multitasking, and dedicated to providing prompt, courteous service. Effective communicator who enjoys working with people and animals and is able to educate owners on protecting their companion animals' health and well-being.

PROFESSIONAL EXPERIENCE

VETERINARY TECHNICIAN
Harrington Animal Clinic, Agawam, MA   *2000 to Present*
Assist 5 veterinarians in providing comprehensive veterinary care. Skilled in performing:

Medical & Surgical Procedures
- Assist in all types of medical treatments (and with restraints), ranging from routine office examinations to critical care, emergency situations, euthanasia, and house calls.
- Set up all equipment and prep animals for surgery: shaving, intubating, inserting IV catheters, and administration of intravenous/intramuscular drugs.
- Assist with surgeries, including spaying/neutering, exploratory, cystotomy, nasal scope, endoscopy, cruciate/luxating patella, abscess, declawing, and other procedures.
- Prepare and sterilize surgical packs in an autoclave; monitor anesthesia and patients' vital signs; administer subcutaneous fluids; perform complete dentistry.
- Accurately document anesthetic drugs used during surgery; handle post-surgical recovery: extubation, patient monitoring, and calling clients to provide follow-up/status reports.
- Prepare vaccines; refill/dispense medications; administer oral medications/vaccines under supervision and provide instructions to clients; assist with administration of chemotherapy.

Tests / Lab Work / Client Education
- Conduct heartworm, Feline Leukemia, and FIV tests. Take glucose and blood (including jugular) samples. Read results of urinalysis and fecal samples.
- Perform and develop radiographs as required. Assist specialists in restraining animals during ultrasounds.
- Educate clients on diseases/preventive care, home care (post surgery, diabetic discharges, administering subcutaneous fluids and medications), grooming, diet, geriatric care, declawing alternatives, and other aspects of animal health care.
- Groom and bathe animals, including fungal baths, lion clips, and reverse sedation according to veterinarian's instruction.

Front Office / Administration
- Cross-trained to perform front office duties, including scheduling routine health exams and surgical appointments, invoicing/cashing out, providing estimates and more. Greet clients and set up patients in exam rooms.
- Place orders for medications and various products per veterinarians' instructions. Sell products to clients.
- Utilize customized computer applications to process payments and enter patient records.
- Serve as resource to new technicians by answering questions on equipment, office, and other procedures.

EDUCATION / TRAINING

A.S., Veterinary Technician; BRIARWOOD COLLEGE, Springfield, MA   2000
Additional Training: Completed intensive on-the-job 3-month training under guidance of licensed veterinarians at Harrington Animal Clinic.

Stephen Reymore

E-mail: sreymore@protypeltd.com

732.555.8113
177 Washington Avenue • Edison, NJ 08818

Career Focus: Sales/Territory Management

Delivering consistent and sustainable revenue gains, profit growth and market-share increases through strategic sales leadership of multi-site branches. Valued offered:

- ✓ Driver of innovative programs that provide a competitive edge and establish company as a full-service market leader.
- ✓ Proactive, creative problem solver who develops solutions that save time, cut costs, and ensure consistent product quality.
- ✓ Empowering leader who recruits, develops, coaches, motivates, and inspires sales teams to top performance.
- ✓ Innovative in developing and implementing win-win solutions to maximize account expansion, retention, and satisfaction.

Experience & Selected Achievements

RANFORD COMPANY • Edison, NJ   1990 to 2004

As Branch Manager, reinvigorated the sales organization, growing company sales from $9MM to $11MM, expanding account base from 450 to 680 and increasing market share 15%. Established new performance benchmark and trained sales force on implementing sales-building customer inventory rationalization programs.

- **Revitalized and restored profitability of 2 underperforming territories** by coaching and developing territory reps.
- **Penetrated 2 new markets and secured a lucrative market niche** in abrasive products. Staffed, opened, and managed the 2 branch locations in New Jersey—one of which alone produced $3MM+ over 3 years.
- **Initiated and advanced the skills of sales force to effectively promote and sell increasingly technical product lines** in response to changing market demands.

Increased profit margins and dollar volume through product mix diversification and expansion. Created product catalogs and marketing literature.

- **Ensured that the company maintained its competitive edge in the marketplace** by adding several cross-functional product lines.
- **Led highly profitable new product introduction with a 40% profit margin** that produced $100K annually in new business.

BERLIN COMPANY • Trenton, NJ   1985 to 1990

As Account Executive, rejuvenated sales performance of a stagnant territory. Turned around customer perception by cultivating exceptional relationships through solutions-based selling and delivering value-added service. Recognized as a peak performer company-wide who consistently ranked #1 in sales and #1 in profits.

- **Positioned and established company as a full-service supplier** to drive sales revenues by translating customer needs to product solutions.
- **More than doubled territory sales from $700K to $1.6MM** during tenure and grew account base from 80 to 125 through new market penetration. **Landed and managed 3 of company's 6 largest accounts** and grew remaining 3.
- **Captured a lucrative account and drove annual sales from $100K in the first year to $400K in 3 years**—outperforming the competition without any price-cutting.
- **Mentored new and existing territory reps** on customer relationship management, solutions-selling strategies, advanced product knowledge, and customer programs.

Education

B.S. in Business Management—Rhode Island University, Providence, RI

MARTIN SHERMAN, C.P.A.

87 Regatta Lane   Mobile: 914.662.7835
Tarrytown, New York 95807   msherman@yahoo.com   Home: 914.618.3499

PROFESSIONAL OBJECTIVE

Certified Public Accountant with a master's degree in accounting and taxation and business management experience.

Proven analytical and financial management skills. Critical thinker and creative problem solver with excellent planning, organizational, and supervisory strengths.

Technical skills: MS Office (Word, Excel, Access and PowerPoint), JD Edwards and Peachtree Accounting.

Key Competencies

General & Cost Accounting
Financial Modeling • Auditing
Financial/Business Analysis
Asset & Liability • Management
Cost/Benefit Analysis • Risk
Assessment • Working Capital

EDUCATION

FORDHAM COLLEGE, NEW YORK, NEW YORK
M.S. in Accounting and Taxation, 2005
B.S. in Business Administration with concentration in **Finance**, 1994

Relevant Courses: Advanced Accounting, Intermediate Accounting, Managerial Accounting, Governmental Accounting, Auditing, Finance, Business Law, Cost Accounting, Tax Accounting

Certified Public Accountant – State of New York, 2005

CAPABILITIES – ACCOUNTING/FINANCE
Education and training provided a solid foundation in:

- Setting up balance sheets, income statements, and cash flow statements in compliance with GAAP.
- Analyzing financial performance of business operations; tracking and analyzing costs; creating and implementing cost control systems to achieve corporate objectives.
- Developing and administering budgets; familiar with capital budgeting process. Versed in the different types of corporations, consolidations, and tax advantages.
- Determining valuation of business assets, stock and bond prices, depreciation schedules, pro forma statements. Creating capital asset pricing models and financial models.
- Calculating P/E ratios, DCF, EPS, discounted cash flow, and beta for equity security analysis.
- Devising portfolio asset allocation strategies and conducting risk assessments; developing business plans.
- Developing financial management and investment strategies for both individuals and companies.

BUSINESS MANAGEMENT EXPERIENCE

Value Stores, Inc., New York, New York (1992 to present)
Manager (1995 to present) / **Assistant Manager** (1992 to 1995)

Promoted to manage the financial and day-to-day operations of $3 million business. Scope of responsibilities encompasses P&L management auditing financial records, payroll, cash management, inventory control, adjusting inventory retail values, account reconciliation, and human resources management. Accomplishments:

- **Significantly improved store's financial performance, bringing it from 10% under budget to 3% above** budget within the first month as manager by:
  - Assessing and realigning employee skills with appropriate tasks/functions.
  - Improving inventory levels and product mix on sales floor.
  - Reducing turnover by recruiting, training, and developing quality candidates.
- **Boosted profits by 20% over prior year, sales by 4% annually** and budgeted profit forecasts by 6% per year.
- **Winner of 3 Paragon Awards out of 15 managers** in the district for achieving excellence in customer service and exceeding profitability/sales targets. Tapped as mentor, developing and training 25 new store managers.

Fred Leonard

89 Lawrence Street • Hopewell, VA 89945 • (765) 344–5559 • fredleonard@aol.com

PROFESSIONAL OBJECTIVE

Offering over 10 years of leadership experience in town government as an elected **Chief Administrative and Fiscal Officer.** Key contributor impacting operational, budgetary, staffing, and resource needs throughout the municipality. Effective leader and consensus builder with planning, organizational, and negotiation strengths, as well as the ability to establish goals and deliver results. Core Competencies:

- **Management/Administration**
- **Economic Development**
- **Public/Private Sector Alliances**
- **Project/Program Management**
- **Fiscal Management/Budgeting**
- **Staff Development/Empowerment**

EXPERIENCE

SELECTMAN / BOARD CHAIR   TOWN OF HOPEWELL, HOPEWELL, VA   1993 to Present

Administration – Proactive executive providing strategic planning and leadership direction to diverse municipal departments as one of 3 elected board members governing the Town of Hopewell. As board member, direct multiple open town meetings, develop and oversee $10 million budget, and administer various projects. Experience includes chairing the Board of Selectmen for the past 3 years. Serve as a Police Commissioner.

Human Resources – Authority for recruitment, promotion, and supervision of the Town Administrator 10 department heads with up to 214 full- and part-time staff, as well as Department of Public Works and Police Department. Personnel functions also encompass recruitment, contract negotiations, benefits administration, employee relations, and policy development and implementation.

Economic Development – Support strong public/private partnership toward diversified growth and prosperity. Source and negotiate with businesses as well as secure agreements to retain and attract new businesses. Develop financial vehicles for public improvements.

Regulatory Affairs – Develop and manage relationships, as well as advocate for municipal affairs, with federal and state regulatory agencies, local business executives, congressional members, and other legislators.

Public Relations – Instrumental in the enhancement of Town's image and building consensus with all boards. Active participant in numerous annual community events; act as spokesperson with the media.

Accomplishments

- Turned around employee morale and productivity, instituted training and employee recognition programs and fostered interdepartmental cooperation, creating a positive work environment while restoring accountability and confidence in the administration. Municipality is recognized for having the "most responsive and best managed administrations statewide."
- Leader in the execution of several town revitalization projects, following failed attempts by prior boards:
  - $2.9 million renovations to Town Hall, Senior Center, and Council on Aging
  - $5 million public safety complex
  - $2.3 million public library project with state library grant offsets of $200,000
  - $15 million sewer project with over $5 million secured in federal grant funding
- Personally negotiated Tax Incentive Financing (TIF) Agreements to retain and attract businesses.
- Effectively negotiated with local executives to relocate their companies back to the Town. Results led to construction of new manufacturing facility for 4 companies employing 550 people combined.

EDUCATION

UNIVERSITY OF VIRGINIA, Charlottesville, VA:
M.B.A. in Finance
B.S. in Business Administration

Don Orlando

MBA, CPRW, JCTC, CCM, CCMC
The McLean Group
E-mail: Yourcareercoach@charterinternet.com
Tel. 334-264-2020
Fax 334-264-9227

One of America's first personal career coaches and a premier resume writer, Don has assisted hundreds of people from all walks of life in finding jobs and changing careers. Professionally active, he is a founding member of Career Masters Institute and he has written the Code of Ethics for that organization. He has developed the exam for the Professional Association of Resume Writers, which is used for certifying resume writing professionals. He has served as a mentor to other career coaches and resume writers.

Don has written numerous articles for trade and professional publications as well as contributed examples of his work to more than 35 books on resume and letter writing. He regularly writes, researches, and teaches in this field.

The following examples showcase Don's unique approach to resume writing. Rather than use an objective, he begins each resume with a powerful employer-focused statement that stresses **benefits** the candidate will likely bring to the position, based upon an understanding of past **patterns of performance**. The Work History sections translate experience into accomplishments, which are stated as outcomes or payoffs for previous employers. His examples represent some of today's most powerful employer-oriented resumes. These resumes speak the language of employers loud and clear.

─────────────────────── **Martin Smith** ───────────────────────
4441 Park Lane Centerville, Alabama 36100
☎ 334.555.5555 (cell) — ✉ ms100@email.com

────────── WHAT I CAN OFFER **TOPLINE** AS YOUR NEWEST **SALES REPRESENTATIVE** ──────────

❏ Established skill at **building** strong, **profitable relationships** with buying decision makers

❏ Tested capability to balance persistence with helpfulness, thus **winning and keeping new customers**

❏ Proven record of **beating the competition** to the sale in a very competitive market

❏ Documented ability in **recapturing lost customers** — even the formerly irate

──────────── RECENT WORK HISTORY WITH EXAMPLES OF PROBLEMS SOLVED ────────────

❏ **Residential Sales Representative** *sought out by our vice-president over 28 tough competitors, several with more years of experience, to be* **Architectural and Commercial Sales Representative**, Acme Building Supply, Pine City, Florida and Centerville, Alabama   Apr 00 – Present

Acme Building Supply manufactures and distributes a full range of brick, tile, and stone. A leader in the industry, our company sells nationwide and our plant runs 24/7.

Bringing in $1.5M annually as the only sales person in my division. Indirectly supervise an administrative assistant.

Recaptured an irate, former, **long-time customer** our company had written off. Overcame his initial resistance by empathizing with him. Customized a product book to meet his specific needs. *Payoffs:* Earned his trust in just six weeks. **He** became, and **remains, one of our top 20 accounts**.

Got a jump on the competition by tracking construction projects long before they became generally known. Found the principal architect and mastered his vision for a very visible city project. Persuaded him to change his plans to showcase one of our lines. Then worked with our vendor to make sure the product enhanced this high-visibility job. *Payoffs:* **Landed $150K contract.**

Rescued a major sale when our client fell in love with our products, but threatened to call off the deal when he found the cost double his original estimates. Got the vendor's rep to drive 300 miles to help explore alternatives. *Payoffs:* Client cut back on every element — from plumbing to air conditioning — to **buy two of our products**.

Turned a cold call into a $20K sale. Worked closely with a consulting architect to go beyond the technical specs of our product. Together, we showed the end user how it could draw customers into his business in a very competitive market. *Payoffs:* Not only pleased the final customer, but **reinforced my relationship with** a leading architect — a **key player in our market**.

CONFIDENTIAL   *More indicators of performance TopLine can use …*

Martin Smith   **Sales Representative**   334.555.5555

Went the extra mile when contractor needed to match products we had delivered more than 10 years ago. Using my strong relationship with our plant manager, we met all the special requirements. *Payoffs:* Made the very tight deadline right on time. Contractor now **calls me, personally, every time**, to supply products for every job.

Transformed an unsatisfied customer into strong account. The day after he originally dropped us for a competitor, I called on him. When I took responsibility for our future performance, he gave me just the chance I needed to recapture his business. *Payoffs:* Using my normal, careful follow up, I made sure the job went off perfectly. Now he "**...won't do anything without calling me.**"

Found, and won over, the key contractor for a major project—the person who would specify the product we manufacture. Located a match for the product the customer specified, then negotiated a reduced price with our vendor. *Payoffs:* **Everybody won**. The customer got a great product. The contractor got a higher profit. We **landed an excellent sale.**

❏ Part-time Laborer *promoted to* Full-time Welder *promoted to* Automation Programmer *promoted to* **Sales Engineer**, J. R. Smith, Centerville, Alabama   89 – 00
J.R. Smith designs and manufactures complete plumbing systems that are sold worldwide.

———————————— EDUCATION AND PROFESSIONAL DEVELOPMENT ————————————

❏ BS, **Marketing**, University of Centerville, Centerville, Alabama   96
Earned this degree while working more than 40 hours a week. My employer paid for my education. Dean's List.

❏ Time Management, American Management Association, 2 days   04
My employer covered the cost of this training.

❏ How to Win Friends and Influence People, Dale Carnegie, Centerville, Alabama   00
Acme Building Supply paid for this 36-contact-hour course.

———————————————— COMPUTER SKILLS ————————————————

❏ Comfortable with Word and advanced techniques to search the Web.
❏ Working knowledge of Excel and PowerPoint.

———————————————— PROFESSIONAL AFFILIATIONS ————————————————

❏ Member, Association of General Contractors   Since 04
❏ Member, Construction Specifications Institute   Since 04

Pete Astrud
inventory manager

4114 North Carlton Street
Kansas City, Missouri 64101
☎ 816.555.5555 (cell) – 816.555.6666 (Home)
✉ peteastrud6290@yahoo.com

MY VALUE TO TOPLINE AS YOUR INVENTORY MANAGER

❏ Proven track record in **maximizing ROI**…in people, software, stock levels, and policies

❏ Documented skill at finding and fixing inventory and logistics problems with **solutions that work over the long haul** ❏ Practiced ability to **train others in best practices**

RECENT WORK HISTORY WITH EXAMPLES OF PROBLEMS SOLVED

❏ Independent **Logistics Contractor**, McConnell Air Force Base, Kansas   Jul 03 – Present

❏ **Logistics Contractor**, BMAR, Inc., McConnell Air Force Base, Kansas   Dec 02 – Jun 03

Helped support a full-service outpatient clinic employing 300 professionals that serves a population of 41,000.

More than 10 years of increasingly responsible logistics-related positions on active duty with the United States Air Force including these most recent assignments:

❏ *Promoted by name at the request of the Chief of Medical Logistics to serve as* **Medical Logistics Manager,** Yigo, Guam   Nov 00 – Oct 02

Served as direct reporting official for eight professionals including an assistant chief of medical logistics, an acquisitions manager, a warehouse manager, warehouse, and purchasing specialists. Took on additional responsibilities as the Director of the Logistics Disaster Team. **Built, defended, and managed an annual budget of $960K.**

Inherited an organization that had needed improvement in accountability and inventory control for two years. Others tried adding more people, but that approach failed. Soon uncovered the real problem: improper training. *Outcomes:* Designed, built, and delivered solid training **without spending an extra dime.** We went from near the bottom of more than 15 organizations **right to the top**—and we stayed there.

Found a much better way to get management the logistics reports they needed to support our mission. Replaced cumbersome text format with an easy-to-use, concise PowerPoint presentation. *Outcomes:* The leadership loved the reports so much, my format **became the corporate standard.** What **once took 40 hours** a month to compile, **now done in an hour.**

Asked to build one of the very first logistics plans in support of homeland defense—after $250K worth of material had already arrived. My baseline audit, done **single-handedly,** corrected dozens of errors in five weeks of nights and weekend work. *Outcomes:* By redistributing several line items, support improved quickly. **Saved $10K a year.**

Did the work of 2 people to get our $1.1M inventory back under control. *Outcomes:* My new policies brought these advantages: **accuracy rose to 99.9 percent** (nearly 5 percent

More indicators of performance TopLine can use …

| Pete Astrud | **Inventory Manager** | 816.555.5555 (Cell) |

above the corporate standard); inventories increased from 1 to 4 times a year; time to complete each inventory fell from 6 man weeks to 12 man hours.

Trained the staff to transition to a much more responsive inventory control—even though I had no experience or training in that system. Mastered the subject so well, I soon trained 54 key customer representatives. *Outcomes:* Organization's **average delivery time fell from 65 to 8 days.**

❑ *Sought out for promotion by senior management to serve as* **Quality Assurance Manager,** United States Embassy, Muscat, Oman   Nov 98 – Oct 00

Helped support 200 directly assigned staff and an additional 40 contractors at four sites spread over hundreds of miles of empty desert in four countries.

Restored accountability measures to the system used to evaluate contractors' performance. *Outcomes:* **Miscalibration rate fell** from 12 percent to 0; **$10K saved** in transportation costs, **availability** of parts **rose 25 percent**—and all this done in 60 days.

Recovered value from expired stock by finding a market for those products. *Outcomes:* **Recovered $75K** in 1 line item category alone.

❑ *Promoted to* **Medical Systems Analyst** and Section Training Manager, Gunter Annex, McConnell Air Force Base, Kansas   Sep 94 – Nov 98

Chosen by the most senior management to **lead a team** that did **breakthrough work on usage rates.** With nothing but the broadest guidance, recruited an interdisciplinary team of 12. *Outcomes:* Our software test produced **such flawless results that it's still in use** today. Brought in this 90-day project **20 days early.** Decorated for this achievement.

EDUCATION AND PROFESSIONAL DEVELOPMENT

❑ Associates Degree, Management, Empire State College of New York, Saratoga Springs, New York   2003

Earned this degree while working 40 hours a week. Completed eight hours toward a B.S. in management at the same school.

❑ Associates Degree in Logistics, Community College of the Air Force, Maxwell Air Force Base, Alabama   98

❑ "Acquisition Planning – Under Development: Determination of Need, Market Research & Analysis Requirements," two days, Federal Acquisition Institute   01

COMPUTER SKILLS

❑ Near expert in a proprietary inventory control, accounting, purchasing, shipping, and report generator **logistics software suite.**

❑ Proficient in Word, Excel, PowerPoint, and advanced Internet search protocols.

❑ Working knowledge of Access and UNIX.

Denise R. Crawford

5400 Willow Lane, #4 – Millbrook, Alabama 36000
ỳ 334.555.5555 (home) – 334.555.6666 (cell) – ✉drcdrc@hotmail.com

What AllSouth Gets When I Join Your Team As An Entry Level Commercial Real Estate Professional

The drive and skill to build and maintain a "pipeline" of potential deals.

The personal contacts among key decision makers statewide including bankers, mayors, city council members, and elected officials.

The vision to see and close deals others have overlooked.

Recent and Relevant Work History with Examples of Problems Solved

Majority Owner, Cornerstone Builders, LLC, Kingly, Alabama   Jul 04 – Present
Cornerstone serves the tri-county area building spec homes 1,800ft² and larger.

Building Relationships with Key Players in Commercial Real Estate

Used my personal contact to persuade a banker to extend a major capital venture loan. Over came a lack of a professional track record in building and limited credit scores my partner had to prove we were a good financial risk. *Payoffs:* **Loan approved** in just two months.

Major, Alabama Army National Guard, serving in a variety of assignments with increasing responsibility in Alabama and Saudi Arabia   Mar 83 – Present

Finding and Serving Customers Others Have Overlooked

Turned around a product that customers didn't like—even though they were a "captive" market: a corporate newspaper. Recruited the right people to help me. Then went to where our readers lived to see what they wanted. Finally, overcame management's resistance to change to roll out an entirely new product. *Payoffs:* **Increased circulation by 100 percent.** We were pressed to keep up with customer demand—the **strongest** it had been **in years.**

Turning Diverse Groups into Solid Supporters

Went beyond changing the group I was asked to lead from dissatisfied strangers into a smoothly running team. Listened carefully, then built their trust through demonstrated fairness every day. *Payoffs:* Retention **grew 15 percentage points. Met** my **goals** in this area for **30 consecutive months**—a rare feat.

District Director *and* **Campaign Manager**, Office of Congressman Martin Kelley, Montgomery, Alabama   Mar 96 – Dec 96 and Dec 01 to Jan 02

Building Coalitions among People Who Drive Commercial Real Estate

Helped our candidate dominate the field by reaching out—personally—to mayors, city council members, and business leaders. Gave them clear and compelling proof that we were ready and able to meet their needs. *Payoffs:* Not only did we build solid support, we came across so powerfully that **not one competitor** from our party **entered the race.**

More indicators of performance AllSouth can use...

Denise Crawford	**Commercial Real Estate Professional**	334.555.5555

Executive Director, Alabama Libertarian Party, Montgomery, Alabama   Aug 97 – Dec 98

PERSUADING BUSINESS LEADERS TO INVEST IN THEIR FUTURE

Found a better way to raise money that aligned our requirements with the business community's needs. Called on committees (you would call them sales forces) in every one of Alabama's 67 counties. Motivated each one to ask businesses to donate goods and services in a fund-raising auction. Drove nearly 4,000 miles in just nine days to make these "warm calls." *Payoffs:* From plan to results—**from $100K in the red to $110K in the black**—in just 5 months.

EDUCATION AND PROFESSIONAL DEVELOPMENT

BS, **Business Administration,** Central University at Montgomery   91
*Granted two **leadership scholarships** under a competitive program that recognized top performers. Earned this degree while working up to 20 hours a week while carrying a full academic load at night.*

AS, **Business Administration,** River City Junior College, River City, Alabama   89
*Granted a one-year scholarship. Held down a 20-hour-a-week job. Served as both Student Government Association Treasurer and **Class President**.*

"How to Generate Leads, Make Cold Calls, and Close Sales," Thomas Nelson, one week, 04

COMPUTER SKILLS

An expert in Word and Adobe PhotoShop; comfortable with advanced Internet search protocols; working knowledge of Excel

LICENSES

Alabama Real Estate License   Granted October 04

COMMUNITY AFFILIATIONS

Member and Treasurer, Delta Nu (an academic honor society), Montgomery Chapter
86 – Present

Former member of the Montgomery Rotary Club   04

Former member of Montgomery Kiwanis   02

Janice M. Shepherd

CPRW, JCTC, CEIP
Write On Career Keys
Top of Alabama Hill
Bellingham WA 98226-4260
Tel. 360-738-7958
Fax 360-738-1189
Website: www.writeoncareerkeys.com
E-mail: janice@writeoncareerkeys.com

With more than 20 years experience crafting targeted resumes for job seekers and career changers, Janice is a recognized expert in the field. She has presented workshops and taught classes on resume writing both at local colleges and for private industry. Her work is featured in more than 20 current career industry publications.

Located in a small community in the Pacific Northwest, she specializes in new grad, blue collar, and career transition resumes. She also provides career transition coaching and interview preparation services to her clients.

As a professional resume writer, Janice has worked with several clients who have diverse occupational backgrounds normally classified as blue collar – refinery workers, mechanics, millwrights, pipefitters, marine workers, heavy equipment operators, construction workers, caretakers, housekeepers, fishermen, and many more. The following resumes showcase the skills and accomplishments of seven blue collar workers. Please note how she incorporates supporting quotes from employers, clients, and others in the resumes on pages 307, 308, 309, and 311. She often uses a Profile and Career Summary in addition to, or in lieu of, an Objective.

Kris Cook

559 Summerland Road, Wellington, WA 98888
Voice: (333) 333-3333 / FAX: (333) 777-777
KCook@yahoo.com

OBJECTIVE

Position as Deckhand on Inland / Near Coastal Marine Vessel

PROFILE

"...hard and vigilant worker... passionate in things he sets out to do...interesting and humorous individual...."
Chef, *Spirit of Discovery,* Cruise West

Possesses great interest in maritime procedures and vessel operation. Demonstrates good understanding of safety and emergency procedures, chemical and sanitation matters. Experienced in basic navigation, lookout, engine rounds, deck maintenance and repair, basic electrical and electronics wiring, operating safety equipment and line handling. Strong problem-solving skills. Proficient—HTML code, Incident Command System; SARA Title3 Tier 2 processing.

QUALIFICATIONS

"...conscientious worker of good character... a credit to his vessel..."
Chief Mate,
M/V Spirit of 98,
Cruise West

+ USA Federal Communications Commission Amateur Radio License
+ Whatcom County Emergency Operations Center Volunteer
+ Red Cross Disaster Services Volunteer / Young Adults Program Coordinator
+ Volunteer, Whatcom County Division of Emergency Management
+ NPFVOA Passenger Vessel Safety Orientation—Safety Equipment and Survival Procedures; Medical Emergencies at Sea; Fire Prevention and Control
+ Federal Emergency Management Agency Emergency Management Institute Courses (FEMA/EMI)

RELEVANT EXPERIENCE

FEMA/EMI *courses completed:*
Emergency Planning
Emergency Management
Exercise Design & Evaluation
Emergency Preparedness
Emergency Program Manager
Radiological Emergency Management
Hazardous Materials Orientation
Disaster Assistance
Orientation to Community Disaster Exercises
EOC Management and Operations

Deckhand, *Columbia Queen,* Delta Queen Steamboat Company, Portland, OR   2/01–present
Columbia and Snake Rivers. Navigational watches, security rounds, line handling including lockages.

Deckhand, *American Queen,* Delta Queen Steamboat Company, New Orleans, LA   1/01–2/01
Mississippi River. Boat maintenance—cleaning, painting—line handling.

Deckhand, *M/V Spirit of 98*, Cruise West, Seattle, WA   4/00–11/00
Contributed to team efforts with basic navigation, lookout, engine rounds, repairing and maintaining equipment, and carrying out other duties as needed.

Galley Assistant, *Spirit of Columbia*, Cruise West, Seattle, WA   seasonal, 1999
Assisted with food prep, service and presentation under pressure—85 meals within 15 minutes.

Galley Prep, *Spirit of Discovery*, Cruise West, Seattle, WA   seasonal, 3/99–5/99
Assisted with food prep, service, and presentation

OTHER EXPERIENCE

Web Developer, Pacific Western Rail System, White Rock, B.C.   8/99–4/00
Created and maintained company web site. Handled shipping and receiving—received product, inventoried to ensure complete order, verified with outstanding packing and shipping orders. Dealt with customers, and Canadian customs computer system for importing goods.

Designed website for Whatcom County Sheriff's Office Division of Emergency Management

Administrative Assistant, Washington State Department of Ecology   temporary 1999
Emergency Appointment to assist with handling of Whatcom Creek disaster. Answered phones, sorted mail, made photocopies, research local newspapers for articles related to pipeline rupture—copied and disseminated to appropriate parties.

EDUCATION

CPR/First Aid
Hazardous Materials Training
Emergency Management, 40 hours, Whatcom Community College, Wellington, WA

Marc Headstrong

1010 E Street, Wellington, WA — (333) 777-0707 — will relocate

- Experienced **HEAVY DUTY DIESEL MECHANIC**—can perform engine overall up to 1000 hp, manual transmissions and rear ends, and all aspects of heavy equipment and truck repair including air, electrical, and fuel problems.

- Hired, trained, and managed up to 32 employees— demonstrated excellent scheduling and prioritizing, and camaraderie resulting in high morale and long-term employees.

- Machine Tool Machinist—operated engine lathe, milling machine, shaper, planer, key-seater, and many others.

- Welder and Welding Operator—all rods, all positions; hard-wire, all positions; dual shield and flux core, flat and horizontal

- Certified WPS

- Top Secret Clearance—Current

"He can build them ... and he can repair them!"

"...our appreciation to you for your timely performance and excellent supply and delivery of structural steel and fabrications ...."

"..maintained high performance standards ... frequently completed work ahead of schedule... maintained constant awareness of safe working practices...."

SUMMARY OF EXPERIENCE

Heavy Duty Diesel Mechanic, 24-HOUR TRUCK REPAIR, Wellington, WA, 1980–present
Spearheaded, established, and maintain 24-hour truck repair service. Timely quality service cultivates loyal customer base and word-of-mouth referrals. Provide on-call repair service for Class 6, 7, and 8 trucks, and all kinds of heavy equipment.

Machinist / Fabricator, ARMSTRONG MANUFACTURING / ARMSTRONG IRON, Lynden, WA, 10 years
Started up and developed manufacturing and fabricating business to build stock handling equipment for manufacturing, build steel buildings and storage tanks up to 300,000 gal. Designed, machined, and fabricated custom equipment including hydraulic for such well-known companies as Snelson-Anvil and Dawson, among others.

- Designed and built all-steel 91x191-foot barn—first of its kind in Whatcom County.

- Received press notoriety as *"cheerful, easy-going welder-machinist"* for *"individual approach ... personalized style of work ... quality of work and huge demand for his services."*

Machinist, GEORGIA-PACIFIC, Wellington, WA, 6 years
Built, maintained, and repaired large acid-resistant stainless steel pumps, compressors, and valves for processing chemicals. Typical projects: compressors that turn 32,000 and run on diamond bearings.

Repair Machinist, CASTLE & COOK, BUMBLE-BEE SEA FOODS, Nack Nick and Dillingham, Alaska, 6 years
Maintained, repaired, and made parts for wide assortment of machinery.

PROFESSIONAL DEVELOPMENT

N-855 Overhaul Class, Cummins Northwest, Inc.
Certificate of Completion, Washington State Machinist Apprenticeship, 4 years
Welding / Diesel Fuel Injection Systems—Wellington Vocational Technical Institute
Graduate, Guardian High School, Wellington, Washington

SHEREN HENDERSEN

22 Dakota Street
Wellington, WA 98333-2222
(333) 444-4444
e-mail: Sheren@email.net

HOUSEKEEPER

"...an absolute model of calm efficiency, adaptability, general competence...." LB, Honokaa, HI

"... remarkable job managing an extremely high-pressure job with a limited budget and staff...quite conscientious and demonstrates personal pride in her work...a self-starter...very good at dealing with conflicting demands of the job...." —JJ, Operations Manager, Bay Resort

PROFILE

Professional housekeeper with adventurous, adaptable nature, and established reputation for reliability, follow-through, and commitment to service. Hands-on management style with proven ability to delegate, organize, and direct the work of others. Creative and innovative problem-solver, exercises good judgment and decision-making, keeps a clear head in times of crises. Easily establishes rapport and productive working relationships with co-workers and guests. Traveled extensively throughout United States.

AREAS OF EXPERTISE

- Housekeeping—cleaning procedures for hotels, motels, lodges, private homes, medical offices.

- Supervision—interview, hire, organize, schedule, train, and evaluate staff.

- Emergencies—trained in procedures to follow in case of fire, flood, broken pipes, etc.— CPR/First Aid Certification

- Inventory—stocking, ordering of linens and cleaning supplies.

- Budget—evaluation and compliance.

SUMMARY OF EXPERIENCE

Executive Housekeeper, Bay Village, Inc., Okay, Washington   1995–present

Oversee daily cleaning and maintenance of 38 cabins, 4 public areas including restrooms and shower houses, and guest kitchen.

Interview, hire, train, schedule, and supervise housekeeping staff. Inspect all cabins and public areas twice daily—before and after cleaning. Wash, dry, fold, and restock, provide hot-tub towels—bundle for delivery to outside laundry. Order cleaning supplies.

Evaluate departmental monthly budget for scheduling and wages—operate consistently within budget.

Assistant Manager, Hoot Owl Lodge, Gato, AK   winter 1994–95

Oversaw housekeeping for busy, well-attended, lodge in remote area of Alaska—consisted of log cabin with bar, restaurant, game area, and six cabins. Occasionally tended bar and cooked meals. Stocked inventory when supplies were delivered. Drove snowmobile.

Executive Housekeeper, Bellingham Travel Lodge, Wellington, WA   1992–1993

Over daily assignments, cleaning, inspection, and laundry for 115 rooms. Substituted for front desk clerk.

Housekeeper, by contract   1989–1990
Wellington News Building and Electric Power Building

EDUCATION

Valley College—Business Machines
Wellington County Vocation School—Word Processing / Secretarial

Carol Henderson

333 West Jones Road
Wellington, WA 77333
(333) 333-3333

OBJECTIVE   Assembler 1

PROFILE

- Amiable
- Dexterous
- Quick to learn new skills
- Strong sense of responsibility

- Dependable
- Organized
- Self-motivated
- Committed team player

WORK HISTORY

Assembly Line Worker   1998 – present
MCE Technical Services, Wellington, Washington
on assignment to: Alpha Tech, Wellington, Washington
After only one week on the job, learned how to build various electronic
components including DCIU and LCM, and hypotting.

Caterer's Assistant   1995 – 1998
Breaktime Mobile Catering, Wellington, Washington
Prepare food for catering service, make sandwiches, wrap, and label. Create
labels on PC computer.

Delivery Driver   1994 – 1995
Orders-to-Go, Puyallup, Washington
Dispatched from Orders-to-Go to pick up food orders from various restaurants
and personally deliver to customers, collect cash payment.

File Clerk   1992 – 1995
Rody Chiropractic, Puyallup, Washington
Filed patient records and miscellaneous correspondence for chiropractic office on
Saturdays.

EDUCATION

Tacoma Technical College, Tacoma, Washington
Cedar Edge High School, Cedar Edge, Colorado

TINA PERSONA

3333 East Jones Street
Hambone, WA 77777
777-777-7777

PROFILE

"...you will not find anyone who will work harder...combines humor with professionalism...key in creating an atmosphere that promotes business and camaraderie among co-workers...."
"...admirable work ethic...creative and artistic...outgoing persona that is infectious and invigorating to all around her." various employers

QUALIFICATIONS

- Cashiering
- Stocking/Inventory
- Customer Service

- Record-Keeping
  Journeyman UFCW
- Machine Operator

- Supervision/Management
- Food Planning/Preparation/Presentation
- Catering/Banquets/Flower Arranging

WORK EXPERIENCE

Kitchen Manager, *Koffee Korner, Hambone, WA, 1997–1998*
Specialized in preparation of Teriyaki/Thai food breakfasts and lunches for 74-capacity restaurant. Managed all areas of kitchen.

Kitchen Manager/Gift Shop Salesperson, *Nelly's O'Deli Airport Bistro, Hambone, WA, 1995–1997*
Managed large volume catering restaurant business and banquet facilities with seating capacity up to 500. Attended to restaurant, breakfast, lunch, and dinner customers. In charge of ordering, stocking, and maintenance. Supervised staff of 10. Opened Gift Shop at 4 a.m., provided customer service and cashiering.

Owner/Floral Designer, *Gifts by Tina, Hambone, WA, 1987–present*
Grow and preserve flowers for wholesale/retail through gift shop. Wholesale jewelry, operate balloon machine, buy and sell baskets and other gift items. Maintain all company records including shipping/receiving. Interview, hire, train, and manage personnel.

Bakery Salesperson, *Jingles, Hambone, WA, 1984–1987*
Assisted in ordering supplies, maintained inventory, provider customer service and production, prepared, decorated, displayed products. Answered 5-line telephone and operated all-department intercom.

Baker's Assistant, *Jazz's Bakery, Hambone, WA, 1983–1984*
Performed as cashier, made bank deposits, assisted in ordering supplies, maintained inventory, provider customer service and production, prepared, decorated, displayed, proofed and baked. Answered 5-line telephone and operated all-department intercom.

Other Experience: Sprew Injection mold machine, forklift, and grip machine operator.

EDUCATION

Hambone Community College, Hambone, WA—
    Accounting, Computers in Business, Database Computing, Business Math, and Typing.
Hambone Vocational College, Hambone, WA—
    Filing, Typing, Record Keeping, and Bookkeeping

Will E. Pommer

50 Woodworker Ave.
Wellington, WA 98225
(360) 738-6838
will@asitis.com

PROFILE

Enthusiastic fast learner with a stable work history and wide range of practical skills.

Exceptional communication and interpersonal skills with ability to relate warmly with people, generating trust and rapport. Hired, trained, supervised employees. Wrote training manuals.

Diplomatic timely sense of humor. Good memory for faces and names; talent for generating new and repeat business.

Proven leader, effective working in self-managed projects and as team member. Good decision-maker, exercises good judgment. Excellent problem-solving and conflict-resolution skills.

Adept at performing routine inventory control warehouse functions; experienced at handling shipping and receiving. Aptitude for numbers.

Added Value—

In-depth knowledge of food handling, OSHA-WISHA, and labor laws.
Food Handler's Permit
Established local network of suppliers for paper and food products.
Forklift / Pallet Jack Operator
Professional Photographer

CAREER SUMMARY

Shipping / Receiving Dock Clerk, Wellington Cold Storage, Wellington, WA   9–12/2005
temporary employment

Shipped and received frozen food products via truck and rail car, making sure items were handled with care and properly placed. Prepared receiving manifests and shipping bills of lading, confirmed orders, and verified inventory using Bar Code Scanner, computer and proprietary software. Enjoyed friendly interface with co-workers and shippers.

Manager/Barrista, Harbor Espresso, Wellington, WA   1997–9/2005

Managed daily operations of espresso stand and deli restaurant. Promoted business. Cultivated and established loyal customer base. Maintained bookkeeping and prepared quarterly taxes. Hired, trained, and supervised employees. Delivered consistent gains in customer satisfaction and retention through top-performing customer service and expertise in work process design, analysis, and improvement.

Manager/Barrista, Coffee Central, Wellington, WA   1996–1997
Manager, Cruisin' Coffee, Wellington, WA   1993–1996
Started businesses from nothing and built to success. Purchased supplies. Hired, trained, and supervised employees.

Freeland Photographer / Various Barrista positions   1990–1992

Traffic Manager, Wellington Cold Storage, Wellington, WA   1962–1989
Scheduled and coordinated shipping and receiving. Received and processed phone orders from customers. Prepared computer-generated paperwork. Operated forklift and pallet jack.

PROFESSIONAL DEVELOPMENT

Business Management Courses, Wellington Community College
History / Education Courses, Valley College / Jikama College

Dan Rowe

76 Bloom Road
Bloom, WA 98230
Telephone: (300) 300-3000; Cellular: (300) 999-9999

Pipe Welder/Fitter
known for quality workmanship, punctuality, dependability

QUALIFICATIONS

Team-spirited, hard-working, open-minded, willing-to-learn, creative problem-solver
presents 9+ years experience as welder/fitter and 5+ years experience as pipe welder/fitter.

- **Certified:**   Carbon Steel, Stainless Steel pipe, 3/8" Aluminum Plate,
  Dual Shield Flux Core Wire Feed on Carbon Steel Pipe

- **Skilled:**   TIG welding—Carbon Steel, Stainless Steel, and Aluminum
  Fabrication, Layout, Blueprint reading

- **Trained:**   EMT / CPR
  Self-contained Breathing Apparatus—Fresh Air A-Suits
  Hazardous Materials Handling
  Working in Confined Spaces and Heights

- **Operate:**   Cranes, Forklifts, Manlifts

CAREER SUMMARY

Pipe Welder/Fitter, Matrix Corp, Bellingham, WA   2002–present

Fabricate truck loading racks for installation in seven California locations—multi-million dollar project.

- Solved problem of failing welds by modifying procedures for positioning pipe during welding process. Greatly improved quality of welds, virtually eliminated re-do's, and saved time, labor, and money.

Pipe Welder/Fitter, IMAC Inc., Higher, WA   1997–2002

Worked in fabrication shop at TOSCO (now Phillips 66) Refinery. Demolished old piping details, fabricated and replaced new piping details. Provided general maintenance and new construction pipe welding/fitting services.

- Designed and fabricated JIGS that saved time and money in processing large projects.

- Solved problem with misalignment in bolt up process on flanges by designing and fabricating tool to align flanges easily. Pending patent application for this innovative design.

Pipe Welder/Fitter, Colt Construction (now Matrix Corp.), Bellingham, WA   (short-term) 1997
Assigned to ARCO Refinery, Cherry Point to structural welding using aluminum wire feed process.

Welder/Fitter, Northwest Marine Service, Bloom, WA   1995–1997

Worked as welder/fitter in shipyard building aluminum catamarans, 55-ft. sport fishing charter boats for the Bay Area. Certified by US Coast Guard for aluminum wire feed welding.

Welder/Fitter, Westman Marine, Bloom, WA   1993–1995

Performed carbon steel, stainless steel, and aluminum welding in maintenance, repair, and new construction of boats.

TRAINING / EDUCATION

Training and certifications through Matrix, Anvil Corp., and U.S. Coast Guard

Graduate, Bloom High School, Bloom, WA

Index

Authors

RONALD L. KRANNICH, Ph.D., is one of America's leading career and travel specialists. He is the principal author of more than 80 books (3+ million copies in print), including such noted career titles as *201 Dynamite Job Search Letters, Nail the Resume!, Nail the Cover Letter!, Discover the Best Jobs for You, The Savvy Networker, Dynamite Salary Negotiations, America's Top Internet Job Sites*, and *Change Your Job, Change Your Life*. He also has written several international-related career guides, including the popular *The Directory of Websites for International Jobs* and *Jobs for Travel Lovers*. In the field of travel, he is author of *Travel Planning on the Internet* and over 20 volumes in the unique "Impact Guides" travel-shopping series. His work is well represented on several websites: www.impactpublications.com, www.winning thejob.com, www.exoffenderreentry.com, and www.ishoparoundtheworld.com. Ron is president of Development Concepts Incorporated, a training, consulting, and publishing firm in Virginia, as well as Vice-President of USA-Global Institutes of Education. A former Peace Corps Volunteer, high school teacher, university professor, and Fulbright Scholar, he received his Ph.D. in Political Science from Northern Illinois University. He can be contacted through the publisher: krannich@impactpublications.com.

WILLIAM J. BANIS, Ph.D., is Vice President for Student Affairs at Northwestern University in Evanston, Illinois. He is the former Director of the Placement Center at Northwestern University and the former Director of Career Development Services at Old Dominion University in Norfolk, Virginia. He earned a Ph.D. in administration from Old Dominion University and an M.A. in speech communication, counseling, and student personnel administration from Penn State University. A noted consultant and public speaker, he has conducted numerous programs on career development and job placement for professional associations, government agencies, community groups, colleges, and corporations as well as appeared on radio, television, and professional conference panels. He is co-author with Ron of *Moving Out of Education: The Educator's Guide to Career Management and Change*.

Career Resources

THE FOLLOWING CAREER RESOURCES are available directly from Impact Publications. Full descriptions of each title, as well as several downloadable catalogs and specialty flyers, can be found on our website: www.impactpublications.com. Complete the following form or list the titles, include shipping (see formula at the end), enclose payment, and send your order to:

IMPACT PUBLICATIONS
9104 Manassas Drive, Suite N
Manassas Park, VA 20111-5211 USA
1-800-361-1055 (orders only)
Tel. 703-361-7300 or Fax 703-335-9486
Email address: query@impactpublications.com
Quick & easy online ordering: www.impactpublications.com

Orders from individuals must be prepaid by check, money order, or major credit card. We accept telephone, fax, and email orders.

Qty.	TITLES	Price	TOTAL
Featured Title			
____	High Impact Resumes and Letters	$19.95	____
Other Titles By Authors			
____	201 Dynamite Job Search Letters	$19.95	____
____	The $100,000+ Entrepreneur	$19.95	____
____	America's Top Internet Job Sites	$19.95	____
____	America's Top 100 Jobs for People Without a Four-Year Degree	$19.95	____
____	America's Top Jobs for People Re-Entering the Workforce	$19.95	____
____	Best Jobs for the 21st Century	$19.95	____
____	Best Resumes and CVs for International Jobs	$24.95	____
____	Best Resumes and Letters for Ex-Offenders	$19.95	____
____	Blue Collar Resume and Job Hunting Guide	$15.95	____
____	Change Your Job, Change Your Life	$21.95	____
____	Complete Guide to Public Employment	$19.95	____
____	Directory of Websites for International Jobs	$19.95	____
____	Discover the Best Jobs for You	$15.95	____
____	Dynamite Salary Negotiations	$15.95	____
____	The Ex-Offender's Job Hunting Guide	$17.95	____
____	Get a Raise in 7 Days	$14.95	____
____	Haldane's Best Answers to Tough Interview Questions	$15.95	____
____	Haldane's Best Cover Letters for Professionals	$15.95	____

_____ I Can't Believe They Asked Me That!	$17.95	_____
_____ I Want to Do Something Else, But I'm Not Sure What It Is	$15.95	_____
_____ Interview for Success	$15.95	_____
_____ The Job Hunting Guide: Transitioning From College to Career	$14.95	_____
_____ Job Hunting Tips for People With Hot and Not-So-Hot Backgrounds	$17.95	_____
_____ Job Interview Tips for People With Not-So-Hot Backgrounds	$14.95	_____
_____ Jobs for Travel Lovers	$19.95	_____
_____ Military Resumes and Cover Letters	$21.95	_____
_____ Military Transition to Civilian Success	$21.95	_____
_____ Nail the Cover Letter!	$17.95	_____
_____ Nail the Job Interview!	$13.95	_____
_____ Nail the Resume!	$17.95	_____
_____ No One Will Hire Me!	$13.95	_____
_____ Overcoming Barriers to Employment	$17.95	_____
_____ Resume, Application, and Letter Tips for People With Hot and Not-So-Hot Backgrounds	$17.95	_____
_____ Salary Negotiation Tips for Professionals	$16.95	_____
_____ Savvy Interviewing: The Nonverbal Advantage	$10.95	_____
_____ The Savvy Networker	$13.95	_____
_____ The Savvy Resume Writer	$12.95	_____
_____ Win the Interview, Win the Job	$15.95	_____

Testing and Assessment

_____ Aptitude, Personality, and Motivation Tests	$17.95	_____
_____ Career Tests	$12.95	_____
_____ Discover What You're Best At	$14.00	_____
_____ Do What You Are	$18.95	_____
_____ I Could Do Anything If Only I Knew What It Was	$16.00	_____
_____ I Don't Know What I Want, But I Know It's Not This	$14.00	_____
_____ I Want to Do Something Else, But I'm Not Sure What It Is	$15.95	_____
_____ I'm Not Crazy, I'm Just Not You	$16.95	_____
_____ Now, Discover Your Strengths	$30.00	_____
_____ The Pathfinder	$16.00	_____
_____ What Should I Do With My Life?	$14.95	_____
_____ What Type Am I?	$14.95	_____
_____ What's Your Type of Career?	$18.95	_____

Attitude and Motivation

_____ 100 Ways to Motivate Yourself	$14.99	_____
_____ Attitude Is Everything	$14.95	_____
_____ Change Your Attitude	$15.99	_____
_____ Reinventing Yourself	$18.99	_____

Inspiration and Empowerment

_____ 7 Habits of Highly Effective People (2nd Edition)	$15.00	_____
_____ The 8th Habit: From Effectiveness to Greatness	$26.00	_____
_____ 101 Secrets of Highly Effective Speakers	$15.95	_____
_____ Awaken the Giant Within	$16.00	_____
_____ Change Your Thinking, Change Your Life	$24.95	_____
_____ Dream It Do It	$16.95	_____
_____ Finding Your Own North Star	$14.95	_____
_____ Goals!	$14.95	_____
_____ It's Only Too Late If You Don't Start Now	$15.00	_____
_____ Life Strategies	$13.95	_____
_____ Magic of Thinking Big	$13.00	_____
_____ Power of Positive Thinking	$12.95	_____
_____ Purpose-Driven Life	$19.99	_____
_____ Self Matters	$14.00	_____
_____ Ten Commandments to Your Success	$11.95	_____
_____ Who Moved My Cheese?	$19.95	_____

Career Exploration and Job Strategies

_____ 5 Patterns of Extraordinary Careers	$17.95	_____
_____ 25 Jobs That Have It All	$12.95	_____
_____ 50 Best Jobs for Your Personality	$16.95	_____
_____ 50 Cutting Edge Jobs	$15.95	_____

_____ 95 Mistakes Job Seekers Make & How to Avoid Them $13.95 _____
_____ 100 Great Jobs and How to Get Them $17.95 _____
_____ 101 Ways to Recession-Proof Your Career $14.95 _____
_____ 200 Best Jobs for College Grads $16.95 _____
_____ 250 Best Jobs Through Apprenticeships $24.95 _____
_____ 300 Best Jobs Without a Four-Year Degree $16.95 _____
_____ America's Top 100 Jobs for People Without a Four-Year Degree $19.95 _____
_____ Best Entry-Level Jobs $16.95 _____
_____ Best Jobs for the 21st Century $19.95 _____
_____ Career Change $14.95 _____
_____ Cool Careers for Dummies $19.99 _____
_____ Directory of Executive Recruiters $49.95 _____
_____ Five Secrets to Finding a Job $12.95 _____
_____ A Fork in the Road: A Career Planning Guide for Young Adults $14.95 _____
_____ Great Careers in Two Years $19.95 _____
_____ High-Tech Careers for Low-Tech People $14.95 _____
_____ How to Get a Job and Keep It $16.95 _____
_____ How to Get Interviews From Classified Job Ads $14.95 _____
_____ How to Succeed Without a Career Path $13.95 _____
_____ Job Search Handbook for People With Disabilities $17.95 _____
_____ Knock 'Em Dead $14.95 _____
_____ Me, Myself, and I, Inc. $17.95 _____
_____ Monster Careers $18.00 _____
_____ Quick Prep Careers $18.95 _____
_____ Quit Your Job and Grow Some Hair $15.95 _____
_____ Rites of Passage at $100,000 to $1 Million+ $29.95 _____
_____ Suddenly Unemployed $14.95 _____
_____ Top 100 Health-Care Careers $24.95 _____
_____ What Color Is Your Parachute? $17.95 _____

Career Directories

_____ Associations USA $75.00 _____
_____ Enhanced Occupational Outlook Handbook $39.95 _____
_____ Job Hunter's Sourcebook $160.00 _____
_____ Occupational Outlook Handbook $17.95 _____
_____ O*NET Dictionary of Occupational Titles $39.95 _____
_____ Professional Careers Sourcebook $150.00 _____
_____ Vocational Careers Sourcebook $150.00 _____

Internet Job Search

_____ 100 Top Internet Job Sites $12.95 _____
_____ America's Top Internet Job Sites $19.95 _____
_____ Career Exploration On the Internet $24.95 _____
_____ Guide to Internet Job Searching $14.95 _____
_____ Job Hunting on the Internet $11.95 _____
_____ Job Seeker's Online Goldmine $13.95 _____

Resumes and Letters

_____ 101 Great Tips for a Dynamite Resume $13.95 _____
_____ 175 Best Cover Letters $14.95 _____
_____ Best KeyWords for Resumes, Cover Letters, & Interviews $17.95 _____
_____ Best Resumes for $75,000+ Executive Jobs $16.95 _____
_____ Best Resumes for $100,000+ Jobs $24.95 _____
_____ Best Resumes for People Without a Four-Year Degree $19.95 _____
_____ Best Cover Letters for $100,000+ Jobs $24.95 _____
_____ Blue Collar Resumes $11.99 _____
_____ College Grad Resumes to Land $75,000+ Jobs $24.95 _____
_____ Competency-Based Resumes $13.99 _____
_____ Cover Letters for Dummies $16.99 _____
_____ Cover Letters That Knock 'Em Dead $12.95 _____
_____ Create Your Own Digital Portfolio $19.95 _____
_____ e-Resumes $16.95 _____
_____ Expert Resumes for People Returning to Work $16.95 _____
_____ Gallery of Best Cover Letters $18.95 _____
_____ Gallery of Best Resumes $18.95 _____
_____ Resume Shortcuts $14.95 _____
_____ Resumes for Dummies $16.99 _____

_____ Resumes That Knock 'Em Dead $12.95 _____
_____ Winning Letters That Overcome Barriers to Employment $17.95 _____
_____ World's Greatest Resumes $14.95 _____

Networking

_____ A Foot in the Door $14.95 _____
_____ How to Work a Room $14.00 _____
_____ Masters of Networking $16.95 _____
_____ Networking for Job Search and Career Success $16.95 _____

Dress, Image, and Etiquette

_____ Dressing Smart for Men $16.95 _____
_____ Dressing Smart for Women $16.95 _____
_____ Power Etiquette $14.95 _____

Interviews

_____ 101 Dynamite Questions to Ask At Your Job Interview $13.95 _____
_____ Job Interviews for Dummies $16.99 _____
_____ KeyWords to Nail Your Job Interview $17.95 _____
_____ Sweaty Palms $13.95 _____

Salary Negotiations

_____ Dynamite Salary Negotiations $15.95 _____
_____ Get a Raise in 7 Days $14.95 _____
_____ Salary Negotiation Tips for Professionals $16.95 _____

Ex-Offenders in Transition

_____ 9 to 5 Beats Ten to Life $15.00 _____
_____ 99 Days and a Get Up $9.95 _____
_____ Best Resumes and Letters for Ex-Offenders $19.95 _____
_____ Ex-Offender's Quick Job Hunting Guide $9.95 _____
_____ Man, I Need a Job $7.95 _____
_____ Putting the Bars Behind You (6 books) $57.95 _____

Government Jobs

_____ Book of U.S. Government Jobs $21.95 _____
_____ FBI Careers $19.95 _____
_____ Post Office Jobs $19.95 _____
_____ Ten Steps to a Federal Job $39.95 _____

International and Travel Jobs

_____ Back Door Guide to Short-Term Job Adventures $21.95 _____
_____ Careers in International Affairs $24.95 _____
_____ Directory of Websites for International Jobs $19.95 _____
_____ International Job Finder $19.95 _____
_____ Jobs for Travel Lovers $19.95 _____
_____ Teaching English Abroad $15.95 _____

VIDEOS/DVDs

Interview, Networking, and Salary

_____ Best 10¼ Tips for People With a Not-So-Hot Past $98.00 _____
_____ Build a Network for Work and Life $69.00 _____
_____ Common Mistakes People Make in Interviews $79.95 _____
_____ Exceptional Interviewing Tips $79.00 _____
_____ Extraordinary Answers to Interview Questions $79.95 _____
_____ Extreme Interview $69.00 _____
_____ Getting Good Answers to Tough Interview Questions $129.00 _____
_____ Make a First Good Impression $129.00 _____
_____ Seizing the Job Interview $79.00 _____
_____ Quick Salary Negotiations $129.00 _____
_____ Why Should I Hire You? $99.00 _____

Dress and Image

____	Head to Toe	$98.00/108.00 ____
____	Tips and Techniques to Improve Your Total Image	$98.00/108.00 ____

Resumes, Applications, and Cover Letters

____	The Complete Job Application	$99.00 ____
____	Effective Resumes	$79.95 ____
____	How Do You Put It On Paper?	$98.00/108.00 ____
____	Ideal Resume	$79.95 ____
____	Quick Cover Letter	$129.00 ____
____	Quick Resume	$129.00 ____
____	Resumes, Cover Letters, and Portfolios	$98.00/108.00 ____

Assessment and Goal Setting

____	Career Assessment	$98.00/108.00 ____
____	Career S.E.L.F. Assessment	$89.00 ____
____	Goal Away	$98.00/108.00 ____
____	Skills Identification	$129.00 ____
____	You DO Have Experience	$69.00 ____

Attitude, Motivation, and Empowerment

____	Down But Not Out	$129.00 ____
____	Looking for Work With Attitude Plus	$99.00 ____
____	A New Attitude	$149.00 ____

SUBTOTAL _____

Virginia residents add 5% sales tax _____

POSTAGE/HANDLING ($5 for first
product and 8% of SUBTOTAL) __$5.00__

8% of SUBTOTAL --- _____

TOTAL ENCLOSED ------------------------------------- _____

SHIP TO:

NAME _____

ADDRESS: _____

_____

_____

PAYMENT METHOD:

❑ I enclose check/money order for $ _____ made payable to IMPACT PUBLICATIONS.

❑ Please charge $ _____ to my credit card:

❑ Visa ❑ MasterCard ❑ American Express ❑ Discover

Card # _____ Expiration date: ____/____

Signature _____